EXCHANGE RATE POLICY

Fluctuations in exchange rates, particularly sterling exchange rates, have troubled policy-makers throughout the 1970s. The papers and comments collected in this volume are the proceedings of a conference on 'Exchange Rate Policy' organised by the Centre for Banking and International Finance at the City University, London, from 30 September to 1 October 1980. They consider what lessons can be drawn for the conduct of policy in the 1980s.

Two types of problem are addressed. One concerns the reaction of policy to factors which have made the United Kingdom increasingly vulnerable to exchange rate changes, notably the removal of exchange controls in 1979, and the exploitation of North Sea oil. The other concerns the very feasibility of intervention, whether it be to stabilise the exchange rate around its trend or to reverse the adverse 'real' effects of natural resource exploitation on the competitiveness of other industries.

Both theory and evidence cast doubts on the value of conventional exchange rate policy. History suggests exchange rates have been most volatile (relative to prices) when intervention was strongest; recent experience shows that markets are highly effective in translating news of economic events into appropriate exchange rate adjustments; and overlaying this news with a series of policy actions serves only to increase confusion in the market about the fundamental value of the currency.

In the next decade, pressures for a firmer exchange rate management are bound to grow. Memories of the recurrent crises of the pegged exchange rate era are fading, and – in spite of its technical imperfections – there is continuous pressure to link sterling with other currencies in the European monetary system. This book delivers a timely reminder on how difficult it is to justify and to operate any positive official policy towards the exchange rate.

Also by Roy A. Batchelor

INDUSTRIALISATION AND THE BASIS FOR TRADE
(*with R. L. Major and A. D. Morgan*)

Also by Geoffrey E. Wood

THE FINANCING PROCEDURES OF BRITISH FOREIGN
TRADE (*with Stephen Carse and John Williamson*)
MONETARY TARGETS (*editor with Brian Griffiths*)

EXCHANGE RATE POLICY

Edited by

Roy A. Batchelor
and
Geoffrey E. Wood

in association with
Centre for Banking and International Finance
The City University, London

First published 1982 by
THE MACMILLAN PRESS LTD
London and Basingstoke
Companies and representatives
throughout the world

ISBN 0 333 29192 1

Printed in Hong Kong

Contents

Contents

Notes on the Contributors

Roy A. Batchelor is Director of Research at the Centre for Banking and International Finance, and editor of the Centre's *Annual Monetary Review*. A graduate of Glasgow University, he has worked in government and in the National Institute of Economic and Social Research. He is co-author of a recent book, *Industrialisation and the Basis for Trade*, and has published many articles on trade and exchange rate policy, monetary control and the problems of inflation and unemployment.

Michael Beenstock is a Senior Research Fellow at the London Business School. A graduate of the London School of Economics, he has worked at HM Treasury and the World Bank. He has published articles and books on macroeconomics, development and energy.

Bruce Brittain is an economist at the Bank for International Settlements in Basle, Switzerland. Formerly employed at Citibank, New York, he has published in the areas of international finance and monetary economics.

Andrew Britton is an Under-Secretary at HM Treasury in charge of the Finance Economic Unit. He joined the Government Economic Service in 1966 and took an MSc at the London School of Economics, before joining the Treasury in 1968. Apart from a spell at the Department of Health and Social Security, he has spent most of his civil service career working on macroeconomics, forecasting and monetary policy.

Alan Budd is Director of the Centre for Economic Forecasting at the London Business School. He graduated from the London School of Economics and has a PhD from Cambridge University. He has taught at Southampton University and has been Visiting Professor at Carnegie-Mellon University, Pittsburgh. He was in HM Treasury, 1970–4. He is the author of *The Politics of Economic Planning*.

Paul de Grauwe is now Associate Professor at the Catholic University of Louvain. He obtained his PhD from the Johns Hopkins University, and worked as an economist at the International Monetary Fund during 1973–4. He was Visiting Professor at the University of Paris (Dauphine). He has published articles in international journals such as the *Journal of International Economics*, the *Journal of Political Economy*, *European Economic Review* and *Weltwirtschaftliches Archiv*.

André Farber is Associate Professor at the University of Brussels and Chairman of the Business School. He has been Visiting Assistant Professor at Cornell University and the University of Chicago. His research interests include international capital markets, microeconomics of uncertainty and innovation. He has published articles in the *American Economic Review*, the *Journal of Monetary Economics* and other various books and reviews.

Desmond Fitzgerald is currently Finance for Industry Senior Research Fellow in the Centre for Banking and International Finance, the City University. He was previously Assistant Professor of Finance at New York University. His current research interests include the structure of UK interest rates, the valuation of commodity options and financial futures contracts, and medieval financial markets.

Alec G. Ford, MA, D Phil (Oxford), has been Professor of Economics at the University of Warwick since 1970 and was previously on the staff at the University of Leicester. He has research interests and publications in the areas of British and international economic history and in macroeconomics.

Jacob A. Frenkel is Professor of Economics at the University of Chicago and a Research Associate of the National Bureau of Economic Research. He is also editor of the *Journal of Political Economy*, a member of the Editorial Board of the *Journal of Monetary Economics*, and a member of the Carnegie-Rochester Conference Series Advisory Council. A graduate of the Hebrew University in Israel and the University of Chicago, he has also taught at the Hebrew University and at Tel-Aviv University. He is the author of numerous articles on international economics and macroeconomics which have appeared, among other places, in the *American Economic Review*, the *Journal of Political Economy*, the *Economic Journal*, *Economica*, the *Quarterly Journal of Economics*, the *Journal of International Economics* and the

Journal of Monetary Economics. He is also a co-author of several books on international economics including *The Monetary Approach to the Balance of Payments* (with H. G. Johnson).

Pieter Korteweg is Professor of Economics at Erasmus University, Rotterdam. He is a member of the Academic Panel of the Group of Thirty and the Shadow European Economic Policy Committee, adjunct scholar of the American Enterprise Institute and Crown-member of the Dutch Social-Economic Council. He is also a member of the Editorial Board of the *Journal of Monetary Economics*, and the North-Holland Studies in Monetary Economics and of the Advisory Committee of the Carnegie-Rochester Conference Series on Public Policy. During the academic year 1974–5 he was Visiting Professor at Carnegie-Mellon University, Pittsburgh. He is the author of numerous books and articles on money and credit, stagflation, exchange rates, the EMS and monetary policy.

George McKenzie is a Senior Lecturer in Economics at the University of Southampton, England. A graduate of Wesleyan University and the University of California at Berkeley, he is author of the *Economics of the Eurocurrency System.* He has published articles in, among other places, the *American Economic Review, Journal of Political Economy, Review of Economic Studies* and *Oxford Economic Papers.* He is currently undertaking research into the effect that the Eurocurrency system has upon the effectiveness of monetary control.

Allan H. Meltzer is Maurice Falk Professor of Economics and Social Science and has been on the faculty of Carnegie-Mellon University since 1957. In 1958 he received a PhD from the University of California, Los Angeles. He is the author of more than 100 articles and books on economics, particularly on money and monetary theory. He is co-director, with Karl Brunner, of the Carnegie-Rochester Conference on Public Policy and co-editor of the Carnegie-Rochester papers on public policy. He is co-chairman, with Karl Brunner, of the Shadow Open Market Committee in the United States and the Shadow European Economic Policy Committee in Europe. He has served as Visiting Professor at Harvard, Chicago, the Yugoslav Institute of Economic Research, the Austrian Institute of Higher Studies and the Hoover Institution. His current research interests include the relation of money to economic activity and prices, the analysis of Federal Reserve monetary policy-making and the relation of private choice to size of government. He has served as a consultant to financial institutions and to government agencies including the Council of Economic Advisers, the Board of Governors of the Federal Reserve System, the US Department of the Treasury and foreign central banks.

Patrick Minford is Professor of Applied Economics at Liverpool University. Before that, in 1975–6 he was editor of the NIESR *Review*. He has also visited Manchester University as a Hallsworth Research Fellow and has been an economic adviser in the external section of HM Treasury. His publications include *Substitution Effects*, *Speculation and Exchange Rate Stability* and articles on trade and macroeconomics.

Milivoje (Mica) Panić is an Adviser, Bank of England, and was previously Chief Economist, National Economic Development Office. He is co-author of *Product Changes in Industrial Countries Trade: 1955–1968*, editor of *The UK and West German Manufacturing Industry 1954–72* and author of *Capacity Utilisation in UK Manufacturing Industry* and articles on inflation, international trade, industrial economics and economic growth.

Ivor Pearce, BA, University of Bristol, PhD (Economics), University of Nottingham, 1953, is Emeritus Professor, University of Southampton. He was Reader in Economics and later Professor, Institute of Advanced Studies, Australian National University, 1951–61, and also Visiting Fellow, Nuffield College, Oxford, and Professor and Head of Department of Economics, University of Southampton, England. He is the author of many papers and a Fellow of the Econometric Society.

Ronald Shone, BSc (Econ), MA, is a Lecturer at the University of Stirling, where he has been for the last four years. He was an undergraduate at Hull and a postgraduate at Essex and Southampton. He spent five years at the University of Sheffield, where he taught and was for part of the time Esme Fairbairn Research Fellow. His interests are divided between microeconomics and international monetary economics, and he has published articles and books in both areas.

Peter Spencer is an Economic Adviser at HM Treasury. He was originally recruited in 1974 to help with the development of an econometric model of the domestic UK financial system. Since 1978 he has been working on the external side, and his responsibilities have included the exchange-rate forecast.

Geoffrey E. Wood is now Senior Lecturer in Banking and International Finance at the City University, London. A graduate of Aberdeen and Essex Universities, he has taught previously at Warwick University, been a member of the Economic Section of the Bank of England, and Visiting Scholar at the Federal Reserve Bank of St Louis. He has published articles in, among others, the *Journal of International Economics*, the *European Economic Review*, and the *American Economic Review*.

Paul van den Bergh obtained his BA (Economics) at the Katholieke Universiteit van Leuven in 1977 and his master's degree at the Université Catholique de Louvain in 1980. After two years as a researcher at the Centre for Economic Research at the Katholieke Universiteit he is now an attaché at the Central Bank of Belgium, economist for international settlements. He is co-author (with Paul de Grauwe) of *Monetary Policies and the Exchange Rates in the EC-countries*.

Introduction

Roy A. Batchelor and Geoffrey E. Wood

Over the past fifty years the United Kingdom government and the Bank of England have regularly been obliged to confront the question of what constitutes an appropriate exchange rate for sterling. In the aftermath of the First World War sterling was pegged to gold, at a rate which was arguably too high[1] and was abandoned in the 1930s. Immediately after the Second World War sterling was again pegged, directly to the dollar and indirectly to gold, at a rate which was clearly above market sentiment,[2] and soon abandoned for a more realistic rate. By the later 1960s, even this rate was proving untenable and, after two major devaluations, sterling embarked in 1973 on a loosely managed float. The initial tendency was for sterling to float downwards, but since 1976–7 it has strengthened markedly. Once again the monetary authorities are under pressure, not for choosing too high a target rate but for not acting so as to bring the rate down.

Complaints about official policy towards the exchange rate presume that there can usefully be such a policy. These complaints nowadays do not generally arise from a belief that pegging the exchange rate is in itself an appropriate objective of policy. They arise rather from the belief that by judicious choice of the exchange rate the government and monetary authority of a country can facilitate the attainment of other objectives.

This belief can have underpinning it several different assumptions. In this introductory essay we set out what these assumptions are, and indicate how the papers in this volume bear on them. The essay concludes with a brief summary of what the analysis and evidence in this volume imply for future policy towards the international monetary system and the exchange rate.

THE CASE FOR OFFICIAL ACTION

Exchange market intervention by the authorities can vary in degree from occasional intervention in the exchanges to firm pegging of the rate. In kind, intervention incorporates not only official transactions in the exchange markets but also the execution of other policies, such as exchange control, designed to affect the rate.

Concern about the rate can arise from three quite different motives. First, it can be believed that the market produces a 'wrong' rate – a rate not fully reflecting all available and relevant information. Second, it can be thought that, while the rate is not 'wrong' in that sense, benefits will accrue to society by shifting it somewhere else. Third, it may be believed not that the average exchange rate is 'wrong' in either of the above senses, but rather that exchange markets are, in the absence of official action, sufficiently volatile that some aspects of economic activity are adversely affected. We consider each of these arguments in turn.

The 'Wrong' Rate

If the statement that the market exchange rate is 'wrong' is to have positive, as opposed to normative, content, what must be shown is that the foreign exchange market is technically inefficient. Market efficiency can be demonstrated if there are no opportunities for trading which yield abnormally high profits. In the context of the exchange market this has two implications – there should be no scope for covered interest arbitrage, and no scope for open speculation. The first of these conditions requires simply that 'interest parity' between low-risk sterling and foreign currency assets be tightly maintained. The second requires that the forward rate – the rate fixed now for exchange of currencies at some future date – be an unbiased predictor of future spot rates, a predictor which generates no systematic – and hence exploitable – pattern in errors over time, and which increases in accuracy the nearer we move to any target date for forward contracts. Note that the accuracy of the forward rate as a predictor of spot rate movements is not at issue here. What is required for market efficiency is evidence that no information relevant to making these predictions has been overlooked by forward speculators.

If the foreign exchange markets persistently produced prices which were 'wrong' in the sense that they displayed inefficiencies, then a good case can be made for official intervention. It is the same case which can be made for intervention in any imperfectly functioning private market – namely that by generating inappropriate prices there is a danger of resource misallocation. Goods would be produced, and capital allocated, in response to prices that do not fully reflect all available information about relative scarcities. Intervention would therefore increase well-being.

That case does not, however, hold if the information is costly to obtain, or otherwise not profitable to exploit. That would imply that the opportunity cost of the resources needed to make the profit exceeded the profit itself and, unless there is a divergence between private and social costs and benefits, resources would be wasted by government intervention just as they would have been by private intervention.

A 'Preferable' Rate

A second case for action by the authorities to affect the exchange rate rests not on any inefficiency in the foreign exchange market but on the belief that the exchange rate is affecting the size of either the tradeable or non-tradeable sector of the economy in an undesirable way. 'Undesirable' can have two meanings in this context. It can mean that the authorities wish to protect one sector of the economy, so that it is larger than it would be under free trade. Motives for this are various. It may be simply that it is thought that the protection-produced production pattern is socially preferable – because, for example, of its effects on the distribution of employment. The motive may be that once the protection has been provided for a time then the sector will expand or recover. This argument is familiar to students of economic development as the case for 'infant industry protection'. In Britain it has been argued, by the Cambridge Economic Policy Group, as a reason to protect long-established, 'senile', industries.

Alternatively, 'undesirable' can mean that it is believed that the exchange rate has moved *temporarily* to a level where it will change the size of a sector, thus requiring the sector first to contract (for example) and then to expand to its original size when the rate reverts to its original value. This temporary movement might not be smoothed out because, although the exchange market is efficient, its maximum time horizon for forward contracts is shorter than the length of the temporary movement. Problems would be caused for the real economy both because of adjustment costs – such as unemployment – and because of the difficulty of recapturing once-lost markets. This argument has some relevance to the United Kingdom if it is believed that the strength of sterling after 1978 was primarily based on the existence of North Sea oil.

This oil will run out before the year 2000, the exchange rate will presumably fall and the tradeable goods sector will once again be profitable.[3]

The second type of argument for an 'exchange rate policy' therefore rests on the desire to provide protection – perhaps over a temporary difficulty – to one sector of the economy.

An argument related to this is that the exchange rate may stay for substantial periods away from Purchasing Power Parity (PPP) with respect to all goods. If this is the case, then countries cannot, even with a floating exchange rate, choose their own rate of monetary expansion and hence underlying inflation rate without a balance of payments crisis – for exchange rates will *not* move to offset price-level movements. If this is correct, then changes in nominal variables – such as the price level – will have temporary real effects, switching goods into and out of foreign trade and imposing unnecessary adjustment costs on the economy under those circumstances. Floating rates would not prevent that, and thus do not bring a benefit often claimed for them.

Excessive Volatility

A traditional argument for pegged rates was that floating rates would inevitably be so volatile they would inhibit international trade.[4] On the basis of this assertion it was then argued that pegged rates, or at any rate 'heavily managed' rates were inherently superior to floating ones.

APPRAISAL AND EVIDENCE

Having set out the various arguments for governments and central banks having a policy towards exchange rates, it is now necessary to appraise these arguments, focusing particularly on how the papers in this volume bear on them.

Market Efficiency

This issue was addressed particularly by Jacob Frenkel. He shows that the foreign exchange markets are efficient; there is no significant amount of wasted information and much of the observed 'noise' in short-run exchange rates is the result of the arrival of 'news' (to use Frenkel's term) – that is, of information which leads to a reappraisal of currency values. This finding is consistent with earlier studies and, in conjunction with work such as Levich (1979), clearly demonstrates that no case for official exchange rate policy can rest on a claim that the foreign exchange markets, by failing to use all available information, produce prices which might cause resource misallocation.

The first argument for the existence of official exchange rate policy does not, then, seem to fit the facts.

Preferred Rates

In the absence of the exchange rate being *in itself* an objective of policy, one exchange rate must be preferred over another because of its effect on the real economy. It must, therefore, be the 'real' exchange rate that the authorities are to have a preference about. A real exchange rate is an exchange rate compensated for price changes; it measures, in other words, the extent to which the price of one country's goods has changed relative to the prices of its trading partners.

This policy of shifting the real exchange rate has been christened, by Max Corden, 'Exchange Rate Protection'. An important aspect of this type of policy was not dealt with at all in the conference. This is whether it is the most efficient way of attaining its objective. Fortunately Corden (1981) has subjected that question to detailed analysis, and has shown that, in this area as in the discussion of infant and senile industry protection (Bhagwati and Ramaswami,1963 and Wood, 1975), direct fiscal measures – use of taxes and subsidies – are more efficient than any other method. Seeking a preferred real exchange rate to protect one sector of an economy is therefore inferior to other means of protecting a sector.

Unfortunately the question cannot be left there. Governments and special interest groups display a persistent fascination with protection by means of the exchange rate, no doubt because the costs imposed on the community by exchange rate protection are less obvious than are the costs of overtly levied taxes. It is therefore necessary to ask both whether the policy is feasible, and whether it has drawbacks other than the efficiency ones analysed by Corden.

Both Batchelor and Wood, and Korteweg, presented results which suggest that there have not been long-lived deviations from PPP. This means that there have not been long-lived changes in the real exchange rate. It is interesting to analyse why this has been so, and to ask whether it is the result of a failure satisfactorily to conduct the policy, or whether it is an inevitable fact of life.

In fact, as Corden (1981) has shown, it is possible for governments and central banks to manipulate the real exchange rates so as to effect exchange rate protection. What they must do is, initially, intervene in the exchange markets by supplying more of their domestic currency than that amount which produced the undesired price level/exchange rate combination and thus the undesired real exchange rate. This would have of itself very limited success, as the larger money stock would drive up domestic prices, thus offsetting the fall in the exchange rate and leaving the real exchange rate unchanged. The government must therefore mop up the monetary effects of their foreign exchange intervention, by sales of long-dated debt. Real exchange rate manipulation is thus possible (though inefficient) – so long as governments are willing to bear the interest rate consequence of a high and increasing real rate of interest on government debt. This price, it would appear, has generally not been accepted.

It is clear that, as a theoretical matter at any rate, one price, the real exchange rate, can be affected only by moving another price, the real rate of interest, in an offsetting direction. Patrick Minford addressed explicitly whether such a policy could be regarded as desirable, setting aside the efficiency arguments advanced by Corden. He concluded that even without these arguments, the case against attempting to manipulate the real exchange rate was very strong. As he pointed out, if the *real* exchange rate is to be affected, many other *real* variables will change. Governments can in principle respond in a stabilising way to such changes. However, individuals can also react to such changes and will adapt their behaviour – the length of wage contracts, for example – until the economy responds in an optimal way to such disturbances. Whether the government's costs in responding are lower than those of the private sector should be considered, but, as Minford points out, since it would be hard for individuals to distinguish such stabilising behaviour from stochastic behaviour, a policy of maintaining pre-announced nominal targets is highly likely to dominate the alternative of real rate management.

Three conclusions emerge, therefore, from analysis of whether exchange rate policy can be justified by arguing that the government should guide the real exchange rate to some 'preferred' level. First, not discussed at the conference but demonstrated by Corden, such manipulation of the exchange rate is inevitably a less efficient means of protecting a sector than some of the available alternatives. Second, an attempt to shift the real exchange rate, although possible in principle, involves real interest rate changes which governments do not seem willing to tolerate. Third, an attempt to maintain a target real exchange rate in the face of shocks to it will, given very reasonable assumptions about the behaviour of the private sector, serve only to impede efficient adjustment by the private sector to these shocks.

On the basis of the conference papars, then, it seems hard to justify an exchange rate policy by arguments that a desirable real exchange rate can be chosen and maintained.

Rate Volatility

It is sometimes asserted that exchange rate volatility since floating has been such as to deter international trade. However, there is very little evidence to support this proposition, perhaps because tests of it have not distinguished between international trade exposed to exchange risk and, quite a large portion of the total, trade not exposed to such risk.[4] Granting the assertion for the sake of the argument, it needs to be asked whether of itself that is an argument for pegging or stabilising rates.

Frenkel's demonstration of the efficiency of the exchange markets bears on this question. He demonstrates that most rate fluctuations are the result of the efficient assimilation of new information. They are not in general speculative bubbles or otherwise irrational price movements, but the rational response of the economy. This in turn means that if these movements are suppressed, something else must adjust. In particular, if exchange rate volatility is to be removed by official intervention it must involve increasing money growth volatility, or interest rate volatility, or both. This shifts the burden of adjustment from international traders to the whole economy, and thus conveys a subsidy to international as against internal trade. No case in general can be made for this.

A second point relevant to this issue emerges from the paper by Batchelor and Wood. This demonstrates that *unpredictable* exchange volatility (relative to price level volatility) *increases* with official intervention – because such intervention diffuses expectations of the future spot rate and thereby creates uncertainty and inhibits private speculation. This indicates that a 'managed' float contributes positively to uncertainty. If 'managed' floating is positively undesirable, then the problem of exchange rate volatility can be solved only by *pegging* the rate. But that solution cannot be supported either, for it implies a subsidy to the traded goods sector without any evidence that such a subsidy is desirable. Further, as is noted in Batchelor and Wood, the speed of convergence to PPP implies that by such pegging countries surrender their ability to choose a preferred inflation rate.

Even if international trade is inhibited by floating rates, then, it appears that this does not constitute a case for exchange rate management or exchange rate pegging. This third case for exchange rate policy does not stand up well in the face of the evidence.

DECISIONS TAKEN

Two of the conference papers have not figured in the above discussion. Both of these papers, by de Grauwe and van den Bergh, and Britton and Spencer, accepted that there had been decisions about exchange rate policy and analysed certain consequences of these decisions.

de Grauwe and van den Bergh analyse certain aspects of the European monetary system. They address the question of the effects of intervention using, alternatively, the dollar or the DM, and of having the ECU as the target for intervention; and they consider the effects of monetary policy in the countries of the EMS when the system is enlarged – by the addition of Britain, for example. In view of the political interest in an EMS these are important questions, fairly readily answered qualitatively (as Michael Beenstock noted in his comments) but much harder to answer quantitatively. Intervention in a non-EMS currency appears to reduce control of rates: targetting the ECU increases the 'symmetry' of the system – in other words, removes one of the weaknesses of Bretton Woods, that it appeared difficult for the 'pivot' currency to adjust; and augmenting the EMS reduces the effectiveness of monetary policy within it. The very considerable interest of this paper lies in its quantification of these answers. It is a major contribution to the analysis of the EMS.

It also linked with some of the other papers in this volume in an interesting way. The papers by Frenkel, Batchelor and Wood, and Minford, all imply that the system will be at best redundant. A critical point in the analysis of all three papers was that expectations were endogenous. de Grauwe and van den Bergh, for empirical tractability, assume exogenous expectations, and the results of future work endogenising expectations in their model will be of considerable interest.

The paper which aroused most critical comment was that by Britton and Spencer. Indeed, one of the authors, Andrew Britton, has written a rejoinder to the two discussants in which he maintains that the difficulties are entirely theirs in that they have failed to understand the paper. The Britton and Spencer paper was motivated by another major act of policy – though whether or not it was directed towards the exchange rate is not clear. This act was the removal of UK exchange controls. The authors argue that this increased the mobility of capital between the UK and the rest of the world, and that this affected, in their words, 'the way the exchange rate is determined'. Their paper does present estimates of the effect increased capital mobility has on the level of the exchange rate, but does not show how the 'way' the rate is determined might be expected to change. Indeed, it is hard to see why it should. A qualitative change might occur had capital mobility been totally restricted before exchange control abolition, but it was not. Accordingly the paper is best viewed as an attempt to estimate the changed effects of policy changes when capital mobility increases. It nowhere, however, presents a demonstration that total capital mobility did increase after the abolition of exchange controls – and after all, UK non-residents, a much larger group than residents, were always free of exchange controls. Nor, as Alan Meltzer notes, is the distinction between real and nominal magnitudes, nor stocks and flows, always clear. The paper may be best regarded as an example of a particular approach to economic modelling.

One theme emerges very strongly from the papers at this conference. It is that there is little reason in principle, or in the practice of the past fifty years, to suppose exchange rate management is an efficient, effective or viable policy weapon. The exchange markets are sufficiently efficient that any government action in them must inevitably move the economy to a situation less desirable to the private sector. All the positive arguments for exchange rate policy were contradicted by the evidence. In a short concluding comment to this volume, Michael Beenstock, elaborating on remarks he made at the conference, goes on to argue that in view of the above-cited evidence, adjustment problems caused by movements in the real exchange rate should be attacked not by a policy towards the demonstrably efficient exchange markets, but by a policy towards the inefficient labour market. And, we would add, goods markets. It is hard to escape from that conclusion.

One final policy implication can be drawn out. Every few years plans are proposed for the 'reform' of the whole international monetary system. On the basis of the evidence reported here and elsewhere, it is hard to see why reform is needed. The exchange markets are efficient; intervention only increases exchange rate unpredictability. With highly flexible exchange rates international reserve shortages cannot exist –real reserves, like real money, are demand-determined and supply cannot affect the real amount. Nor is there any case for an international vehicle currency to facilitate trade and international investment. The rapidity of convergence to PPP, and the methods available to traders to protect themselves against exchange risk during the transition period, mean that exchange risk is not such as to have to make the world as a whole seek some vehicle free of exchange risk.[5]

There is abundant evidence from the behaviour of price levels in most developed economies, that domestic monetary control could benefit from reform; and there is equally abundant evidence that the international monetary system does not need reforming.

NOTES

1. An extensive discussion of this period, and a survey of contemporary opinion, can be found in D. E. Moggridge, *British Monetary Policy 1924–31* (Cambridge University Press, 1972), particularly Chapters 3 and 4.
2. In his speech (12 December 1945) recommending the Bretton Woods Agreements to the House of Commons, the Chancellor of the Exchequer, Hugh Dalton, was interrupted first by Mr Robert Boothby and then by Mr W. J. Brown.

> *Mr Dalton:*   We shall go into Bretton Woods with the existing rate of 4.03 dollars to the pound. There has to be an initial rate, and my advisers in the Treasury and the Bank of England are satisfied that 4.03 dollars is as good a rate as you can fix now. There is no reason to suppose it is too high or too low, in relation to the probable course of events.
>
> *Mr Boothby:*   Is there any reason to suppose that the Treasury is now in a position to know any of the governing factors which should settle the rate of exchange?
>
> *Mr Dalton:*   They do not decide these matters entirely out of their own inner consciousness. They take counsel with other people, and, in stating the advice given to me, I have associated with the Treasury the Bank of England – not yet nationalised. If my hon. Friend will adduce any substantial reason why 4.03 dollars is wrong, of course I will give it most careful consideration.
>
> *Mr Brown:*   That is far too high. In Portugal, or wherever there is a free market, the rate is nearer 2.50 dollars to the pound.

3. A brief statement of this view, and a proposed policy response, can be found in 'What Should be Done about the Overvalued Pound'? by David T. King, *The Banker*, November 1980.
4. This possibility is discussed in more detail in 'Floating Exchange Rates in the 1970s: A Discussion of the Heller Paper', by Geoffrey E. Wood, in *Stabilisation Policies: Lessons from the 1970s and Implications for the 1980s* (St Louis, Washington University, Centre for the Study of American Business, 1980).

5. The methods used by international traders to protect themselves against exchange risk are examined in some detail in *The Financing Procedures of UK Foreign Trade*, by Stephen Carse, John Williamson and Geoffrey E. Wood (Cambridge University Press, 1980).

REFERENCES

Bhagwati, J. and V. K. S. Ramaswami (1963), 'Domestic Distortions, Tariffs, and the Theory of the Optimum Subsidy', *Journal of Political Economy* (February).
Corden, W. M. (1981). 'The Exchange Rate, Monetary Policy and North Sea Oil: The Economic Theory of the Squeeze on Tradeables', Centre for Banking and International Finance Discussion Paper, The City University and Oxford Economic Papers.
Levich, R. (1979). 'The Efficiency of Markets for Foreign Exchange' in R. Dornbusch and J. A. Frenkel, *International Economic Policy: Theory and Evidence* (Johns Hopkins, Baltimore).
Wood, G. E. (1975). 'Senile Industry Protection', *Southern Economic Journal* (January).

1 Floating Exchange Rates: the Lessons of Experience

Roy A. Batchelor and Geoffrey E. Wood

INTRODUCTION

Economists often make bad predictions and hand out bad advice. As often, their excuse is that the world never stands still long enough to allow current theories to bear fruit in the fields of prediction and policy-making. This excuse can, however, hardly be advanced in discussions of exchange rate theory or policy; our experience of exchange rate regimes has been extraordinarily rich, and the changes in those regimes have followed a clearly discernible pattern: In the twentieth century alone, international trade and payments among developed nations have been conducted in three periods under fixed exchange rates – the pre-1914 gold standard, the resurrected gold standard of the late 1920s and early 1930s, and the *de facto* dollar standard of the 1950s and 1960s – and in the three succeeding periods of floating exchange rates – in the 1920s, the mid-1930s, and the 1970s.

Both regimes have operated during times of rapid growth, and both have also operated throughout periods of general recession. The striking alternation in exchange rate regime is thus not obviously associated with cycles in real economic activity. Nor is it obviously associated with changes in monetary conditions. Both fixed and floating regimes have been sustained through years of general monetary deflation, in the 1930s, through the general inflation in the period 1960–80, and through a period of peculiarly diverse monetary experience in the 1920s.

Our inference is that the pendulum swings in exchange market regime are not attributable to objective economic conditions. They are, rather, due to the ambivalent attitudes of national monetary authorities, who desire stability in international exchanges but at the same time make independent discretionary interventions in the domestic economy. It is technically impossible to meet both objectives. At times the desire for stability has asserted itself, exchange rates have been pegged, and monetary pressures have been allowed to accumulate. These pressures ultimately make the political balance between the desirability of stable exchange rates and the desirability of monetary independence swing towards floating the exchange rate. During floating, however, a nostalgia for stability returns, and grows as memories of the costs of exchange rate pegging recede year by year, and so the extent of intervention increases once more.

The strength of current nostalgia for a return to fixed rates in the United Kingdom and in the developed world as a whole may be gauged from the two recent quotations below, the first from the Governor of the Bank of England, the second from the Annual Report of the Bank for International Settlements:

Exchange market expectations are on occasions clearly extrapolative, feeding on themselves. At such times official intervention may be the only way of avoiding extreme and unnecessary instability.
. . . . . Moreover while, in my view, the influence of the authorities in stabilising expectations is likely to be greater if they are ready, and seen to be ready, to ride out, in the short run, conflicts between domestic and external objectives, a certain amount of elasticity in the pursuit of both may be the best way to permit temporary disturbances to wash through without prejudice to either. (The Rt. Hon. Gordon Richardson, 1979)

The other additional element of strength [in the world economy] lies in the revised attitudes of most industrial countries towards exchange rate fluctuations. The western industrial world confronted the 1974 oil crisis with the newly acquired belief that floating exchange rates were better suited to the 1970s than the Bretton Woods system of pegged but adjustable rates. We now know that this change of mind did a lot of damage in its exaggeration. . . . the new attitude of authorities in several countries towards exchange rate developments was partially responsible for the 'vicious circle' developments in Europe and for the repeated dollar crises of more recent years. This attitude has now been revised. There is a formal commitment to ensuring exchange rate stability within the EMS; and, while no such commitment has been undertaken outside the EMS, domestic monetary measures explicitly taken with balance of payments considerations in mind clearly show the authorities *do* care about the exchange rate. (Bank for International settlements, 1980)

The balance of evidence thus appears, to the agents of intervention at least, to be delicately poised and they seem to infer from this that the most desirable exchange rate regime is some compromise system of 'managed floating'. But the evidence adduced in these current arguments relates to the short span of recent experience with floating. Actions taken from such a narrow perspective clearly run the risk of perpetuating the swings in fashion which have characterised the past sixty years. Our view is that we should consider all of the lessons of the twentieth-century history of foreign exchanges, and that only on that basis is it possible to decide whether the present aspirations of central banks are sensible or even practicable.

The lessons have been of two kinds. First, we have accumulated many theoretical insights into exchange rate determination and balance of payments movements. Second, we have accumulated a mass of empirical evidence against which theory and policy proposals can be tested. We therefore start our investigations below by setting out a fairly general and widely acceptable view of how in principle exchange rates are determined, and examine within this framework what precise motives central bankers and others have for wishing to fix exchange rates. The model is described in more detail in Batchelor and Horne (1980). We then carry out a series of statistical tests on the trends, variability and stability of floating exchange rates, using data from the 1920s, 1930s and 1970s, to decide whether current dissatisfaction with the workings of exchange markets is justified. Finally we consider whether, in the light of our results, the workings of these markets could be improved by an increase in official intervention of the kind advocated by central bankers.

EXCHANGE RATES IN THEORY

A number of apparently distinctive theories of the behaviour of flexible exchange rates have been developed over the past decade. Much of this work builds on ideas first articulated in the 1920s by Cassel (1922), Keynes (1923) and others. Among the modern presentations a distinction must be drawn between theories which view the exchange rate as a mechanism for equilibrating goods, capital and money flows between pairs of countries, and theories which view the exchange rate as a measure of the terms on which agents who hold stocks of currencies as assets are prepared to trade one against another. Overlapping these so-called 'structural' and 'asset-pricing' theories, a number of other conceptions of exchange rate determination have developed, most notably the 'monetary approach', the 'purchasing power parity' and 'interest parity' relationships, and pure 'currency substitution' models.

Our interpretation of these developments is that the *asset pricing model* dominates the *structural model* in terms of the insights it gives into exchange rate behaviour. In principle, both approaches should give equivalent results, since equilibrium in the balance of payments requires that net goods flows and capital flows be exact offsets to any changes in the stocks of national currencies held abroad. In practice, however, the current and capital accounts of the balance of payments are scarcely ever considered as passively adjusting to changes in currency preferences. Quite the opposite is true. Further, to implement the structural approach, we require a detailed understanding of the behaviour of the various heterogeneous components of current and capital accounts. The structural approach to exchange rate determination thus appears an unreliable and unnecessarily oblique approach to what is, after all, the relative price of two moneys. The asset demand approach determines such relative prices directly.

This advantage of directness is also claimed as the main virtue of the *monetary approach to the balance of payments* under fixed exchange rates over its main rival, the absorption approach. The monetary approach to exchange rate determination is not, however, the same thing as the full asset-pricing approach. Standard portfolio theory suggests that assets are held for the returns they yield, for their intrinsic lack of risk, and for the contribution they make to hedging the risks inherent in the rest of the portfolio. The monetary theory considers only the first of these factors. It asserts that currencies are held only because of the real purchasing power they command over goods produced in the issuing country and, further, that monetary growth is the main source of change in real purchasing power. A permanent rise in the rate of money growth in one country relative to money growth in the world as a whole will raise the relative prices of that country's goods, and so reduce the relative real value of the stocks of domestic currency held internally and externally. In other words, the monetary approach is concerned exclusively with changes in the rate of return to currency holdings. This means that in circumstances where currencies are marked down because of, say, an increase in the variability of monetary policy or an increase in the synchronisation of one country's inflation rate with the world inflation rate, the monetary theory has no explanatory power. This is why most primitive theories of sterling's behaviour broke down after 1978. The existence of North Sea oil effectively insulated the United Kingdom economy from the inflationary or recessionary impacts of oil price shocks on the rest of the developed world. The reduced covariance of the real value of sterling with the real purchasing power afforded by other currencies caused investors to raise substantially the terms on which they traded it against other components of their currency portfolios.

The *purchasing power parity* relationship is simply a shorthand way of expressing the idea that currencies are valued only for their relative purchasing power over currently produced goods, without necessarily assuming a monetary basis for inflation. It asserts that

$$P = SP^f \tag{1}$$

where S is the spot exchange rate expressed as the domestic price of foreign currency, and P and P^f are domestic and foreign price levels averaged over some period long enough for investors to distinguish permanent changes in prices from transitory fluctuations. From our arguments above, this should be considered as a special case of the portfolio relationships

$$S = (1 + Q)(P/P^f) \tag{2}$$

$$Q = a(\text{Var } P - \text{Var } P^f) + b \text{ Cov } (P, P^f) \tag{3}$$

where the subjective 'risk premium' Q depends on the variability of domestic inflation and the covariance of domestic with world inflation. Alternatively it can be regarded as a factor which corrects any bias due to the omission of asset prices from the indexes P and P^f. Turning equation (2) around, the factor $1 + Q$ can be seen to measure the ratio of prices of domestic and foreign national products when these prices are expressed in terms of a common currency. This is often termed the '*real exchange rate*'. Purchasing power parity clearly holds in an absolute sense only if $a = b = 0$, and explains movements over time only if the relative variance and covariance terms in (3) are constant.

Purchasing power parity is a long-run *behavioural* relationship which holds only on average over time, and only then if no changes occur in the risk premium. There are in addition *arbitrage* relationships which may affect real resource allocation and make spot exchange rates deviate from purchasing power parity in the short run. Conditions for no arbitrage (equilibrium) in the goods account and capital account of the balance of payments are expressed, respectively, in the 'law of one price' and the 'interest parity' conditions:

$$P^T = SP^{fT} \tag{4}$$

$$(1 + R^f) = (1 + R)S/F \tag{5}$$

where P^T and P^{fT} are the prices of domestic and foreign tradeable goods (exports and import substitutes), R and R^f are rates of return on domestic and foreign bonds and F is the forward exchange rate appropriate to the common maturity of these bonds.

Two points should be noted about the law of one price. First, since goods flows take time to respond to competitive pressures, it does not hold from day to day but more probably from year to year. Second, in contrast to the purchasing power parity relationship, it is a statement about traded goods prices, not about exchange rate behaviour. Putting (4) together with the purchasing power parity theory of exchange rate behaviour in fact yields

$$\frac{P^T}{P} = (1 + Q)\frac{P^{fT}}{p^f} \tag{6}$$

This shows that the price of domestic traded goods relative to domestic prices in general will move proportionally with these prices in the rest of the world. However, the factor of proportion $(1 + Q)$, the real exchange rate, may vary. If the risk premium on the domestic currency is raised, then tradeable goods prices will rise relative to non-tradeable goods prices, attracting resources into the tradeable goods sector; if the risk premium falls, then the tradeable goods sector will be squeezed, as its prices must in the long run fall relative to non-tradeable goods prices.

Two points should also be made about the interest parity relationship (5). First, capital markets are highly responsive to competitive pressures, and their efficiency is such that this interest parity relationship holds from day to day. Short-run exchange rate movements must therefore be dominated by movements in the elements of this equation – that is, by movements in interest rates and forward exchange rates. Second, if the forward market is, like the spot market, composed of risk-averse agents evaluating the properties of future stocks of currencies as assets, then the forward rate F will settle at the average expected future spot rate plus a risk premium. That is:

$$F = S^e + cQ^e \tag{7}$$

Short-run changes in exchange rate expectations or in perceptions of risk will therefore have the effect of changing the actual current spot rate by the same amount, assuming relative interest rates are fixed.

As shown in Batchelor (1980), further analysis of the interest parity relationship lets us distinguish four sources of possible spot rate volatility in a flexible exchange rate system. The volatility may be *extrinsic* due to fluctuations in F which are in turn due to uncertainties about the mean long-term future spot rate S^e, changes in its variability, or changes in its covariance with other rates. Since these depend in turn on the combination of real and monetary conditions which determine price movements, extrinsic volatility may be further broken down into that part which is genuinely *autonomous*, due to the possibility of changes in tastes or technologies, or to resource discoveries, and that part which is *induced* by uncertainties over the authorities' monetary policy or their attitude to exchange market intervention.

Alternatively, short-run fluctuations in spot exchange rates may be *intrinsic*. Even if expectations are fully *rational* in the technical sense, so that S^e is certainly an unbiased prediction of future spot rates, spot exchange rates may deviate from the equilibrium in the short run. This would happen when, following a monetary expansion, domestic interest rates fell at the same time as the expected spot rate rose (depreciated). If expectations are *extrapolative* an extra degree of intrinsic volatility is introduced into the short-run exchange rate, since the fact of a movement in the expected spot rate will in itself cause a further movement in the same direction, even though this may carry the rate beyond that which would be rationally expected. Only if exchange rates overshoot their equilibrium value as a result of this last kind of behaviour can we properly blame 'destabilising speculation' for observed fluctuations in currency values.

We conclude that the theorising of the past decade, building on foundations laid in the interwar period, reduces to two statements about exchange rate behaviour. The trend in any exchange rate is dominated by movements in relative rates of inflation, modifed by changes in a risk premium. The volatility of any exchange rate in the short term can be attributed to real and monetary factors impinging on interest rates, and to the simultaneous effects of these factors on exchange rate expectations.

EXCHANGE RATE MANAGEMENT

Management of exchange rates can be effected at various levels and in various ways. The strongest degree of control occurs as a result of multilateral agreement to defend a stable set of parities. This principle governed international settlements for two decades following the Bretton Woods agreement of 1944, and was also enshrined in the network of parallel national legislation which governed central bank operations under the pre-1914 gold standard, and in the late 1920s. In other periods a range of weaker attempts to manage exchange rates has been made by monetary authorities. These have consisted either of unilateral policies, or of multilateral policies built around a shifting set of parities. The 'snake' arrangement, and the current European Monetary System, are representative of this latter group of policies. The behaviour of the United States in the early 1930s, or of the United Kingdom in the mid-1970s, in trying to maintain 'constant competitiveness', is typical of the former.

In this paper we are interested in comparing the performance of an essentially flexible exchange rate regime subject to these weak, stabilising or targetting, forms of intervention, with the performance of the regime with no intervention. Although no stretch of years has ever been completely free from central bank intervention in the foreign exchanges, the low level of reserves in most countries – except perhaps, the Netherlands – in the years following the end of the 1914–18 war make the early 1920s the closest approximation to a free float. By contrast policies in the 1970s were moderately interventionist, and the 1930s strongly so, as a result of the operations of the massive stabilisation funds operated by the major economies from the late 1920s onwards. Note that the degree of intervention during the 1920s and 1930s was largely pre-determined by the circumstances of the world economy at the very start of each decade.

The motives for weak forms of intervention are in part similar to those used to justify pegging exchange rates completely. Freely floating exchange rates are alleged to confer one benefit and incur one cost in terms of economic efficiency. They confer the benefit of 'monetary independence', in the sense that the rate of domestic inflation can be tailored to domestic objectives without fear that any deviation from the world rate of inflation will trigger a balance of payments crisis. This relies on compensating movements of the spot exchange rate maintaining the purchasing power parity condition (1), thereby ensuring that no net money flows occur in response to changes in the price ratio P/P^f. The efficiency cost of flexible exchange rates is that traders are made uncertain as to the value, in terms of its domestic purchasing power, of expected future receipts of or payments in foreign currency. At a cost, they can buy insurance cover against this uncertainty in the forward exchange market (or by invoicing strategy (Carse, Williamson and

Wood, 1980),) but still run the risk that the future spot rate will differ from the current forward rate.

Critics of freely floating exchange rates argue that in practice, because of lags in adjustment to purchasing power parity, monetary independence is not achieved, so that these benefits of floating are illusory. Moreover, they argue that the various intrinsic or autonomous sources of instability in the spot exchange market make the insurance and forecasting problems of traders very costly indeed. Action to *stabilise* exchange rates would therefore involve little sacrifice in terms of general inflation objectives while, by relieving traders of exchange risk and pooling these risks centrally, a policy of exchange rate management would contribute to economic efficiency. By extension, further gains could be captured by pooling central bank risks through some stronger multilateral swap arrangements. A different case for exchange rate policy is often made, on distributional rather than allocative efficiency grounds. As we have seen, changes in the exchange rate not associated with relative price changes – that is, changes in the real exchange rate – act as subsidies to or taxes on the tradeable goods sector. If the authorities wish to expand that sector beyond the size which its competitive position justifies, then a subsidy to the sector can be conferred by defending an exchange rate below purchasing power parity. Such a policy of *targetting* the exchange rate might seem desirable if, say, export growth was thought to be particularly valuable in promoting growth in general, or if tradeable goods industries were having trouble in adjusting to an appreciation in the real exchange rate. Two points should be noted about such a policy of 'exchange rate protection'. First, it has to be compared with alternative fiscal means of achieving the same distributional objective (Corden, 1980). Second, if purchasing power parity holds in the long run, the policy eventually must consist of either a more expansionary monetary policy (which raises P) or a more erratic monetary or fiscal policy (which raises Q). Neither of these options seems particularly attractive, and a high price may be involved in sustained exchange rate targetting.

Two empirical aspects of floating exchange rate systems appear crucial to any assessment of the value of stabilising or targetting exchange rate policies.

The first is the length of time taken for purchasing power parity to be re-established after any disturbance. If this lag in adjustment is long, then balance of payments imbalances will persist long enough to cause real resources to be temporarily shifted between tradeable and untradeable sectors. If the lag is short, then no real allocative disturbances will be implied by exchange rate fluctuations. Moreover, if the lag in adjustment to purchasing power parity is long, the undesirable corollaries of exchange rate targetry – the pursuit of inflationary or erratic domestic policies – need not emerge for some time.

The second empirical question concerns the size and nature of exchange rate volatility. If volatility is large and intrinsic in any flexible exchange rate system, then continuous stabilising official intervention may be useful and effective. If volatility is due to extrinsic, autonomous, features of the world economy, then stabilising intervention may also be justified when occasion demands. The drawback in such stabilising policies is that, by misleading or diffusing exchange rate expectations, they may lead to a degree of induced exchange rate instability. If volatility proves to be induced by confusions sown by the intervention policy itself, then attempts at stabilisation are clearly self-defeating.

The two succeeding sections consider in turn historical evidence on the speed of convergence to purchasing power parity, and on the size and origins of exchange rate volatility.

CONVERGENCE TO PURCHASING POWER PARITY

A number of studies have formally investigated the validity of the assumption that purchasing power parity is maintained by floating exchange rates in the long run (Officer, 1976). Most start from the regression

$$\ln (S_t) = d_0 + d_1 \ln (P_t/P_t^f) + u_t \qquad (8)$$

and test whether the elasticity term d_1 is unity, and whether the residual u_t is small. Results on monthly data from the 1920s, the 1930s and the mid-1970s indicate that $d_1 = 1$ as required, but that u_t varies systematically in the short run, so that purchasing power parity is not continuously maintained. This means that the periods considered have not been subjected to any large systematic shifts in the real exchange rate $(1 + Q)$, but that purchasing power parity is in no sense a complete theory of what did cause exchange rate fluctuations. Our theoretical contention that interest parity is continuously maintained within narrow limits – and that exchange rate fluctuations can be understood in terms of the dynamics of this relation – is, however, supported by the findings of Einzig (1937) on the 1920s and 1930s, and those of Frenkel and Levich (1975) and Aliber (1978) in the 1970s.

For purposes of assessing whether monetary independence is achievable under floating, the studies of purchasing power parity cited above have one major shortcoming. They tell us only whether exchange rates offset relative price movements over the sample period of the regression taken as a whole. A regression like equation (8) cannot tell us with what rapidity this offsetting behaviour occurred – the crucial issue for monetary independence. Only one study, by Hodgson and Phelps (1975) on 1920s data, investigates the dynamics of the purchasing power parity relationship, and that study assumes a smooth lagged adjustment of exchange rates to price movements. Our theory suggested, however, that convergence would not be smooth, and that if anything spot rates were liable to lead to price changes in time, because of the impact of exchange rate expectations on forward exchange rates.

To assess whether short-run deviations from purchasing power parity can persist long enough to cause real effects, we therefore run a series of regressions of the form

$$\ln(S_t) - \ln(S_{t-1}) = e_0 + e_1\{\ln(P_t/P_t^f) - \ln(P_{t-1}/P_{t-1}^f)\} + v_t \quad (9)$$

where v_t is a zero-mean disturbance term. The time period t is taken, successively, as one month, one quarter, one half-year, and one year, and the spot rates and prices are measured as averages within these periods. If $e_0 = 0$ there is no systematic trend from period to period other than that due to relative price movements. If $e_1 = 1$, then as relative prices change from one period to the next the spot rate also changes by an exactly offsetting amount. Test of $e_0 = 0$ and $e_1 = 1$ constitute, respectively, tests of the long-run and short-run (within-period) validity of the purchasing power parity constraint.

The results of estimating these parameters from *monthly* data on six sterling exchange rates in the three floating rate periods 1921–6, 1931–6, and 1973–8 are shown on Table 1.1. The parameter e_0 has been multiplied by 12×100 to convert it into a percentage per annum measure of exchange rate 'drift'. Beneath the estimated coefficients are t-statistics testing whether $e_0 = 0$ and $e_1 = 1$; given the large size of our monthly data sample these t-statistics must be at least 1.64 if the constraints are to be rejected at the 5 per cent significance level. Alongside the estimated coefficients we also show two measures of the explanatory power of the purchasing power hypothesis with respect to changes in exchange rates: $\overline{R}^2$ measures the percentage of the total variation in these month-to-month changes explained by current relative price movements, while s, the standard error of the regression, measures the average absolute size of the residual term v. No significant low-order

TABLE 1.1 Monthly Exchange Rate Changes and Relative Inflation[a]

Country	1921–6 Coefficients e_0	e_1	1921–6 Statistics $\overline{R}^2/s$	1931–6 Coefficients e_0	e_1	1931–6 Statistics $\overline{R}^2/s$	1973–8 Coefficients e_0	e_1	1973–8 Statistics $\overline{R}^2/s$
Belgium	−11.0 (1.5)	1.5 (2.7)	0.51 / 4.60	2.2 (0.6)	2.2 (7.7)	0.73 / (2.56)	−8.1 (1.6)	0.2 (2.8)	0.00 / 2.78
France	−3.3 (0.5)	1.4 (2.7)	0.55 / 4.45	−0.0 (0.1)	1.4 (2.6)	0.52 / 2.98	0.5 (0.1)	0.6 (2.0)	0.10 / 2.56
Germany	7.5 (0.3)	1.0 (1.8)	0.98 / 12.89	–	–	–	−17.1 (2.4)	−0.5 (2.9)	0.00 / 3.01
Netherlands	3.5 (1.2)	0.2 (6.2)	0.01 / 2.01	−0.1 (0.0)	1.4 (2.0)	0.39 / 2.87	−10.6 (2.3)	0.0 (4.4)	0.01 / 2.87
Sweden	0.2 (0.1)	−0.1 (8.5)	0.00 / 1.42	13.3 (0.7)	0.6 (2.8)	0.15 / 1.34	−2.9 (0.7)	0.3 (2.3)	0.01 / 2.83
United States	2.3 (0.6)	0.6 (2.6)	0.14 / 2.51	0.1 (0.2)	1.4 (1.6)	0.30 / 3.00	−2.3 (0.6)	0.1 (3.7)	0.02 / 2.43

Source: data from Tinbergen (1934), Derksen (1938), International Monetary Fund (1973–9).

[a] Figures in parentheses are *t*-statistics testing the restrictions $e_0 = 0$, $e_1 = 1$; the estimated parameter e_0 has been multiplied to give a *per cent per annum* figure.

serial correlation was detected in any of the regressions, so the test statistics for this are not reported.

Three interesting differences between the two earlier periods, the 1920s and 1930s, and the 1970s, are revealed by the regressions of Table 1.1. First, the independent trend terms e_0 are invariably insignificant in the interwar periods, whereas the mark rate and the guilder rate show signs of non-price-related trends in the 1970s. With these exceptions exchange rate movements have succeeded in offsetting relative price movements over six-year periods of floating, a finding in conformity with the results of the earlier studies cited above.

Second, in statistical terms none of the slope coefficients e_1 is close to unity. In other words, floating exchange rates have failed to offset month-to-month movements in relative prices in all periods. In the 1920s, the French and Belgian francs moved more than proportionately: in the 1930s, this is also true of the sterling-dollar and -guilder rates: but in the 1970s exchange rates have moved only slowly towards their long-run equilibrium and show none of this anticipatory behaviour.

Third, short-run price movements explain hardly any of the month-to-month exchange rate changes in the recent float, $\overline{R}^2$ being at most 0.1. In the 1920s and 1930s, however, the non-inflation-related fluctuations are much less dominant, and the $\overline{R}^2$ correspondingly higher. The exceptions are the heavily managed Dutch guilder and the relatively thinly traded Swedish kronor, currencies which would not be regarded as unstable on more conventional criteria.

Table 1.2 lists the regression results which emerged by the stage of using *annual* average data. As aggregation over time proceeds, it becomes progressively more difficult to reject the hypothesis $e_1 = 1$. This is only marginally due to the fact that the progressive fall in the number of data points raises the critical value of the t-statistic from 1.64 towards 2.01. By the time we consider changes in annual averages only one spot rate – the Dutch guilder – has failed to display convergence to purchasing power parity in the 1920s, and all currencies except the Belgian franc converged satisfactorily in the 1930s and 1970s.

Monetary shocks and other factors which cause changes in the trend of relative prices will thus be offset by exchange rate movements within about a year. Is this compensating movement sufficiently rapid to ensure that no significant real resource movements are caused by unilateral changes in monetary policy? We have little evidence on the lags between prices and international goods flows in the 1920s and 1930s. A typical investigation of trade elasticities in the 1960s and 1970s by Dornbusch and Krugman (1976) found that the total size of responses was modest

TABLE 1.2 Annual Exchange Rate Changes and Relative Inflation

Country	1921–6 Coefficients		1921–6 Statistics	1931–6 Coefficients		1931–6 Statistics	1973–8 Coefficients		1973–8 Statistics
	e_0	e_1	$\overline{R}^2 / s$	e_0	e_1	$\overline{R}^2 / s$	e_0	e_1	$\overline{R}^2 / s$
Belgium	9.0	0.7	0.24	2.8	1.7	0.97	7.4	0.2	0.00
	(0.2)	(0.9)	15.80	(2.1)	(4.7)	2.97	(1.2)	(1.8)	5.66
France	−6.2	1.6	0.66	−1.0	1.3	0.64	2.1	0.7	0.65
	(1.2)	(1.1)	7.59	(0.3)	(0.8)	7.57	(0.6)	(1.6)	5.24
Germany	−14.4	1.0	0.99	n.a.	—	—	−8.1	0.3	0.01
	(0.3)	(0.5)	4.56				(0.7)	(0.9)	5.88
Netherlands	2.4	0.1	0.01	3.3	2.2	0.66	0.1	0.9	0.13
	(1.5)	(3.3)	3.56	(0.7)	(1.6)	6.78	(0.0)	(0.2)	4.44
Sweden	0.7	1.0	0.50	1.5	0.3	−0.26	2.3	1.0	0.16
	(1.4)	(0.1)	3.48	(1.3)	(1.1)	2.71	(0.4)	(0.0)	9.44
United States	2.2	0.6	0.85	0.9	1.7	0.41	4.7	1.1	0.10
	(0.7)	(0.4)	2.49	(0.2)	(0.8)	13.70	(0.5)	(0.2)	10.23

See notes to Table 1.1

and that it took 12–18 months for half of the real effects of deviations from purchasing power parity to become apparent. Even longer, three-year, average lags have been found by Junz and Rhomberg (1973). Since much of the data used in these studies came from fixed rate periods, when most changes in price competitiveness could be considered permanent, it is extremely unlikely that they could overestimate the slowness of adjustment of trade flows under a pure floating exchange rate regime.

Taken in conjunction with such estimates our findings suggest that, with few exceptions, it was possible to pursue independent monetary policies under the conditions of floating in the 1920s, 1930s and 1970s. Conversely, the practice of defending exchange rates at artificial parities would only temporarily redistribute income between tradeable and untradeable goods sectors, and would within a year involve substantial accommodating changes in monetary policy. The benefits adduced for flexible exchange rates thus appear genuine.

EXCHANGE RATE VOLATILITY

We turn now to a consideration of the size and origins of the costs which they impose. Our first problem is to measure the volatility of exchange rates in an appropriate way. By far the simplest measure is the root mean square deviation of rates from their average value in each period of floating, that is

$$I(S) = (100/\overline{S}) \left\{ \sum_{t-1}^{T} (S_t - \overline{S})^2 / (T-1) \right\}^{\frac{1}{2}} \qquad (10)$$

where $\overline{S}$ is this average rate, and t relates to the finest possible division of the period.

For the purpose of assessing the seriousness of exchange rate fluctuations this index has the desirable property that large deviations from the mean give a disproportionately large boost to the index. In other words, a quadratic loss function is imputed to traders. The formula has the serious disadvantage, however, that no allowance is made for whether the exchange rate deviation was predictable or unpredictable. Thus a steady trend in the exchange rate will produce a larger index $I(S)$ the larger the trend. But a rapid trend in an exchange rate may be no more difficult for traders to anticipate than a mild trend, and so be no more costly in terms of uncertainty and the cost of cover.

A more appropriate index, developed in Batchelor (1979), is the measure

$$J(S) = (100/\overline{S}) \left\{ \sum_{t-1}^{T} (S_t - S_t^e)^2 / (T-1) \right\}^{\frac{1}{2}} \qquad (11)$$

where S_t^e is the traders' expectations of the exchange rate. The exact size of the instability measure then depends (other things being equal) on the sophistication which we impute to traders. The series S_t^e may be derived from a simple time trend, from a more complicated time-series rule such as an ARIMA model, or from some structural model.

Table 1.3 displays the $I(S)$ indexes, and the $J(S)$ indexes derived from simple trend estimates of S^e and from an ARIMA $(2, 1, 1)$ model of S^e. These indexes have been computed from monthly data for all currencies in the floating rate periods. The measures of unpredictability, the $J(S)$, clearly give a more sanguine picture of exchange rate volatility than do the unadjusted measures of volatility $I(S)$. Indeed if we are prepared to impute sophisticated forecasting behaviour to traders, only around 3 per cent of observed exchange rate fluctuations were unanticipated in each historical period.

The general patterns of volatility across periods and across currencies are rather similar irrespective of whether expectations are assumed to follow a simple trend or the more complex ARIMA model. Currency values were on average less predictable in the 1930s than in the 1920s and 1970s. The ranking of currencies is not, however, maintained over time. The relatively volatile rates in the 1920s were the Belgian and French francs – and of course the German mark under hyperinflation. In the 1930s uncertainty was also concentrated around the dollar-sterling rate. But in the 1970s all rates have proved equally unpredictable.

By measuring volatility in terms of unpredictability we have moved closer to assessing the seriousness of exchange rate flexibility for resource allocation. However, the general level of uncertainty in the economy may have been different in the 1920s, the 1930s and the 1970s, and in such circumstances these absolute measures of volatility tell us little about the contribution of exchange rate uncertainty to the general level of uncertainty. We have therefore developed a *relative* measure of volatility, by taking the ratio of measured exchange rate volatility to the similarly measured volatility of relative goods prices.

Assuming a simple trend method of exchange rate and price forecasting, the figures shown on Table 1.4 are obtained for the three periods of floating. In the 1920s, the ratio of exchange rate to relative price volatility is 1.1; in the 1930s it is as high as 2.1; and in the 1970s the

TABLE 1.3 Alternative Measures of Exchange Rate Volatility

Country	1921–6		1931–6		1973–8	
	Absolute *I(S)*	Relative *Trend ARIMA*	Absolute *I(S)*	Relative *Trend ARIMA*	Absolute *I(S)*	Relative *Trend ARIMA*
Belgium	23.5	11.9 3.5	16.0	15.7 5.0	18.4	4.9 2.7
France	21.9	11.5 3.9	18.1	11.7 4.2	12.0	6.0 2.7
Germany	507.9	382.3 55.2	n.a.	n.a. n.a.	20.9	5.3 3.0
Netherlands	8.3	3.0 1.7	17.8	10.5 3.6	19.8	5.1 2.8
Sweden	11.7	3.4 2.2	3.2	2.5 1.5	13.3	9.0 4.1
United States	10.7	5.3 2.0	14.2	13.0 3.4	14.0	8.3 2.6
Unweighted average	15.2	7.0 2.7	13.9	10.7 3.5	16.4	6.4 3.0

Source: Data as in Table 1.1

TABLE 1.4 The Volatility of Exchange Rates and Relative Prices

Country	1921–6 Exchange rate	1921–6 Relative price	Ratio	1931–6 Exchange rate	1931–6 Relative price	Ratio	1973–8 Exchange rate	1973–8 Relative price	Ratio
Belgium	11.8	9.9	1.2	15.7	8.4	1.9	4.9	3.5	1.4
France	11.5	6.4	1.8	11.7	6.5	1.8	6.0	5.7	1.1
Germany	382.3	387.4	1.0	n.a.	n.a.		5.3	2.7	2.0
Netherlands	3.0	4.1	0.7	10.5	3.8	2.8	5.1	2.0	1.8
Sweden	3.4	2.9	1.2	2.5	1.8	1.4	9.0	6.2	1.5
United States	5.3	7.1	0.7	13.0	5.7	2.3	8.3	4.1	2.0
Unweighted average	7.0[a]	6.1[a]	1.1	10.7[a]	5.2[a]	2.1	6.4	4.2	1.6

[a] Excluding Germany.

mean ratio falls midway between these extremes at 1.6. There is little disparity across countries in this ranking. Only in France were exchange rates in the 1920s more volatile relative to price movements than in the 1930s and 1970s. It is evident that the volatility of exchange rates in the 1920s constitutes a better advertisement for floating exchange rates than does the superficially similar experience of the 1970s, in that it was achieved against a background of less stable price movements.

The Sources of Volatility

Our theoretical model indicated that, if exchange rate volatility were due to intrinsic 'overshooting', we should observe much greater volatility in spot exchange rates than in relative prices. The experience of the 1920s should therefore lead us to conclude that such intrinsic overshooting in exchange markets is not a universal feature of flexible rate regimes. Since the evidence on purchasing power and interest parity suggests that essentially the same model operated in all the periods considered, the volatility observed in the 1930s and the 1970s must be regarded as extrinsic, imposed by conditions peculiar to these periods. The issue is, then, whether the relatively greater extrinsic volatility of the 1930s and 1970s was autonomous, due to a great degree of monetary and real disturbance, or whether it was induced by the authorities' exchange rate policy.

Some summary statistics on the variability of monetary and real conditions in the 1920s, the 1930s and the 1970s are given in Table 1.5. The 1920s saw by far the highest and most variable rates of real growth. The 1970s saw the highest rates of monetary growth, but in terms of its variability this period was no more unsettled than the 1920s or 1930s. The qualitative characteristics of this table have been collected in Table 1.6, along with our earlier judgement that exchange rate management was most strict in the 1930s, less strict in the 1970s, and weakest in the 1920s. These rankings of autonomous and policy factors are set against our findings on absolute and relative exchange rate volatility.

Three conclusions stand out from the Table 1.6. First, on any measure exchange rate volatility is not correlated with real economic disturbances. The 1920s was much the most unsettled period for all countries except, perhaps, the United States. Yet in the 1920s absolute exchange rate volatility was low, and compared to the large disturbances in relative prices could be considered very low.

Second, while there is no congruence between the average rate of monetary expansion and either measure of exchange rate volatility,

TABLE 1.5 Trends and Fluctuations in Real and Monetary Growth[a]

Country	Measure	1921–6		1931–6		1973–8	
		Real growth	Monetary expansion	Real growth	Monetary expansion	Real growth	Monetary expansion
Belgium	mean	8.7	9.0	-0.8	3.1	1.8	8.4
	s.d.	13.0	5.9	9.5	4.4	5.9	3.1
France	mean	14.0	8.7	-3.8	2.4	2.4	11.3
	s.d.	17.3	8.5	9.3	6.1	4.6	2.4
Germany	mean	n.a.	n.a.	5.9	1.9	1.7	9.5
	s.d.			16.3	7.1	4.6	5.0
Netherlands	mean	n.a.	-0.7	-1.8	-1.7	2.6	9.5
	s.d.		2.1	6.1	4.0	4.0	6.1
Sweden	mean	5.1	-3.0	5.1	1.6	0.6	12.4
	s.d.	13.3	2.4	10.3	3.2	4.4	6.0
United Kingdom	mean	2.1	-1.1	4.4	6.5	1.3	14.0
	s.d.	11.3	1.6	5.9	4.9	4.4	5.4
United States	mean	5.6	4.2	3.7	1.2	3.6	5.6
	s.d.	14.5	5.5	17.6	9.5	6.5	1.3
Unweighted	mean	7.1	2.9	1.4	2.1	2.0	10.1
Averages	s.d.	13.9	4.3	10.7	5.6	4.9	4.2

Source: Data from Mitchell (1975); International Monetary Fund (1979).
[a] Per cent per annum.

TABLE 1.6 Autonomous and Induced Factors in Relative Exchange Rate
                                Volatility

Factor	Period		
	1921–6	*1931–6*	*1973–8*
Real growth	fast	slow	moderate
variability	high	moderate	low
Monetary growth	moderate	slow	fast
variability	moderate	high	low
Management	low	high	moderate
Absolute exchange rate instability	moderate	high	low
Relative exchange rate instability	low	high	moderate

there is a positive association between the variability of monetary
growth and the absolute level of exchange rate volatility. A superficial
comparison of performance in the 1920s, the 1930s and the 1970s might
therefore suggest that the stability of domestic monetary policy is more
important than the nature of exchange rate intervention in reducing
short-run fluctuations in exchange rates. This would not, however,
explain why, in the relatively calm monetary conditions of the 1970s,
exchange rate fluctuations have not been reduced even more, to the same
dimensions as fluctuations in goods prices.

This may be explained by our third observation on the contents of
Table 1.6. It is that there is an exact match between the ranking of
periods according to the degree of intervention, and their ranking
according to the critical measure of relative exchange rate volatility.
Correlation does not, of course, indicate what is cause and what is effect.
It could conceivably be argued that it was the high relative volatility of
exchange rates which excited a high degree of exchange market
intervention by national governments. However, history argues against
this interpretation. As we noted earlier, exchange rate policy in the 1920s
and 1930s was determined by initial economic and political conditions –
the shortage of reserves after 1918, and the growth of stabilisation funds
in the late 1920s and early 1930s. Subsequent events during these
decades did not change the tenor of intervention policy. Our interpretation of the correlation between relative exchange rate instability and the
degree of intervention is, then, that the latter causes the former – that
exchange rate instability is to a large extent induced. Conversely, while
stable domestic monetary policies can help to stabilise exchange rates,
our reading of history suggests that volatility will not be minimised
unless intervention is also reduced to a minimum.

CONCLUSION

We began with a description of the cycles in official attitudes to exchange rate management. We suggested that this cycle was due to the persistently short perspective in which the merits and demerits of floating were considered. On a longer perspective the empirical evidence shows that the benefits of floating are genuine, and that its main efficiency cost – short-term exchange fluctuation – need not be paid to the extent observed in the 1930s and the 1970s. These short-run fluctuations are in large part associated with the pursuit of exchange rate management policies. To the extent that such policies are aimed at stabilising rates the evidence is, then, that they are in practice self-defeating. To the extent that management is aimed at a target depreciation, to subsidise producers of exports or import substitutes, the costs of induced exchange rate volatility must be recognised, and subtracted from the benefits of any temporary income redistribution which the policy might achieve.

REFERENCES

Aliber, R. Z. (1978). *Exchange Risk and Corporate International Finance* (Macmillan, London).
Bank for International Settlements (1980). *Annual Report* (Basel).
Batchelor, R. A. (1979). 'Must Floating Exchange Rates be Unstable?', Centre for Banking and International Finance, *Annual Monetary Review*, No. 1.
Batchelor, R. A. (1980). 'Independence and Uncertainty under Managed Floating: A Historical Perspective', paper presented to SSRC Quantitative Economic History Study Group, Annual Conference, University of Newcastle-upon-Tyne.
Batchelor, R. A. and Horne, J. (1980). 'Money, Expectations and Exchange Market Adjustment: A Survey', unpublished.
Cassel, G. (1922). *Money and Foreign Exchange after 1914* (London, Constable).
Carse, S., Williamson, J. and Wood G. E. (1980). *The Financing Procedure of British Foreign Trade* (Cambridge University Press).
Corden, W. M. (1981). 'The Exchange Rate, Monetary Policy and North Sea Oil: The Economic Theory of the Squeeze on Tradeables', Centre for Banking and International Finance Discussion Paper, The City University and Oxford Economic Papers.
Derksen, J. B. D. (1938). *International Abstract of Economic Statistics, 1931– 1936*, Permanent Office of the International Statistical Institute (The Hague, 1938).
Dornbusch, R. and Krugman, P. (1976). 'Flexible Exchange Rates in the Short Run', *Brookings Papers in Economic Activity*, no. 3.
Einzig, P. (1937). *The Theory of Forward Exchange* (Macmillan, London).

Frenkel, J. A. and Levich, R. M. (1975). 'Covered Interest Parity: Unexploited Profits?', *Journal of Political Economy*, 83, no. 2, April.

Hodgson, J. S. and Phelps, P. (1975). 'The Distributed Impact of Price Level Variations on Floating Exchange Rates', *Review of Economics and Statistics*, 62, no. 1, February.

International Monetary Fund, *International Financial Statistics?*, various issues 1973-9.

Junz, M. B. and Rhomberg, R. R. (1973) 'Price Competitiveness in Export Trade Among Industrial Countries', *American Economic Review*, 63, Papers and Proceedings.

Keynes, J. M. (1923). *Tract on Monetary Reform*, Chapter 3 (Macmillan, London: Royal Economic Society Edition 1971).

Mitchell, B. R. (1975). *European Historical Statistics 1750-1970* (Macmillan, London).

Officer, L. M. (1976). 'The Purchasing Power Parity Theory of Exchange Rates: A Review', *International Monetary Fund Staff Paper*, 23, no. 1, March.

Richardson, G. (1979). *The Prospects for an International Monetary System*, The Henry Thornton Lecture (The City University, London), November.

Tinbergen, J. (ed.) (1934). *International Abstract of Economic Statistics, 1919-1930*, International Conference of Economic Services (M. Hayez, Brussels).

Comments on 'Floating Exchange Rates: the Lessons of Experience'

B. Brittain

In their paper Roy Batchelor and Geoffrey Wood have discussed a problem which perennially has been at the centre of the economic policy debate. The question is whether monetary policy ought to be encumbered by a commitment to intervene in the foreign exchange market; or, expressed in a way more relevant to the current British policy debate, should monetary policy, already encumbered by a commitment to achieve a monetary target, be further encumbered by a commitment to stabilise the exchange rate; and, if it should, which encumbrance should be thrown off when the two cannot be carried simultaneously?

This question, whether in the general or in the more specific form, transcends the experience of major economies since 1973, the beginning, as defined by Batchelor and Wood, of the most recent period of exchange rate flexibility. Therefore, it is entirely appropriate for the authors to seek to apply the lessons of twentieth-century experience to the current policy debate. The paper is all the more interesting because its conclusion, that *unlimited* exchange rate flexibility is everywhere desirable, even today, belies the choice of British policy-makers in at least 78 of the 110 years since the end of the Franco-Prussian War.

In my brief comment on this paper, I shall summarise the principal points of Batchelor and Wood but I shall spend most of the comment making the two following points of my own. Firstly, evidence presented in the paper does, to be sure, support the contention that exchange rates should be flexible. In my opinion, however, the evidence is equally consistent with precisely the opposite conclusion as well. The second point I should like to make is that the historical evidence capable of allowing one to discriminate between the two positions seems, for at least the continental European economies, to favour some subordination of domestic monetary policy to external considerations. On the basis of these two points, I shall conclude by arguing that the Bank of England might find it worthwhile to consider an upward revision of their monetary target in order to remove some of the pressure from sterling.

It would, of course, be foolish to argue that the recent growth of sterling M3 by almost 20 per cent in the year to mid-August would leave the monetary aggregate within an acceptable upper bound of a revised monetary target. Instead, I would prefer to argue that should the British authorities be seen successfully to be stabilising and then reducing money growth rates, demand for the currency could be perceptibly increased by international diversification into sterling and sterling should be stronger than any model based on purely domestic considerations would predict.

Furthermore, if the Swiss and German experience and subsequent policy actions of 1978–79 were to be taken as a guide, the British authorities should revise their monetary targets to accommodate this shift in money demand.

I would now like to turn to the paper itself. In the paper the authors offer us an adumbrated version of a popular monetarist model of the exchange rate and of prices. The model has the following principal features. Firstly, the money stock is assumed to be the principal source of inflation and is, in addition, assumed to be controlled by the monetary authorities. Therefore, the assumed flow of causality in the model is from money to prices and thence to the exchange rate. If one invokes rational expectations, as the authors sometimes do, the flow of causality is from money to the exchange rate and to prices simultaneously. The second principal feature of the model is that domestic prices, expressed in terms of the local currency, are assumed to equal prices abroad also expressed in the domestic currency once correction is made for certain risk factors that may keep the currency at a premium over its level as implied by cross-country price comparisons. This is the purchasing power parity condition.

The authors test the model principally by testing whether the purchasing power parity condition holds. They undertake this test using bilateral comparisons of the sterling exchange rate with relative prices in France, Germany, the Netherlands, Sweden and the United States. They run the tests on monthly and annual data for the three periods 1921–26, 1931–36 and 1973–78 and conclude that purchasing power parity holds when exchange rates are flexible. Standard errors of regressions of the rate of change of the sterling exchange rate against inflation differentials show that, two-thirds of the time, rates of currency change diverge from inflation differentials by less than about 6 per cent per annum.

In addition to conducting this principal test, the authors attempt to measure unexpected variations in exchange rate. They do this in order to assess the costs of exchange rate flexibility. These costs are found to be small and are asserted to be the result of variable monetary policy. The principal conclusion of the first test and also of the paper is on page 24:

> Monetary shocks and other factors which cause changes in the trend of relative prices will thus be offset by exchange rate movements within about a year.

My criticism of this conclusion and my major criticism of the paper is based on a different reading of the historical evidence, particularly as regards the flow of causality among money, prices and the exchange rate. One could conclude both from the historical record, and from the results of the authors' tests, that exchange rate movements which cause changes in the trend of relative prices will be offset by changes in monetary policy within about a year.

In other words, I am prepared to argue for all countries other than Germany, particularly in the period 1921–26, that causality may at times be better characterised as flowing from the exchange rate to prices and to money than from money to prices and to the exchange rate.

In reaching this conclusion, I am explicitly excluding the case of Germany since my interpretation is the same as the authors' – regarding the flow of causality. One need only read, for example, Bergmann's *History of Reparations* (1927) to see that the Reichsbank's policy before and during the hyperinflation was one of interest stabilisation with a vengeance, and stabilisation at far below the prevailing rate of inflation. To quote briefly from page 185 of Bergmann:

> During the Decline of the Mark, commercial and industrial interests had learned . . . that no more profitable business existed than to obtain a credit from the Reichsbank in paper Marks by discounting Treasury bills, promptly to invest the proceeds of the credits in commodities or, if possible, in foreign exchange and then to repay the debt to the Reichsbank at maturity, at a handsome profit in paper Marks which in the meantime had further declined.

But for other countries and time periods than Germany in 1921–26, my conclusions are the opposite of the authors' as regards the flow of causality. A reasonable interpretation of 1931–36, in particular, is clearly that the authorities played some role in re-establishing purchasing power parity after deviations had emerged. Thus had the establishment of parity been left to the market in those years, it is conceivable that more serious divergences among national price levels expressed in some common currency could have persisted for longer than the authors believe. To see this point it is useful to consider the case of sterling between 1931 and 1936 and thus all of the bilateral comparisons made by the authors for that period.

1. Throughout 1931 parity had held between British prices and foreign prices expressed in sterling; but in 1931 sterling was forced off the gold standard and was devalued substantially against other currencies.

The proximate source of devaluation appears to have been the capital flows induced, in part, by the French gold purchase policy of 1929. That policy had, among its objectives, first to see that marginal increments to French foreign exchange reserves were accumulated not in sterling but in gold; a second objective was in 1930 and 1931 to convert the remaining sterling balances outstanding at the Bank of France into gold.

The purchasing power disparity that was induced by sterling's fall in 1931 appears to have persisted in some degree until 1936, when by the terms of the Tripartite Agreement among the United Kingdom, France and the United States, the French franc was devalued with respect to the dollar and the pound. This conscious act of policy to devalue the franc, rather than market forces alone, appears, in part, responsible for the return to purchasing power parity.

2. My reading of the situation in the period since 1973 is somewhat different from that of the authors as well; and here as regards the flow of causality among money, prices and the exchange rate. This time I refer to the experience of Germany and Switzerland between 1976 and 1979; and by virtue of referring to Germany I am referring also to the experience of Germany's continental partners in the European Monetary system; or four of the six cases cited by Batchelor and Wood.

The German mark and the Swiss franc both began strongly to appreciate in 1978. The appreciation of the two was held by authorities there to be an unanticipated growth in the demand for their currencies particularly on the part of organisations holding internationally diversifiable portfolios. The increased demand seemed to be based on a fundamental reassessment of monetary policy in Switzerland and Germany on the one hand, and the United States on the other. As policy in the United States was judged increasingly to be erratic and on average more expansionary than had been anticipated, particularly by comparison with policy in Germany and Switzerland, diversifiable portfolio holders came increasingly to favour the Deutsche Mark and the Swiss franc. Given the increase in demand for the currency, the two monetary authorities were faced with choosing between the encumbrance of their monetary target and the encumbrance of a commitment to exchange rate stability. As is already history, the exchange rate encumbrance remained; the Germans redefined their targeted money growth rate, the Swiss abandoning it altogether for a time. When the Swiss subsequently readopted a monetary target, they made it contingent upon certain behaviour of the exchange rate. To have done otherwise would have proved deflationary in the monetarist sense of the term.

I believe that this rough description of German and Swiss central-bank behaviour is enough to demonstrate that at times between 1973 and 1978 the flow of causality is not from money, to prices and the exchange rate but rather from the exchange rate to money. Again, purchasing power parity seems for a time not to have been restored by market forces but sustained rather by the activity of the central bank. It is therefore difficult to argue that, because over the sample period, purchasing power parity held, the central bank should not intervene. Indeed one might argue the opposite, that purchasing power parity held because the central bank intervened.

To conclude my comment, I would like to ask, of what relevance are these points to the United Kingdom? I think their principal point of relevance is the demonstration that monetary authorities who embark on policies that will both stabilise their money growth rates and lower them somewhat more quickly than in other countries should expect to see shifts in internationally diversified portfolios towards their own currencies. As the United Kingdom appears to be in precisely this situation, the Bank of England should be cognisant of this potential movement of money demand in setting its monetary growth targets. The degree to which they should adapt the target is, in some ways, reflected by the strength of sterling. Thus, as the Swiss, the British authorities might want to consider setting contingent money targets, that is targets which will reduce the variability of the pound vis-à-vis the continental currencies.

Comment on 'Floating Exchange Rates: the Lessons of Experience'

Alec G. Ford

In this comment on 'Floating Exchange Rates: the Lessons of Experience' I wish to concentrate on two of the historical episodes dealt with in this interesting paper and to approach them in a more explicit historical way – the 1919–25 period which saw the return of the £ to the gold standard as the old parity, and the 1931–6 behaviour of the £ after it had left gold. In each of these periods we find the £–$ exchange rate depreciating at first and then appreciating but with very different public policies and background conditions. It is, indeed, helpful to realise that in each period the British monetary authorities appeared to have a distinct economic policy objective for the £ exchange rates and thus for their monetary policies too. While the authors use the asset-pricing approach to the balance of payments to explain how changes in pairs of relative prices feed through to subsequent changes in the relevant exchange rate to vindicate the purchasing power parity approach, I shall adopt a different method of approach which would emphasise the aspect of exchange rates being determined by flows of foreign currency receipts and payments as distinct from equilibrating demands to hold particular *stocks* of assets in optimum portfolios.

Indeed the differences between these approaches may be more apparent than real in so far as time dimensions are involved which, until specified, may cloud the issues. Certainly stock equilibria must involve flow equilibria, and as Lal has said:

> The exchange-rate is the price of foreign money in terms of national money and is determined within a simultaneous-equation system in which there will be both stock and flow equilibria in the monetary (asset) and real (goods) markets.[1]

In my comments I shall be looking at the influences of relative price movements *and* relative income movements on the £–US$ exchange rate (implicitly on flows).

1919–25: 'ELEMENTARY DECENCY'

It is important for an understanding of this period to recall that the pound sterling before 1914 was a proud currency which had been linked internally and externally to gold at face value for almost a century, a feature which was basic for British banking and finance at home and abroad – meeting one's obligations in full. However, it was realised towards the end of the First World War that the parity (which had been sustained by wartime pegging and the submarine menace) could not be sustained with peace because British prices had broadly doubled whereas American prices had risen by 50 per cent as compared with 1914. The Cunliffe Committee on Currency and Foreign Exchanges had been set up to advise how to get back at the *old* parity with gold – there was no thought of stabilising the £–gold or £–US$ rate at some *de facto* parity: 'elementary decency' and banking propriety dictated that the old parity should be attained. With peace these fears were realised with the US dollar retaining its old gold parity, while the £ (shamefully) had to become 'inconvertible' along with other European currencies. This enforced free float was seen as a regrettable phase by the British authorities whose policy aim was to use monetary policy to deflate British prices relatively to American prices so that on purchasing power parity grounds the £–gold and £–US$ exchange rates would appreciate upwards to the old mint par (£1 = 4,8665 US$).

What then was the size of the task? Wholesale prices had risen some 37 per cent more in Britain than in the United States over the period 1913–20, while the consumers' expenditure average value indexes showed a rise of 50 per cent for Britain over the United States. This does indicate the importance for puchasing power parity tests of the choice of price series for calculating relative prices. The authors have opted for wholesale prices whereas a good case can be made for using cost-of-living indices or GDP deflators, as Keynes had argued in his *The Economic Consequences of Mr. Churchill* (1925). Keynes was concerned to measure the degree of overvaluation of the pound against the dollar on its return to gold at the pre-1914 parity in April 1925 and to emphasise his view that the use of wholesale price index numbers was inappropriate for purchasing power parity comparisons. Wholesale prices were then dominated by internationally traded raw materials, whose national currency prices would be closely linked by exchange rates and adjustment would be rapid ('the law of one price'). In such circumstances exchange rate movements and relative price movements might be expected to show strong conformity and *vice versa*. However, other more sticky prices would not have adjusted so that an appreciation such as for 1925 would thrust a squeeze on profit margins of exporters and others, and if the pressure on 'sheltered' prices and wages were resisted, then the pressure on manufacturers would remain and cost-of-living indices would record overvaluation persisting. Cost-of-living index numbers would prove better indicators of purchasing-power-parity exchange rates than wholesale prices (which might underestimate the degree of domestic adjustment), under the assumption of no necessity for subsequent deflationary pressure. I can do no better than quote:

> His [sc. the Chancellor of the Exchequer] experts made, I think, two serious mistakes. In the first place, I suspect that they miscalculated the degree of the maladjustment of money values which would result from restoring sterling to its pre-war gold parity, because they attended to index numbers of prices which were irrelevant or inappropriate to the matter in hand. If you want to know whether sterling values are adjusting themselves to an improvement in the exchange, it is useless to consider, for example, the price of raw cotton in Liverpool. This *must* adjust itself to a movement of the exchange, because, in the case of an imported raw material, the parity of international values is necessarily maintained almost hour by hour. But it is not sensible to argue from this that the money wages of dockers or of charwomen and the cost of postage or travelling by train also adjust themselves hour by hour in accordance with the foreign exchanges. Yet this, I fancy, is what the Treasury did. They compared the usual wholesale price index numbers here and in America, and – since these are made up to the extent of at least two-thirds from the raw materials of international commerce, the prices of which necessarily adjust themselves to the exchanges – the true disparity of internal prices was watered down to a fraction of its true value. This led them to think that the gap to be bridged was perhaps 2 to 3 per cent, instead of the true figure of 10 or 12 per cent, which was the indication given by the index numbers of the cost of living, of the level of wages, and of the prices of our manufactured exports – which indexes are a much better rough-and-ready guide for this purpose, particularly if they agree with one another, than are the index numbers of wholesale prices.[2]

The £–$ exchange rate which had been freed in 1919 fell steadily to a low point of 3.378 in 1920, with an annual average figure of 3.661 for 1920, which implied a depreciation of 33 per cent as compared with pre-1914 mint par.[3] Thereafter the pound–dollar exchange rate appreciated, reaching within 10 per cent of the mint par by 1922 at 4.427 (annual average), under the influence of a restrictive monetary policy in Britain which was causing British prices and incomes to fall relatively to American prices and incomes. Between 1920 and 1925 as the £ price of a dollar fell by 25 per cent wholesale prices in Britain fell by 23 per cent relatively to America, while the GNP deflator exhibited an 18 per cent relative fall; again, GNP at constant prices in Britain fell by 12 per cent relatively to American GNP. I would, therefore, suggest that declines both in relative prices and in relative real incomes contributed to the appreciation of the pound (via the current account), such that it could resume its pre-1914 mint par, and that the latter relative income decline (holding down UK imports) was one reason why the parity could have been achieved with incomplete price adjustment and why economists ever since have complained of the overvaluation of the £ by this move. For if we compare British and American wholesale prices 1913 to 1925 we find that British prices had risen by 58 per cent and American by 48 per cent (a relative rise of 6.8 per cent) whereas in Britain the consumers'[3] expenditure average value index had risen by 90 per cent, but by 59 per cent in the United States (a relative rise of 20 per cent). A contributory feature in the appreciation of the pound 1920–5 may well have been switching into the £ from foreign currencies in the belief that it was going to rise, but direct evidence of this is not available.

In this episode we have had the pound floating freely but the authorities pursuing an 'independent' monetary policy to appreciate sterling to its pre-1914 parity. This appreciation was achieved by a decline in British prices *and* real incomes relatively to the United States such that the old parity was achieved although relative prices had incompletely adjusted, leading thereby to charges of overvaluation of sterling, whose size clearly depended on the price series chosen for comparisons.

1931–6 'NO ONE TOLD US WE COULD DO THAT!'

(One ex-minister from the minority 1929–31 Labour government commenting on the National government's action in taking the £ off gold on 21 September 1931.) The pound was indeed forced off gold in September 1931 by the critical *proximate* factor of London's quick international illiquidity as short-term foreign-held £ liabilities considerably exceeded the UK's short-term international assets and overseas holders sought to liquidate their £ holdings as confidence waned, while a considerable current account deficit had emerged in 1931. However, certain other European currencies remained on gold for

most of this 1931–6 period (notably the French franc and the Belga) so
that there is differing individual exchange rate behaviour in this period,
but we shall concentrate on the £–US$ relationship. It should also be
remembered that the Empire (less Canada) and some other countries
followed the £ and left gold to form the Sterling Bloc.

After September 1931 the £ depreciated sharply against the US$,
reaching a low of 3.372$ (as compared with the old mint par of 4.8665$).
The British authorities seem to have become disillusioned with gold as
the 1925 prospectus had not been fulfilled and to have realised that now
there was a chance to pursue more independent policies designed to
benefit the domestic economy.[4] A cheap money policy was initiated in
1932 with Bank Rate down to 2 per cent (and remaining there until 1939)
and both short- and long-term interest rates showing marked falls (the
Treasury Bill rate reached 0.546 per cent on average in 1935 and the long
yield fell to 2.89 per cent) while the monetary base was expanded. High-
powered money showed a 17.5 per cent rise from 1932 to 1936, while in
the same period the money stock (bank deposits *plus* currency) rose by
19.5 per cent. One initial element here had been to achieve the
conversion of the 5 per cent War Loan to $3\frac{1}{2}$ per cent *1952 or after* in
1932, but the main aim of the authorities' easy money policy was to help
raise home prices, profits and hence activity from the Depression. Again
a floating exchange rate permitted an independent monetary policy, but
of a different character to the earlier episode.

A second distinct policy emerged: to use the newly founded Exchange
Equalisation Account to affect the exchange rates to help the depressed
export trade. Indeed, a target rate of US$ 3.40 had been set by Treasury
officials in 1932, only to be overtaken by events. However, a distinct
policy did emerge of longer-term EEA intervention in foreign exchange
markets to hold the £ down as much as possible (by stopping it
appreciating so much) to benefit British exports.

And appreciate it did despite the cheap money policy! The £–US$
exchange rate rose from a 1932 annual average of 3.504$ to a 1936
annual average of 4.971 – and a 29.5 per cent fall in the sterling price for
a dollar – while the £–French franc showed a sterling depreciation of 7
per cent. At the same time as this appreciation of the £ (the effective
exchange rate for the £ rose by 12.3 per cent)[5] we find a cumulative
British current account deficit of £114 million for the years 1932–6 and
British quick international asset/liability position improving by some
£250 million,[6] as the EEA sought to prevent yet more appreciation. This
appreciation very much reflected a net inflow on capital account into
Britain on a substantial scale, despite the lower interest rates, while

Britain continued to lend abroad on a modest, controlled, scale to the £-bloc countries. The sources of this inflow are less clear but must include refugee or 'hot' money from Europe, foreign investment in the growing 'new' British industries (for example, Ford, Vauxhall and oil companies) and financial asset changes as predicated by the asset-model of Batchelor and Wood.

In terms of the current account adjustment variables we find that the 29.5 per cent fall in the £ price of dollars between 1932 and 1936 was associated with a 10 per cent fall in British GNP as compared with US GNP; with a 10.5 per cent fall in relative wholesale prices, a 6.7 per cent fall in relative GNP deflators, and a 5.7 per cent fall in relative consumers' expenditure average value indices. This appreciation of the £ against the US$ over the period 1932–6 would appear to exceed by far more than 1920–5 the relative price changes, but it should be mentioned that the £–$ exchange rate had fallen excessively in 1931–2, and that Britain had imposed import duties and imperial preference after 1931, each of which might be expected to have caused the £–$ rate to appreciate with unchanged relative prices. In the 1932–6 period we find relative prices and relative income movements contributing towards an appreciation of the pound against the dollar, but we must emphasise too the role of the influx of capital from abroad.

The model presented by the authors has emphasised the 'Asset' mechanism of adjustment to bring about the purchasing power parity response of exchange rates to relative price disturbances over a time-span of up to one year. There are, indeed, attractions of this direct method, but is directness always a virtue if it might be obscuring a more oblique underlying mechanism? One element stressed in favour of the 'Asset' approach has been the (alleged) slowness of trade items (and hence the exchange rate) to react to (prior) relative price changes – but what if relative price movements are reinforced by relative income, movements, as we have shown for the appreciations of 1920–5 and 1932–6? For income changes historically have operated speedily on traded items (for example, in the 1870–1914 British economy[7]). Indeed, in considering responses of exchange rates to relative price changes I would suggest that there are various elements to bear in mind:

(a) the effects of changes in relative prices on current account items;
(b) the possible associated relative income effects on current account items;
(c) the effects of changes in relative prices on asset holdings in various currencies.

My historical account leads to me to think that one major issue is how much influence to attribute to each of these (complementary) elements. A second issue which emerges for the purchasing power parity approach and which has a Keynesian ancestry is the choice of price indices to represent relative price changes – was the pound overvalued in 1925? It all depends on the price indices chosen for comparison. In such studies it is important to discuss more the appropriateness (or otherwise) of the choice of, say, wholesale prices, as compared with cost-of-living indices. A third point to note is that in each of these historical episodes we have an appreciating pound but in the earlier period UK monetary policy has a restrictive stance, while in the later period it has a relaxed and easy stance, and to repeat that in each instance the pound appreciates.

SOURCES OF CITED STATISTICS

£–$ exchange rates ⎫
UK and USA consumers' expendi- | *The British Economy Key*
  ture average value index numbers ⎬   *Statistics 1900–1970*
UK wholesale prices | (LCES/Times, 1972).
UK Balance of Payments ⎭

UK GNP at constant prices, C. Feinstein, *National Income Expenditure*
    and Output of the UK 1855–1965
    (Cambridge, 1972).

USA GNP at constant prices ⎫   *Historical Statistics of the*
USA Wholesale Prices   ⎬   *U.S. Colonial Times to 1957*
    (US Dept. of Commerce,
    1961).

NOTES

1. Deepak Lal, *A Liberal International Economic Order: The International Monetary System and Economic Development*, Essays in International Finance No. 139 (Princeton, 1980), p. 14. Compare also R. Shone, 'The Monetary Approach to the Balance of Payments: Stock-Flow Equilibria', *Oxford Economic Papers*, July 1980, pp. 200–9, and J. A. Frenkel, T. Gyffason and J. F. Helliwell, 'A Synthesis of Monetary and Keynesian Approaches to Short-Run Balance-of-Payments Theory', *Economic Journal* (September 1980), pp. 582–92.
2. J. M. Keynes, *The Economic Consequences of Mr. Churchill*, as reprinted in S. Pollard (ed.), *The Gold Standard and Employment Policies between the Wars* (London, 1970), pp. 30–1.
3. This is calculated as a rise in the £ price of a dollar by 33 per cent.

4. This account follows Susan Howson's work in 'The Management of Sterling 1932–9', *Journal of Economic History* (March 1980), pp. 53–60, and *Domestic Monetary Management in Britain 1919–38* (Cambridge, 1975).
5. See J. Redmond, 'An indicator of the Effective Exchange Rate of the Pound in the 1930s', *Economic History Review* (February 1980), pp. 83–91.
6. £ balances rose from £468 million (end-'32) to £721 million (end-'36) while gold and foreign exchange holdings rose from £206 million (end-'32) to £703 million (end-'36).
7. See, for example, A. G. Ford, *The Gold Standard 1880–1914: Britain and Argentina* (Oxford, 1962), *passim*.

2 Flexible Exchange Rates, Prices and the Role of 'News': Lessons from the 1970s

Jacob A. Frenkel

1 INTRODUCTION

Recent experience with flexible exchange rate systems has led to renewed interest in the operation of foreign exchange markets as reflected in many recent studies of the principal determinants of exchange rates. The 1970s witnessed the dramatic alteration of the international monetary system from a regime of pegged exchange rates which prevailed for about a quarter of a century (since the Bretton Woods conference) into a regime of flexible (though managed) rates. As a consequence of the emergence of the new legal and economic system traders, national governments and international organisations were confronted with new economic problems, choices and instruments. During the 1970s exchange rates fluctuated widely and inflation rates accelerated. The international monetary system had to accommodate extraordinarily large oil-related shocks which affected trade flows in goods and assets. Huge oil payments had to be recycled. Uncertainties concerning future developments in international politics reached new heights and the prospects for the world economy got gloomier. These developments placed unprecedented pressures on the markets for foreign exchange as well as on other asset markets. They were associated with a large slide in the value of the US dollar, and resulted in speeding up the creation of new institutions like the European monetary system which provided the formal framework for the management of exchange rates among members. The increased interdependence among countries and the realisation that exchange rate policies by one national government exert influence on other economies have also induced legal responses from international organisations. For example, in late April 1977 the Executive Board of the International Monetary Fund approved the details of the second amendment to Article IV of the amended Articles of Agreement dealing with the principles and procedures for surveillance of exchange rate policies of member countries.

These developments provide the background for this paper which is intended to sum up the relevant evidence bearing on a set of related questions and to present a brief survey of key issues and lessons from the experience with floating rates during the 1970s. The main orientation of the paper is empirical and the analysis is based on the experience of three exchange rates involving the dollar/pound, the dollar/French franc and the dollar/DM. Section 2 provides an analysis of the efficiency of foreign exchange markets by examining the relationship between spot and forward exchange rates. The extent of exchange rate volatility is also examined. This analysis of the foreign exchange markets sheds light on several questions including (i) whether exchange rates fluctuate 'excessively'; (ii) whether speculation in the foreign exchange markets is destabilising; (iii) whether there is 'insufficient' speculation in the foreign exchange markets; (iv) whether there is evidence for market failure in the sense that there are unexploited profit opportunities. These issues are significant in assessing the performance of floating rates as well as in evaluating the need for government intervention in the foreign exchange markets. The analytical framework that is used for interpreting the volatility of exchange rates and the association between spot and forward rates is the modern theory of exchange rate determination. Within this framework exchange rates are viewed as the prices of assets that are traded in organised markets and, like the prices of other assets, are strongly influenced by expectations about future events.

The relationship between exchange rates and interest rates is analysed in Section 3. One of the key issues that is raised in this section is the distinction between anticipated and unanticipated changes in rates of interest. As an analytical matter this distinction is important because the modern approach to exchange rate determination implies that exchange rates are strongly influenced by 'news' which by definition is unpredictable. Therefore, it is unanticipated rather than anticipated changes in interest rates that should be closely associated with changes in exchange rates. This prediction is tested empirically.

Section 4 analyses the relationship between exchange rates and prices by examining the patterns of deviations from purchasing power parities. The main point that is being emphasised is that there is an important intrinsic difference between exchange rates and national price levels. Exchange rates are more sensitive to expectations concerning future events than national price levels. As a result, in periods which are dominated by 'news' which alter expectations, exchange rates are likely to be more volatile and departures from purchasing power parties are likely to be the rule rather than the exception. The analysis of the relationship between exchange rates and prices is relevant for assessing whether the flexible exchange rates system was successful in providing national economies with an added degree of insulation from foreign shocks, and whether it provided policy-makers with an added instrument for the conduct of macroeconomic policy. The evidence regarding deviations from purchasing power parities is also relevant for determining whether there is a case for managed float. Section 5 contains concluding remarks.

2 THE EFFICIENCY OF THE FOREIGN EXCHANGE MARKET AND THE MOVEMENT OF EXCHANGE RATES

In this section I analyse the principal characteristics of the relationship between spot and forward exchange rates which seem to emerge from the experience of the 1970s. Following an analysis of the efficiency of the foreign exchange market I discuss the more general issues underlying the relationships between spot and forward rates and their volatility.

2.1 The Efficiency of the Foreign Exchange Market

One of the central insights of the monetary (or the asset market) approach to the exchange rate is the notion that the exchange rate, being a relative price of two assets, is determined in a manner similar to the determination of other asset prices and that expectations concerning the future course of events play a central role in affecting current exchange rates.[1]

If the foreign exchange market is efficient and if the exchange rate is determined in a fashion similar to the determination of other asset prices, we should expect current prices to reflect all currently available information. Expectations concerning future exchange rates should be incorporated and reflected in forward exchange rates. To examine the efficiency of the market I first regress the logarithm of the current spot exchange rate, $\ln S_t$, on the logarithm of the one-month forward exchange rate prevailing at the previous month, $\ln F_{t-1}$, as in equation (1).[2]

$$\ln S_t = a + b \ln F_{t-1} + u_t \tag{1}$$

If the market for foreign exchange is efficient so that prices reflect all relevant available information, then the residuals in equation (1), u_t, should contain no information and therefore should be serially uncorrelated. Further if the forward exchange rate is an unbiased forecast of the future spot exchange rate (as should be the case under an assumption of risk neutrality), then the constant term in equation (1) should not differ significantly from zero,[3] and the slope coefficient should not differ significantly from unity. I examine three exchange rates: the dollar/pound, the dollar/franc and the dollar/DM. Equation (1) was estimated using monthly data for the period June 1973–July 1979 (data sources are listed in the Appendix). The beginning of the period was set so as to concentrate on the experience of the current exchange rate regime (following the initial post-Bretton-Woods transition period). The resulting ordinary least squares estimates are reported in Table 2.1. Also reported in Table 2.1 are additional regressions which will be analysed shortly. As may be seen for the dollar/DM exchange rate the hypotheses that (at the 95 per cent confidence level) the constant term does not differ significantly from zero and that the slope coefficient does not differ significantly from unity cannot be rejected. These hypotheses are rejected for the dollar/franc exchange rate and are rejected (marginally) for the dollar/pound exchange rate. The joint hypotheses, however, that the constant is zero *and* that the slope coefficient is unity cannot be rejected at the 95 per cent for the dollar/pound and the dollar/DM exchange rates and at the 99 per cent for the dollar/franc exchange rate. The test statistics for testing the joint hypotheses are reported in the column headed by F in Table 2.1. These results are relevant for assessing whether the forward rate is an unbiased forecast of the future spot rate. We turn next to the question of efficiency.

It was argued above that in an efficient market, expectations concerning future exchange rates are reflected in forward rates and that spot exchange rates reflect all currently available information. If forward exchange rates prevailing at period $t-1$ summarise all relevant information available at that period, they should also contain the information that is summarised in data corresponding to period $t-2$. It thus follows that including additional lagged values of the forward rates in equation (1) should not greatly affect the coefficients of determination and should

TABLE 2.1 Efficiency of Foreign Exchange Markets Monthly Data: June 1973–July 1979
(standard errors in parentheses)

Dependent variable: $\ln S_t$	Estimation method	Constant	$\ln F_{t-1}$	$\ln F_{t-2}$	R^2	s.e.	D.W.	F	m
Dollar/pound	OLS	0.033 (0.017)	0.956 (0.024)		0.96	0.027	1.72	1.86	
	OLS	0.031 (0.018)	1.047 (0.116)	−0.088 (0.113)	0.96	0.027	1.94		
	IV	0.030 (0.018)	0.961 (0.025)		0.95	0.027	1.74		2.01
Dollar/franc	OLS	−0.237 (0.078)	0.843 (0.051)		0.79	0.029	2.23	4.83	
	OLS	−0.225 (0.082)	0.706 (0.117)	0.146 (0.117)	0.79	0.029	1.90		
	IV	−0.236 (0.080)	0.844 (0.053)		0.78	0.030	2.24		2.26
Dollar/DM	OLS	−0.023 (0.027)	0.971 (0.032)		0.93	0.032	2.12	0.51	
	OLS	−0.019 (0.028)	0.913 (0.119)	0.063 (0.122)	0.93	0.032	1.96		
	IV	−0.021 (0.027)	0.973 (0.032)		0.93	0.032	2.10		0.91

Note: s.e. is the standard error of the equation and R^2 is the coefficient of determination; in the case of instrumental variables estimation the R^2 was computed as $1 - \text{Var}\,(\hat{u}_t)/\text{Var}\,(\ln S_t)$. The F statistic tests the joint restriction that the constant equals zero and the slope/equals unity. The test statistic is distributed as $F\,(2, 71)$. Critical values for $F\,(2, 71)$ are 3.13 (95 per cent) and 4.92 (99 per cent). The instrumental variable (IV) estimation method is used in order to allow for the possibility of errors in variables arising from using $\ln F_{t-1}$ as a proxy for the expected future spot rate; the instruments are a constant, time, time-squared and lagged values of the dependent and the independent variables. The m-statistic which tests for the absence of errors in variables is distributed χ^2 with two degrees of freedom. The critical value for $\chi^2(2)$ is 5.99 (95 per cent).

not yield coefficients that differ significantly from zero. The results reported in Table 2.1 are consistent with this hypothesis; in all cases the coefficients of $\ln F_{t-2}$ do not differ significantly from zero and the inclusion of the additional lagged variables does not improve the fit. Most importantly, in all cases the Durbin–Watson statistics are consistent with the hypothesis of the absence of first-order autocorrelated residuals and an examination of higher order correlations (up to 12 lags) shows that no correlation of any order is significant.[4]

To examine further the relationship between the various exchange rates we note that one of the assumptions underlying equation (1) was that the forward exchange rate measures the unobservable value of the *expected* future spot exchange rate. This assumption provided the justification for using equation (1) instead of the explicit specification of the rational expectations hypothesis that is embodied in equation (2):

$$\ln S_t = E_{t-1} \ln S_t + \varepsilon_t \tag{2}$$

where $E_{t-1} \ln S_t$ denotes the expected (logarithm of the) spot exchange rate for period t based on the information available at period $t-1$. If, however, the forward exchange rate at $t-1$ is a 'noisy' proxy for the expected future value of the spot rate (i.e. it measures it with a random error) then we would obtain

$$a + b \ln F_{t-1} = E_{t-1} \ln S_t + v_{t-1}; E(v_t) = 0 \tag{3}$$

and substituting equation (3) into equation (2) yields:

$$\ln S_t = a + b \ln F_{t-1} + (\varepsilon_t - v_{t-1}). \tag{4}$$

In this case the error term in equation (1) would be $u_t = \varepsilon_t - v_{t-1}$, the assumption that the covariance between $\ln F_{t-1}$ and u_t is zero would entail a specification error, and the application of the ordinary-least-squares (OLS) procedure would yield biased estimates due to the classical errors in variables bias.

In order to examine the possibility that the OLS estimates might be subject to the errors in variables bias, one needs to test the hypothesis that $\text{cov}(u_t, \ln F_{t-1}) = 0$. This test follows the specification test outlined by Hausman (1978).[5] To perform the test equation (1) was estimated by applying the OLS procedure as well as by using an instrumental variables (IV) estimation method. Under the null-hypothesis of no misspecification the OLS coefficients vector $\hat{b}_0$ is an efficient and an unbiased estimate of the true coefficient vector. Under the alternative hypothesis of misspecification the vector $\hat{b}_0$ is biased and an unbiased coefficient vector $\hat{b}_1$ can be obtained by applying an instrumental variables estimation procedure. The test-statistic relevant for testing the null-hypothesis can be written as

$$m = (\hat{b}_1 - \hat{b}_0)' \, (\text{var} \, \hat{b}_1 - \text{var} \, \hat{b}_0)^{-1} \, (\hat{b}_1 - \hat{b}_0) \tag{5}$$

where var $(\hat{b}_1)$ and var $(\hat{b}_0)$ denote the variance-covariance matrices of $\hat{b}_1$ and $\hat{b}_0$, respectively. Under the null-hypothesis m is distributed (in large samples) as χ^2 with two degrees of freedom. Table 2.1 reports the results of estimating equation (1) by applying the instrumental variables estimation method. As may be seen for all exchange rates the two vectors of coefficients $\hat{b}_1$ and $\hat{b}_0$ are very close to each other. For example for the dollar/pound exchange rate, the constants are 0.033 and 0.030 and the slopes are 0.956 and 0.961 – consequently, the resulting m statistic is 2.01 which is well below 5.99 – the critical value of $\chi^2(2)$ at the 95 per cent confidence level. The m statistics corresponding to the other exchange rates are also below this critical value. It is concluded, therefore, that the use of the forward exchange rate as a proxy for expectations does not introduce a significant errors-in-variables bias and thus the use of the OLS estimation procedure seems appropriate.[6]

The principal conclusions that may be drawn from the previous discussion are that the behaviour of the foreign exchange market during the 1970s has been broadly consistent with the general implications of the efficient market hypothesis.

2.2 Exchange Rate Movement: Volatility and Predictability

In this section I analyse the volatility of exchange rates and the extent to which this volatility is predictable. As is well known, during the same period exchange rates have been very volatile. The standard errors of the monthly percentage changes of the three exchange rates have been about 3 per cent per month. Further, the standard errors of the regressions in Table 2.1 indicate that the forecasts of future spot exchange rates based on the forward rates are very imprecise: the standard errors of the equations are about 3 per cent per month.

These characteristics of price changes (volatility and unpredictability) are typical of auction and of organised asset markets. In such markets current prices reflect expectations concerning the future course of events, and new information which induces changes in expectations is immediately reflected in corresponding changes in prices, thus precluding unexploited profit opportunities from arbitrage. The strong dependence of current prices on expectations about the future is unique to the determination of durable asset prices; it is not a characteristic of price determination of non-durable commodities. The strong dependence of asset prices on expectations also implies that periods which are dominated by uncertainties, new information, rumours, announcements and 'news', which induce frequent changes in expectations, are likely to be periods in which changes in expectations are the prime cause of fluctuations in asset prices. Further, since the information which alters expectations must be *new*, the resulting fluctuations in price cannot be predicted by lagged forward exchange rates which are based on past information.[7] Therefore, during such periods, one should expect exchange rates (and other asset prices) to exhibit large fluctuations. When the prime cause of fluctuations is new information, one may expect that lagged forward exchange rates (which are based on past information) are imprecise (even though possibly the best unbiased) forecasts of future spot rates.

To gain further insights into the implications of this perspective on the relationship between predicted and realised changes in exchange rates, Figures 2.1–2.3 present plots of predicted and realised percentage changes in exchange rates for the three pairs of currencies where the predicted change is measured by the lagged forward premium. Also presented in these figures are the differentials in national inflation rates which are discussed in Section 4. The key fact which emerges from these figures is that predicted changes in exchange rates account for a very small fraction of actual changes.[8] This phenomenon is also reflected in the comparison between the variances of actual and predicted changes in exchange rates: in all cases the variances of monthly percentage changes in exchange rates exceed the variances of monthly forward premia by a factor that is larger than twenty.[9] This fact suggests that the bulk of exchange rate changes seem to be due to 'new information' which, by definition, could not have been anticipated and reflected in the forward premium or discount which prevailed in the previous period.

This view of the foreign exchange market can be exposited in terms of the following simple model.[10] Let the logarithm of the spot exchange rate on day t be determined by

$$\ln S_t = z_t + b E_t(\ln S_{t+1} - \ln S_t) \qquad (6)$$

where $E_t(\ln S_{t+1} - \ln S_t)$ denotes the expected percentage change in the exchange rate between t and $t + 1$, based on the information available at t, and where z_t represents the ordinary factors of supply and demand that affect the exchange rate on day t. These factors may include domestic and foreign money supplies, incomes, levels of output, etc. Equation (6) represents a sufficiently general relationship which may be viewed as a

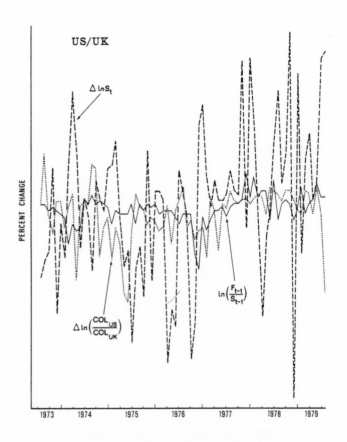

FIGURE 2.1 Monthly percentage changes of the US/UK consumer price indices
[$\Delta(\ln \text{COL}_{US}/\text{COL}_{UK})$], of the $/£ exchange rate, ($\Delta \ln S_t$), and
the monthly forward premium; [$\ln (F_{t-1}/S_{t-1})$] July 1973–July
1979

'reduced form' that can be derived from a variety of models of exchange
rate determination. These models may differ in their emphasis of the
determinants of $z(t)$ but they all are likely to share a similar reduced
form.[11] Assuming that expectations are rational in that equation (6)
applies to expectations of future exchange rates, it follows, by forward
iteration, that

$$E_t \ln S_{t+j} = \frac{1}{1+b} \sum_{k=0}^{\infty} \left(\frac{b}{1+b} \right)^k E_t z_{t+j+k}. \tag{7}$$

Thus, the current exchange rate ($j = 0$) and current expectations of

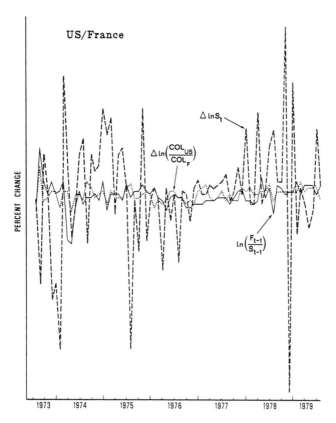

FIGURE 2.2 Monthly percentage changes of the US/France consumer price indices, $[\Delta(\ln \mathrm{COL_{US}}/\mathrm{COL_F})]$, of the \$/F.fr. exchange rate, $(\Delta \ln S_t)$, and the monthly forward premium; $[\ln(F_{t-1}/S_{t-1})]$ July 1973–July 1979

future exchange rates $(j > 0)$ are linked because both depend on expectations concerning the future zs. The strength of the link depends on the magnitude of b which characterises the dependence of the current exchange rate on the expected percentage change thereof.[12] The presumption is that due to profit opportunities from arbitrage this link is strong at least for the exchange rates expected in the near future. Hence, the current exchange rate, $\ln S_t = E_t \ln S_t$, should be closely linked to the current expectation of the next period's exchange rate, $E_t \ln S_{t+1}$, which in turn should be closely linked to the exchange rate expected for the following period, $E_t \ln S_{t+2}$, and so on.

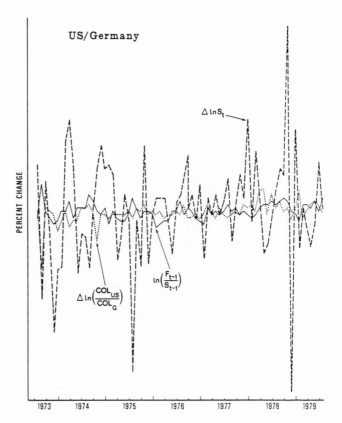

FIGURE 2.3 Monthly percentage changes of the US/German consumer price
indices, $[\Delta \ln (COL_{US}/COL_G)]$, of the \$/DM exchange rate,
$(\Delta \ln S_t)$, and the monthly forward premium; $[\ln (F_{t-1}/S_{t-1})]$ July
1973–July 1979

In order to examine this hypothesis I present in Figures 2.4–2.6 plots
of the spot and the contemporaneous forward exchange rates for the
three pairs of currencies. Also presented are the ratios of national price
levels which are discussed in Section 4. If the dominant factor underlying
changes in rates is new information which alters views about current and
expected future exchange rates by approximately the same amount, then
one should expect a high correlation between movements of spot and
forward rates. This fact is clearly demonstrated by Figures 2.4–2.6 where
it is seen that spot and forward exchange rates tend to move together and
by approximately the same amount (the vertical difference between the

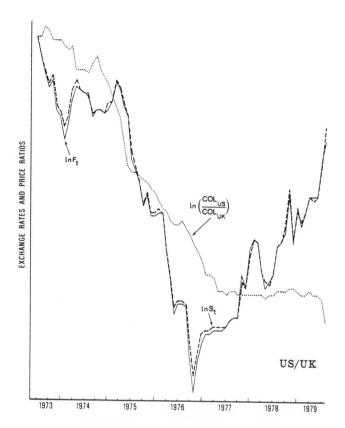

FIGURE 2.4 Monthly observations of the dollar/£ spot ($\ln S_t$) and forward ($\ln F_t$) exchange rates and the ratio of the US/UK cost of living indices [$\ln (COL_{US}/COL_{UK})$ (scaled to equal the spot exchange rate at the initial month)]: June 1973–July 1979

two rates corresponds to the percentage forward premium or discount on foreign exchange). The correlations between the spot and the forward exchange rates for the three pairs of currencies exceed 0.99 and the correlations between the corresponding percentage changes of the spot and forward rates exceed 0.96. The high correlation between movements in spot and forward rates is expected since the two rates respond at the same time to the same flow of new information (which is presumed to affect the rate for more than one period). In general, the details of the relationship between spot and forward exchange rates depend on the time series properties of the zs in equation (7) and in particular on

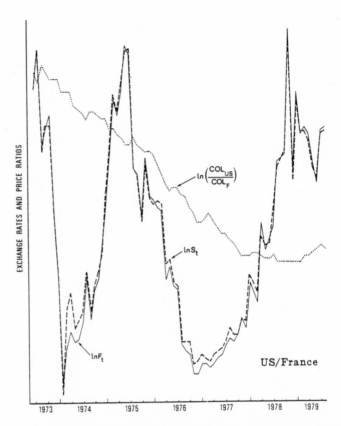

FIGURE 2.5 Monthly observations of the dollar/F.fr. spot ($\ln S_t$) and forward ($\ln F_t$) exchange rates and the ratio of the US/French cost of living indices $[\ln(\text{COL}_{US}/\text{COL}_F)$ (scaled to equal the spot exchange rate at the initial month)]: June 1973–July 1979

whether the new information is viewed as permanent or transitory.[13]

The comovement of spot and forward rates is evidence of the close link between current and expected future exchange rates which is illustrated by equation (7). This characteristic is typical of the foreign exchange market and is also shared by prices of many assets and commodities traded in organised markets. The recent pattern of gold prices provides a useful example of this general principle. Table 2.2 reports the spot and the futures prices of gold as recorded recently in the International Money Market (IMM) at the Chicago Mercantile Exchange on five consecutive days. The two key facts which are illustrated by this table are

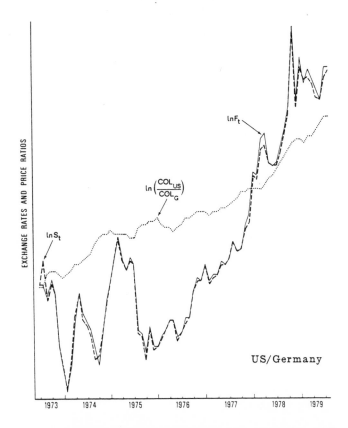

FIGURE 2.6 Monthly observations of the dollar/DM spot (ln S_t) and forward
(ln F_t) exchange rates and the ratio of the US/German cost of
living indices [ln(COL$_{US}$/COL$_G$) (scaled to equal the spot
exchange rate at the inital month)]: June 1973–July 1979

(i) the extent of day-to-day volatility in gold prices and (ii) the general
uniformity by which these changes are reflected in the price of gold for
immediate delivery as well as in the prices for the eight future delivery
dates.

Another feature which is revealed by Figures 2.4–2.6 is that the
contemporaneous spot and forward exchange rates are approximately
equal, thus indicating that the market's best forecast of the future spot
rate is (approximately) the current spot rate. This phenomenon reflects
the fact that, as an empirical matter, exchange rates have followed
(approximately) a random walk process. For such a process current

TABLE 2.2 Futures Price of Gold on Consecutive Days Daily Data: 1 May 1980–7 May 1980

Delivery date	Price (per ounce) and change from previous day									
	May 1	Change	May 2	Change	May 5	Change	May 6	Change	May 7	Change
1980 May	516.0	14.4	511.0	−5.0	519.0	8.0	506.5	−12.5	512.0	5.5
June	517.0	10.5	575.5	−1.5	523.7	8.2	510.3	−13.4	516.0	5.7
September	536.0	10.5	533.5	−2.5	540.7	7.2	527.0	−13.7	531.5	4.5
December	554.0	9.5	551.0	−3.0	558.0	7.0	541.5	−16.5	547.0	5.5
1981 March	571.5	9.5	568.0	−3.5	574.7	6.7	557.0	−17.7	561.5	4.5
June	588.5	10.5	585.0	−3.5	591.0	6.0	571.5	−19.5	576.0	4.5
September	605.3	10.3	602.0	−3.3	607.0	5.0	585.5	−21.5	590.0	4.5
December	622.0	11.0	619.0	−3.0	623.0	4.0	599.5	−23.5	604.0	4.5
1982 March	638.5	11.5	636.0	−2.5	693.0	3.0	613.5	−25.5	618.0	4.5

Note: These prices are settlement prices at the International Money Market (IMM) at Chicago Mercantile Exchange as reported in the *Wall Street Journal* 2 May–8 May 1980.

prices are indeed the best forecasts of future prices (and to the extent that the exchange rate had some drift, the above statement should be interpreted in reference to that drift). It is relevant to note, however, that while the random walk phenomenon seems to correspond to the actual paths of exchange rates it does not reflect a theoretical necessity.

The final characteristic of the foreign exchange market is described by Figures 2.7–2.9 which plot for the three pairs of currencies the spot exchange rate and the forward premium on forward exchange. Since the spot rate and the forward premium are expressed in terms of different

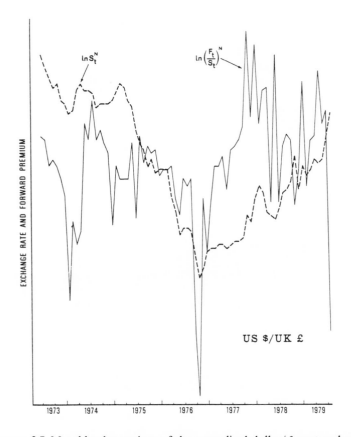

FIGURE 2.7 Monthly observations of the normalised dollar/£ spot exchange rate ($\ln S_t^N$) and the normalised forward premium $\left[\ln (F_t/S_t)^N\right]$. Both series are normalised by subtracting from each series its mean and by dividing by the corresponding standard error: June 1973–July 1979

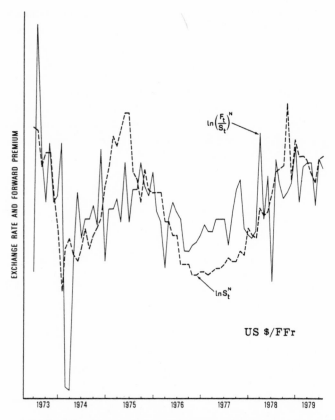

FIGURE 2.8 Monthly observations of the normalised dollar/F.fr. spot exchange rate (ln S_t^N) and the normalised forward premium $[\ln (F_t/S_t)^N]$. Both series are normalised by subtracting from each series its mean and by dividing by the corresponding standard error: June 1973–July 1979

units (where the latter is expressed as percentages per month), the two series were normalised for the purpose of the plots by subtracting from each series its mean and by dividing by the corresponding standard error.[14] The fact which emerges from these figures is that generally (though not always) there is a positive correlation between the expected depreciation of the currency (as measured by the forward premium on foreign exchange) and the spot exchange rate. This positive correlation may be rationalised by noting that currencies which are expected to depreciate are traded at a discount in the forward market and, on

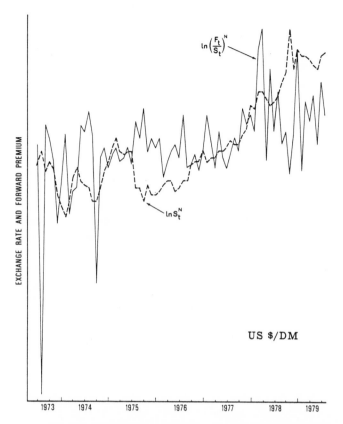

FIGURE 2.9 Monthly observations of the normalised dollar/DM spot $(\ln S_t^N)$ and the normalised forward premium $[\ln (F_t/S_t)^N]$. Both series are normalised by subtracting from each series its mean and by dividing by the corresponding standard error: June 1973–July 1979

average, these currencies also command a lower foreign exchange value in the spot market.[15] This relationship is embodied in the specification of equation (6) and is interpreted further in the next section.

3 EXCHANGE RATES, INTEREST RATES AND INNOVATIONS

This section contains an analysis of the relationship between exchange rates and interest rates from the perspective of the monetary (or the asset market) approach to the exchange rate. Following a discussion of the broad facts, the analysis proceeds with an empirical examination of the role of 'news'.

3.1 Exchange Rates and Interest Rates: The Broad Facts

To set the stage for this section it is useful to recall the analysis which predicts a negative association between the rate of interest and the exchange rate. According to that analysis a higher rate of interest attracts foreign capital which induces a surplus in the capital account of the balance of payments and thereby induces an appreciation of the domestic currency (i.e. a *lower* spot exchange rate). Another variant of this approach states that the higher rate of interest lowers spending and thus induces a surplus in the current account of the balance of payments which results in a *lower* spot exchange rate. A third variant claims that the higher rate of interest implies (via the interest parity theory) a higher forward premium on foreign exchange; and to the extent that at a given point in time the forward exchange rate which represents the expected future spot rate is predetermined by past history, as would be the case under the adaptive expectations hypothesis (which is clearly rejected by the evidence on the comovements of spot and forward rates), the required rise in the forward premium will be brought about by a *lower* spot rate (i.e. by an appreciation of the domestic currency). Whatever the route, by ignoring the distinction between nominal and real rates of interest, this approach predicts a *negative* relationship between the rate of interest and the spot exchange rate (or, alternatively, a positive relationship between the rate of interest and the foreign exchange value of the domestic currency).

While such a prediction might be appropriate for non-inflationary environments, it might be entirely inappropriate for inflationary environments (like the one prevailing in the US in recent years). In such periods variations in rates of interest are most likely to be dominated by variations in inflationary expectations rather than by liquidity effects associated with changes in the ratio of money to bonds. In such an environment the rate of interest is expected to be *positively* correlated with the exchange rate. The broad facts are consistent with this hypothesis. Over the recent period the rise in the rate of interest in the US (relative to the foreign rate of interest) has been associated with a rise in the spot exchange rate (i.e. with a depreciation of the dollar) rather than with a fall in the spot rate. Figure 2.10 illustrates the point by plotting the foreign exchange value of the US dollar against the interest rate differential. As is evident, the higher (relative) rate of interest in the US

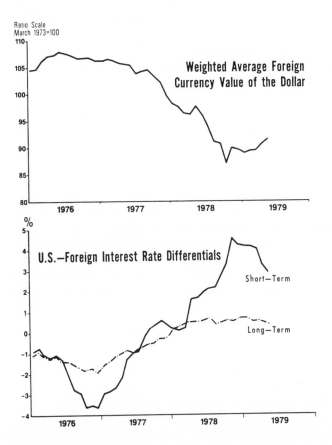

FIGURE 2.10 Foreign exchange value of the US dollar and interest rate differentials

Sources: Federal Reserve Statistical Release H. 13; Federal Reserve *Bulletin*; International Monetary Fund, *International Financial Statistics*.
[1] Secondary market rates for 90-day large certificates of deposit in the United States less the weighted average of foreign three-month money market rates.
[2] US long-term government bond yields less the weighted average of foreign long-term government bond yields.
Latest data plotted: May

Source: D. R. Mudd (1979)

has been associated with a higher exchange rate (i.e. with a lower foreign exchange value of the dollar).

The positive association between the rate of interest and the exchange rate in the context of the US dollar and the inflationary environment can be accounted for by the monetary (or the asset market) approach to the exchange rate which puts a special emphasis on the influence of the expectations on current exchange rates.[16] For example, according to the monetary approach, a rise in the domestic (relative) rate of interest which is primarily dominated by a rise in the expected (relative) rate of inflation induces a decline in the demand for real cash balances; for a given path of the nominal money supply asset market equilibrium requires a price level which is higher than the price which would have prevailed otherwise. When the domestic price level is linked to the foreign price through some form of purchasing power parity, and when the path of the foreign price is assumed to be given, the higher domestic price can only be achieved through a *rise* in the spot exchange rate (i.e. through a depreciation of the currency).[17]

This explanation of the positive association between interest rates and exchange rates has an intuitive appeal in that it implies that in an inflationary environment a relatively rapid rise in prices is associated with high *nominal* rates of interest as well as with a depreciation of the currency in terms of foreign exchange. This relationship is embodied in equation (6) which states that an expected depreciation of the currency (which in our case is associated with inflationary expectations and high nominal rates of interest) results in an immediate depreciation.[18]

The foregoing analysis also provides the explanation for the observation (which was noted in Section 2.2) that generally there is a positive correlation between the forward premium on foreign exchange and the level of the spot rate. Since during inflationary periods the spot rate is expected to be positively correlated with the interest rate differential and since according to the interest parity theory that differential must equal the forward premium on foreign exchange, it follows that the forward premium is also expected to be positively correlated with the level of the spot rate.[19]

3.2 Exchange Rates and News

One of the central implications of the rational expectations hypothesis is that unanticipated events, 'news', play a predominant role in affecting real variables and asset yields. This implication is embodied in many expositions of modern macroeconomics and its empirical content has been the subject of numerous recent studies.[20] In the context of exchange rate determination the discussion in Section 2 and in particular the contributions by Mussa (1977, 1979a) and Dornbusch (1978) emphasised that the predominant cause of exchange rate movements is 'news' which could not have been anticipated.[21] Expressing the spot exchange rate at period t as the sum of factors which were anticipated from the past as well as factors which represent 'news', Dornbusch (1978) decomposes the effects of 'news' into those which alter the expected future spot rate between the last period and the present and those which lead to a reassessment of the one-period interest rate differential starting at the present, that is 'news' about the term structure. Both of these white-noise serially uncorrelated components play a role in determining the spot exchange rate in Dornbusch's analysis.

The evidence presented in Section 2 suggests that the forward rate summarises the information that is available to the market when the forward rate is being set, and in equation (3) it was assumed that the expected exchange rate can be written as $a + b \ln F_{t-1}$ plus a serially uncorrelated error. We may therefore express the spot rate at period t as a function of factors which have been known in advance and are summarised by the lagged forward rate, as well as a function of the 'news'.

$$\ln S_t = a + b \ln F_{t-1} + \text{'news'} + w_t. \tag{8}$$

In what follows this notion is applied to an empirical analysis of the role of 'news' as a determinant of the exchange rate. The key difficulty lies in identifying the variable which measures the 'news'. Since quite frequently it is difficult to observe and quantify the 'news', it is convenient to examine the relationship between the exchange rate and a variable whose time series is likely to *manifest* the 'news' promptly. Assuming that asset markets clear fast and that the 'news' are immediately reflected in (unexpected) changes in the rates of interest, equation (8) may be written as

$$\ln S_t = a + b \underbrace{\ln F_{t-1}}_{\substack{\text{'expected'} \\ \text{exchange rate'}}} + \alpha \underbrace{\left[(i - i^*)_t - E_{t-1}(i - i^*)_t \right]}_{\text{'news'}} + w_t \tag{9}$$

where the bracketed term denotes the innovation in the (one-month) interest differential and where $E_{t-1}(i - i^*)_t$ denotes the interest differential which was expected to prevail in period t based on the information available at $t - 1$. The expected interest rate differential was computed from a regression of the interest differential on a constant, on two lagged values of the differential and on the lagged forward exchange rate $\ln F_{t-1}$.

As was argued above, the association between exchange rates and interest rates is likely to be positive during periods in which most of the variations in nominal rates of interest are dominated by variations in inflationary expectations – a characteristic which seems to fit the inflationary environment of the 1970s. Under such circumstances, when the unexpected interest differential reflects 'news' concerning inflationary expectations, the coefficient α in equation (9) is likely to be positive.[22] Table 2.3 reports the two-stage least squares estimates of equation (9) for the three exchange rates over the period June 1973–July 1979.[23] As may be seen in all cases the coefficients of the expected interest differential are positive and in the case of the dollar/pound exchange rate the coefficient is statistically significant. In order to verify the importance of using the series of innovations in the interest differential, Table 2.3 also reports estimates of regressions which replace the innovations by the actual series of the interest differential. In all cases the coefficients of the actual interest differential do not differ significantly from zero. Table 2.4 describes analogous two-stage least squares estimates of regressions which include both the actual interest rate differential and the innovation in the differential.[24] Again, in all cases the coefficients on the actual differential do not differ significantly from zero while the coefficients on the innovations are all positive and are significant for the dollar/pound and the dollar/franc exchange rates.

One possible interpretation of the positive coefficient on the (unexpected) interest differential may be given in terms of the prediction of the monetary approach to the exchange rate in which case the estimate of the coefficient α in equation (9) might be interpreted as an estimate of a structural parameter. Under an alternative interpretation the innovations in the interest differential belong in equation (9) only as far as they *manifest* 'news' which are relevant for exchange rate determination. If, for example, the dominant element of 'news' were variations in inflationary expectations, then one could also use the innovations in other time series as long as they reflect these relevant 'news'. To examine this possibility the same regressions as in Tables 2.3–2.4 were estimated using the 12-month interest differential and the results are reported in Tables 2.5–2.6. As before in all cases the coefficients on the actual differential do not differ significantly from zero while in all cases the coefficients on the innovations in the differential are positive and significant for the dollar/pound and the dollar/franc exchange rates.[25]

On the whole the record shows that during the 1970s exchange rates and the interest rate differential have been associated positively, thus indicating that during that inflationary period the same factors which

TABLE 2.3 One-month Interest Rate Differentials and Exchange Rates; Instrumental Variables Monthly Data: June 1973–July 1979 (standard errors in parentheses)

Dependent variable ln S_t	Constant	ln F_{t-1}	$(i-i^*)_t$	$[(i-i^*)_t - E_{t-1}(i-i^*)_t]$	s.e.	R^2	D.W.
Dollar/pound	0.021 (0.020)	0.965 (0.026)	−0.152 (0.118)		0.028	0.95	1.69
	0.031 (0.017)	0.959 (0.024)		0.432 (0.181)	0.026	0.96	1.78
Dollar/franc	−0.024 (0.181)	0.992 (0.124)	−0.462 (0.324)		0.034	0.71	2.21
	−0.246 (0.077)	0.837 (0.051)		0.245 (0.167)	0.029	0.80	2.17
Dollar/DM	0.004 (0.064)	0.997 (0.064)	−0.180 (0.394)		0.033	0.93	2.12
	−0.022 (0.026)	0.972 (0.031)		0.413 (0.347)	0.031	0.93	2.05

Note: Interest rates are the one-month (annualised) Euromarket rates. The expected interest rate differential $E_{t-1}(i-i^*)_t$ was computed from a regression of the interest differential on a constant, two lagged values of the differential, and the logarithm of the lagged forward exchange rate. Two-stage least squares estimation method was used. The instruments for the interest differential were a constant, two lagged values of the differential, and the logarithm of the lagged forward exchange rate; the instruments for the unexpected differential were a constant, Durbin's rank variable, and the logarithm of the lagged forward exchange rate. $(i-i^*)_t$ denotes the actual interest rate differential where i denotes the rate of interest on securities denominated in US dollars and i^* denotes the rate of interest on securities denominated in foreign currency. $[(i-i^*)_t - E_{t-1}(i-i^*)_t]$ denotes the *unexpected* interest rate differential. s.e. is the standard error of the equation. A quasi-R^2 was computed as $1 - \text{Var}(u_t)/\text{Var}(\ln S_t)$.

TABLE 2.4 One-month Interest Rate Differentials and Forecast Errors of Exchange Rates; Instrumental Variables Monthly Data: June 1973–July 1979 (standard errors in parentheses)

Dependent variable $\ln S_t$	Constant	$\ln F_{t-1}$	$(i - i^*)_t$	$[(i - i^*)_t - E_{t-1}(i - i^*)_t]$	s.e.	R^2	D.W.
Dollar/pound	0.018	0.969	−0.156	0.562	0.023	0.97	1.81
	(0.017)	(0.022)	(0.100)	(0.191)			
Dollar/franc	−0.136	0.915	−0.312	0.547	0.031	0.75	2.19
	(0.112)	(0.076)	(0.209)	(0.282)			
Dollar/DM	0.002	0.996	−0.173	0.599	0.032	0.93	2.07
	(0.044)	(0.045)	(0.286)	(0.457)			

Note: Interest rates are the one-month (annualised) Euromarket rates. The expected interest rate differential $E_{t-1}(i - i^*)_t$ was computed from a regression of the interest differential on a constant, two lagged values of the differential, and the logarithm of the lagged forward exchange rate. Two-stage least squares estimation method was used. The instruments were a constant, two lagged values of the interest differential, Durbin's rank variable of the unexpected differential, and the logarithm of the lagged forward exchange rate. $(i - i^*)_t$ denotes the actual interest rate differential where i denotes the rate of interest on securities denominated in US dollars and i^* denotes the rate of interest on securities denominated in foreign currency. $[(i - i^*)_t - E_{t-1}(i - i^*)_t]$ denotes the *unexpected* interest rate differential. s.e. is the standard error of the equation. A quasi-R^2 was computed as $1 - \text{Var}(u_t)/\text{Var}(\ln S_t)$.

TABLE 2.5 Twelve-month Interest Rate Differentials and Exchange Rates; Instrumental Variables Monthly Data: June 1973–July 1979 (standard errors in parentheses).

Dependent variable ln S_t	Constant	ln F_{t-1}	$(i-i^*)_t$	$[(i-i^*)_t - E_{t-1}(i-i^*)_t]$	s.e.	R^2	D.W.
Dollar/pound	0.027 (0.019)	0.960 (0.025)	-0.083 (0.147)		0.027	0.95	1.71
	0.031 (0.017)	0.959 (0.024)		0.887 (0.291)	0.025	0.96	1.81
Dollar/franc	-0.152 (0.155)	0.904 (0.107)	-0.230 (0.320)		0.030	0.77	2.32
	-0.246 (0.077)	0.837 (0.051)		0.729 (0.342)	0.029	0.80	2.10
Dollar/DM	-0.012 (0.063)	0.982 (0.063)	-0.074 (0.395)		0.032	0.93	2.11
	-0.022 (0.026)	0.972 (0.031)		0.979 (0.663)	0.031	0.94	2.07

Note: Interest rates are the twelve-month Euromarket rates. The expected interest rate differential $E_{t-1}(i-i^*)_t$ was computed from a regression of the interest differential on a constant, two lagged values of the differential, and the logarithm of the lagged forward exchange rate. Two-stage least squares estimation method was used. The instruments for the interest differential were a constant, two lagged values of the differential, and the logarithm of the lagged forward exchange rate; the instruments for the unexpected differential were a constant, Durbin's rank variable, and the logarithm of the lagged forward exchange rate. $i-i^*$, denotes the actual interest rate differential where i denotes the rate of interest on securities denominated in US dollars and i^* denotes the rate of interest on securities denominated in foreign currency. $[(i-i^*)_t - E_{t-1}(i-i^*)_t]$ denotes the *unexpected* interest rate differential. s.e. is the standard error of the equation. A quasi-R^2 was computed as $1 - \text{Var}(\hat{u}_t)/\text{Var}(\ln S_t)$.

TABLE 2.6 Twelve-month Interest Rate Differentials and Exchange Rates; Instrumental Variables Monthly Data: June 1973–July 1979 (standard errors in parentheses)

Dependent variable ln S_t	Constant	ln F_{t-1}	$(i - i^*)_t$	$[(i - i^*)_t - E_{t-1}(i - i^*)_t]$	s.e.	R^2	D.W.
Dollar/pound	0.024 (0.016)	0.965 (0.021)	-0.087 (0.121)	0.978 (0.286)	0.022	0.97	1.82
Dollar/franc	-0.180 (0.118)	0.884 (0.181)	-0.184 (0.245)	0.915 (0.432)	0.029	0.79	2.16
Dollar/DM	-0.013 (0.053)	0.981 (0.054)	-0.063 (0.338)	1.031 (0.752)	0.031	0.93	2.08

Note: Interest rates are the twelve-month Euromarket rates. The expected interest rate differential $E_{t-1}(i - i^*)$ was computed from a regression of the interest differential on a constant, two lagged values of the differential, and the logarithm of the lagged forward exchange rate. Two-stage least squares estimation method was used. The instruments were a constant, two lagged values of the interest differential, Durbin's rank variable of the unexpected differential, and the logarithm of the lagged forward exchange rate. $(i - i^*)_t$ denotes the actual interest rate differential where i denotes the rate of interest on securities denominated US dollars and i^* denotes the rate of interest on securities denominated in foreign currency. $[(i - i^*)_t - E_{t-1}(i - i^*)_t]$ denotes the unexpected interest rate differential. s.e. is the standard error of the equation. A quasi-R^2 was computed as $1 - \mathrm{Var}(\hat{u}_t)/\mathrm{Var}(\ln S_t)$.

induced a rise in the interest differential also induced a rise in the spot exchange rates. Furthermore, consistent with the hypothesis that current changes in exchange rates are primarily a response to new information, the evidence shows the importance of the innovations in the interest differential.

The principle that current exchange rates already reflect expectations concerning the future course of events implies that unanticipated changes in exchange rates are primarily due to innovations. Since the empirical work suggests that most of the actual changes in exchange rates are unanticipated, it follows that most of the actual changes in exchange rates are due to 'news'. In the present section this principle was applied to the analysis of the relationship between exchange rates and interest rate differentials. The principle however is general. For example, it implies that the relationship between a deficit in the balance of trade and the exchange rate depends crucially on whether the deficit was expected or not. A deficit that was expected may have no effect on the exchange rate since the latter already reflected these expectations. In contrast, an unexpected deficit in the balance of trade may contain significant new information that is likely to be accompanied by large changes in the exchange rate.[26] This distinction might be useful in interpreting the weak and unstable relationship between the balance of trade and the exchange rate without having to rely on explanations like the J-curve or on variable import and export elasticities.

4. EXCHANGE RATES AND PRICES

One of the striking facts concerning the relationship between prices and exchange rates during the 1970s has been the poor performance of the predictions of the simple versions of the purchasing power parity doctrine. The originators and proponents of the purchasing power parity doctrine (Wheatley and Ricardo during the first part of the nineteenth century and Cassel during the 1920s) have viewed the doctrine as an extension of the quantity theory of money to the open economy. By now the consensus seems to be that, when applied to aggregate national price levels, purchasing power parities can be expected to hold in the long run if most of the shocks to the system are of a monetary origin which do not require changes in relative prices. To the extent that most of the shocks reflect 'real' changes (like differential growth rates among sectors), the required changes in sectoral relative prices may result in a relatively loose connection between exchange rates and aggregate price levels. The experience during the 1970s illustrates the extent to which real shocks (oil embargo, supply shocks, commodity booms and shortages, shifts in the demand for money, differential productivity growth) result in systematic deviations from purchasing power parities. As illustrated in Figures 2.1–2.3, short-run changes in exchange rates have not been closely linked to short-run differentials in the corresponding national inflation rates as measured by consumer price indices. Furthermore, this loose link seems to be cumulative. As illustrated in Figures 2.4–2.6 divergences from purchasing power parities, measured in terms of the relationship between exchange rates and the ratio of consumer price indices, seem to persist.

The link between prices and exchange rates is illustrated in Table 2.7 which reports the results of regressions of the various exchange rates on

TABLE 2.7 Purchasing Power Parities: Instrumental Variables Monthly Data: June 1973–July 1979
(standard errors in parentheses)

Dependent variable $\ln S_t$	Constant	$\ln(P_w/P_w^*)$	$\ln(P_c/P_c^*)$	s.e.	D. W.	ρ
Dollar/pound	0.712 (0.149)	0.165 (0.507)		0.027	1.63	0.963
	2.982 (2.978)		1.070 (0.897)	0.029	1.66	0.998
Dollar/franc	−1.521 (0.027)	0.184 (0.374)		0.029	2.26	0.863
	−1.570 (0.047)		−1.070 (0.817)	0.029	2.30	0.901
Dollar/DM	−0.900 (0.018)	1.786 (0.230)		0.034	1.69	0.739
	−0.908 (0.175)		2.217 (0.263)	0.031	1.96	0.759
Pound/DM	−1.668 (0.041)	0.821 (0.144)		0.027	1.60	0.895
	−1.666 (0.048)		0.965 (0.197)	0.027	1.57	0.909
Franc/DM	0.863 (0.143)	−0.026 (0.487)		0.020	1.61	0.981
	0.602 (0.048)		1.180 (0.327)	0.019	1.48	0.929

Note: $\ln S_t$ denotes the logarithm of the spot exchange rate; $\ln(P_w/P_w^*)$ and $\ln(P_c/P_c^*)$ denote respectively, the logarithms of the ratios of the wholesale price indices and the cost of living indices. Cochrane–Orcutt iterative technique with two-stage least squares estimation method was used; the instruments are a constant, time, time-squared, and lagged values of the dependent and independent variables. s.e. is the standard error of the equation.

the corresponding ratios of wholesale and of cost of living price indices. As may be seen the results of the regressions which involve the US dollar are extremely poor. For the dollar/pound and the dollar/franc exchange rates the estimates of the coefficients of the price ratios are insignificant and for the dollar/DM exchange rate the estimates differ significantly from unity. In contrast the results of the regressions of exchange rates that do not involve the US dollar or the US price level (the pound/DM and the franc/DM exchange rates) are superior: except for the wholesale price indices in the franc/DM regression all the coefficients are highly significant and the elasticities of the exchange rates with respect to the various price indices do not differ significantly from unity.

The vast difference in the performance of the regressions for the various currencies can be explained by noting that first, due to transport cost, purchasing power parities are expected to hold better among the neighbouring European countries than among each of these countries and the US; second, changes in commercial policies and non-tariff barriers to trade seem to have been more stable within Europe than between Europe and the US; third, within Europe the snake agreement and later on the European monetary system have resulted in a reduced degree of intra-European flexibility of exchange rates; and fourth, there seem to have been large changes in the equilibrium *real* exchange rate between the US dollar and the European currencies.[27] It should be noted, however, that to some extent the overall poor performance of the purchasing power parities doctrine is specific to the 1970s. During the floating rates period of the 1920s, the doctrine seems to have been much more reliable.[28]

The preceding discussion accounted for the persisting deviations from purchasing power parities in terms of changes in real factors which affect equilibrium relative price structure. It should be noted, however, that even in the absence of such changes there is a presumption that, at least in the short run, exchange rate fluctuations would not be matched by corresponding fluctuations of aggregate price levels. The discussion in Section 2 emphasised that in periods which are dominated by 'news' which alter expectations, exchange rates (and other asset prices which are traded in organised markets) are expected to be highly volatile. Aggregate price indices, on the other hand, are not expected to reveal such a degree of volatility since they reflect the prices of goods and services which are less durable and therefore are likely to be less sensitive to the news which alter expectations concerning the future course of events. It follows therefore that in periods during which there are ample 'news' which cause large fluctuations in exchange rates there will also be large deviations from purchasing power parities.[29]

TABLE 2.8 Mean Absolute Percentage Changes in Prices and Exchange Rates Monthly Data: June 1973–July 1979

				Variable		
				Exchange rates Against the dollar		
Country	WPI	COL	Stock market	spot	forward	COL/COL_US
US	0.009	0.007	0.037	–	–	–
UK	0.014	0.012	0.066	0.021	0.021	0.007
France	0.011	0.009	0.054	0.020	0.021	0.003
Germany	0.004	0.004	0.030	0.024	0.024	0.004

Note: All variables represent the absolute values of monthly percentage changes in the data. WPI denotes the wholesale price index and COL denotes the cost of living index. Data on prices and exchange rates are from the IMF tape (May 1979 version). The stock market indices are from *Capital International Perspective*, monthly issues.

The difference between the characteristics of exchange rates and national price levels is also reflected in their time series properties and is fundamental for interpreting the deviations from purchasing power parities. The monthly changes in exchange rates exhibit little or no serial correlation while national price levels do exhibit a degree of serial correlation. The 'stickiness' exhibited by national price levels need not reflect any market imperfection but rather it may reflect the costs of price adjustment which result in the existence of nominal contracts of finite length. Likewise, it may reflect the results of confusion between relative and absolute prices and confusion between permanent and transitory changes. This difference between the time series properties of exchange rates and prices is reflected in the low correlation between the practically random month-to-month exchange rate changes and the serially cor-related differences between national rates of inflation.

The different degrees of volatility of prices and exchange rates are illustrated in Table 2.8 which reports the average absolute monthly percentage changes in the various exchange rates and prices. As is evident, the mean absolute change in the various spot exchange rates has been about 2 per cent per month (and even slightly higher for the changes in the forward rate). The magnitudes of these changes have been more than double the magnitudes of the changes in most of the various price indices as well as in the ratios of national price levels. For example, the mean monthly change in the cost of living price index was 0.4 per cent in Germany, 0.7 per cent in the U.S., 0.9 per cent in France and 1.2 per cent in the UK. These differences are even more striking for the detrended series.

The notion that exchange rates have been volatile is clearly illustrated by Figures 2.1–2.3 and by Table 2.8. The comparison of the magnitudes of the changes in the exchange rates with the magnitudes of the changes in the price indices and in the ratios of national price levels may suggest, according to a narrow interpretation of the purchasing power parity doctrine, that exchange rate fluctuations have been 'excessive'. The previous discussion, however, has emphasised that exchange rates, being the relative prices of assets, are fundamentally different from the price indices of goods and services and therefore are expected to exhibit a different degree of volatility in particular during periods that are dominated by 'news'. An alternative yardstick for measuring the degree of exchange rate fluctuations would be a comparison with prices of other assets. Indeed, while exchange rate changes have been large relative to changes in national price levels, they have been considerably smaller than changes in the prices of other assets like gold, silver, many other commodities that are traded in organised markets, and common stocks. For example, Table 2.8 also reports the mean absolute monthly percentage change in stock market indices. As may be seen, the mean monthly change in these indices ranged from over 3 per cent in Germany to over 6 per cent in the UK. By these standards it is difficult to argue that exchange rates have been excessively volatile.

Given the short-run deviations from purchasing power parities, it is relevant to explore whether these deviations tend to diminish with time or tend to persist or even grow in size. In order to examine the patterns of the deviations the autocorrelation functions and the partial autocorrelation functions of these deviations for the wholesale and the cost of living price indices have been computed. The deviation from purchasing power parities during month t is denoted by Δ and is defined as:

$$\Delta_t = \ln S_t - \ln (P/P^*)_t. \qquad (10)$$

Figures 2.11, 2.12 and 2.13 illustrate the patterns of the deviations for the three exchange rates. As may be seen the general pattern is very similar for the three exchange rates and for the two price indices. In all cases the autocorrelation function tails off at what seems to be an exponential rate and in all cases the partial autocorrelation function shows a spike at the first lag. This pattern seems to indicate (as might have been expected on the basis of the time series properties of exchange rates and price indices) that the deviations from purchasing power parities follow a first-order autoregressive process. It is noteworthy, however, that in all cases the value of the autoregression term is about 0.9, indicating the possibility that the series may not satisfy the stationarity requirement. To allow for

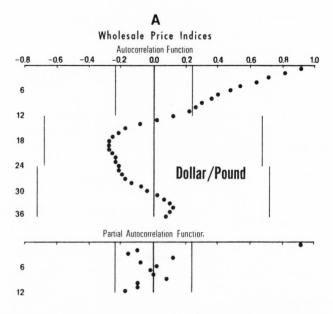

The dollar/pound: deviations from PPP with Cost of Living Indices

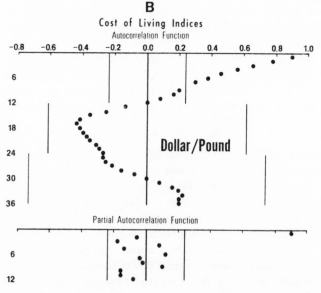

FIGURE 2.11 The dollar/pound: deviations from PPP with Wholesale Price Indices

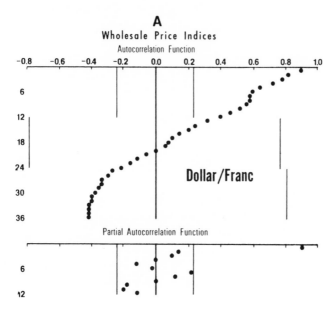

The dollar/franc: deviations from PPP with Cost of Living Indices

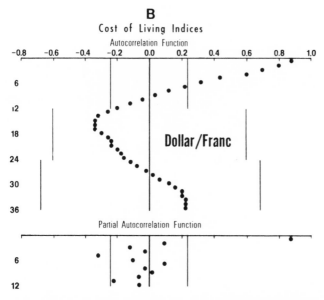

FIGURE 2.12 The dollar/franc: deviations from PPP with Wholesale Price Indices

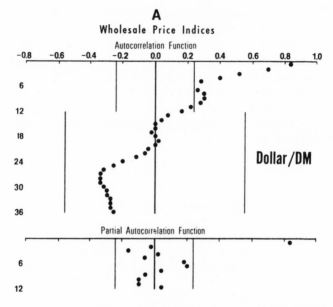

The dollar/DM: deviations from PPP with Cost of Living Indices

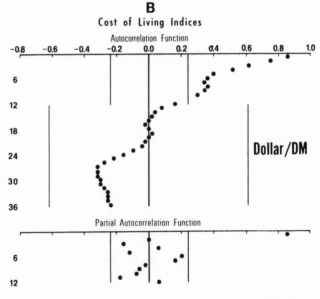

FIGURE 2.13 The dollar/DM: deviations from PPP with Wholesale Price
             Indices

this possibility the autocorrelation functions and the partial autocorrelation functions of $\Delta_t - \Delta_{t-1}$, that is of the first difference of the deviations from purchasing power parities, have also been examined. The results indicate that these differences are serially uncorrelated and thus imply that the deviations Δ_t follow a random walk process. In view of this possibility it is concluded that the deviations from purchasing power parities seem to follow a first-order autoregressive process but that the data do not provide sufficient evidence to reject the alternative hypothesis of a random walk.[30]

5 CONCLUDING REMARKS

This paper has examined some aspects of the operation of flexible exchange rates. The analysis was based on the experience of the 1970s. The principal conclusions which may be drawn from the empirical work are:

(1) In spite of the extraordinary turbulence in the markets for foreign exchange, it seems that to a large extent the markets have operated efficiently. It should be emphasised, however, that the concept of 'efficiency' that is being used in this context is somewhat narrow in that it refers only to the notion that the markets do not seem to entail unexploited profit opportunities. A broader perspective should deal with the social cost of volatility in terms of the interference with the efficiency of the price system in guiding resource allocation as well as with the cost of alternative outlets for the disturbances that are currently reflected in the volatility of exchange rates. As for the choice among alternative outlets for the disturbances, one may argue that since the foreign exchange market is a market in which risk can be bought and sold relatively easily, it may be reasonable to concentrate the disturbances in this market, rather than transfer them to other markets, such as labour markets, where they cannot be dealt with in as efficient a manner.

(2) The high volatility of exchange rates (spot and forward) reflects an intrinsic characteristic of the relative price of monies and other assets that are traded in organised exchange. The price of gold, and the price of stocks as well as exchange rates between national monies, depend critically on expectations concerning the future course of events, and adjust rapidly in response to new information. In this perspective the exchange rate (in contrast with the relative price of national outputs) is

being viewed as a financial variable which is determined in a macroeconomic setting.

(3) During inflationary periods variations in nominal rates of interest are dominated by changes in inflationary expectations; as a result, high nominal rates of interest are associated with high exchange rates (a depreciated currency). This relationship was supported by the empirical work.

(4) The asset view of exchange rate determination implies that 'news' are among the major factors which influence changes in exchange rates. In this context the key finding was the dependence of exchange rate changes on the unexpected changes in the rates of interest. This finding is in accord with the analytical prediction that current exchange rates already reflect current expectations about the future while changes in the current exchange rates reflect primarily changes in these expectations which, by definition, arise from new information.

(5) The experience of the 1970s does not support the predictions of the simple version of the purchasing power parity doctrine which relates the values of current measured prices to current exchange rates. The empirical work showed that deviations from purchasing power parities can be characterised by a first-order autoregressive process.

(6) One of the key analytical insights that is provided by the monetary (or the asset market) approach to the exchange rate is that exchange rates reflect not only current circumstances but also those circumstances which are expected to prevail in the *future*. This anticipatory feature of the exchange rate (which is emphasised by Mussa, 1979b) does not characterise (at least to such a degree) the prices of national outputs which reflect to a large extent *present* and *past* circumstances as they are embedded in existing contracts. Consequently, periods which are dominated by large and frequent changes in expectations are likely to be periods in which the future is expected to differ greatly from the present and the past. Under such circumstances one may expect to find frequent deviations from purchasing power parities when the latter are computed using current prices. These deviations reflect the intrinsic difference between asset prices and national price indices.[31]

(7) Since commodity prices do not adjust fully in response to exogenous shocks it seems that intervention in the foreign exchange market which ensures that exchange rates conform with purchasing power parities would be a mistaken course of policy. When commodity prices are slow to adjust to current and expected economic conditions, it may be desirable to allow 'excessive' adjustment in some other prices. Further, changes in real economic conditions requiring adjustment in

the equilibrium *relative* prices of different national outputs occur continuously. An intervention rule which links changes in exchange rates rigidly to changes in domestic and foreign prices in accord with purchasing power parity ignores the occasional need for equilibrating changes in relative prices.

NOTES

An earlier version of this paper was prepared for a conference on Stabilization Policy: Lessons from the 1970s and Implications for the 1980s, sponsored by the Federal Reserve Bank of St Louis and the Center for the Study of American Business at Washington University, held at the Federal Reserve Bank of St Louis on 19–20 October 1979. I am indebted to Lauren J. Feinstone for helpful suggestions and efficient research assistance and to the National Science Foundation grant SOC 78–14480 for financial support. I have benefited from useful comments by Andrew Abel, William Branson, Sebastian Edwards, Stanley Fischer, Craig S. Hakkio, Edi Karni, Paul Krugman, Leonardo Leiderman, Robert E. Lucas, Jr., Allan Meltzer, Michael L. Mussa, Sam Peltzman, Nasser Saidi and Roland Vaubel, as well as by participants in seminars held at the NBER, Columbia University, New York University, Harvard University, the University of Virginia, the University of Rochester, Oxford University, Tel-Aviv University and the International Monetary Fund. This research is part of the NBER's Program in International Studies. The views expressed are those of the author and not necessarily those of the NBER, Inc.

1. For collections of articles summarising this approach see the *Scandinavian Journal of Economics*, no. 2 (1976) and Frenkel and Johnson (1978).
2. For an application of the same methodology in analysing the efficiency properties of the foreign exchange market during the German hyperinflation of 1921–3 see Frenkel (1976, 1977, 1979). For an application to other exchange rates during the 1920s see Frenkel and Clements (1981), for an application to the 1920s and the 1970s see Krugman (1977); for an interesting analysis using time series and cross-section data see Bilson (1979), for an analysis of market efficiency using novel econometric techniques see Hakkio (1979), and Hansen and Hodrick (1980), and for surveys see Levich (1978, 1979).
3. More precisely, if (assuming risk neutrality) the forward rate measures the expected value of the future spot rate, then the constant term in the logarithmic equation (1) should be $-0.5\sigma_u^2$; see Frenkel (1979). The statement that under risk neutrality the forward rate equals the expected future spot rate neglects the effects of the stochastic elements in prices. As an empirical matter this neglect does not seem to be consequential; see Frenkel and Razin (1981).
4. Since $\ln F_{t-1}$ is highly correlated with $\ln S_{t-1}$ the Durbin–Watson statistic may not be appropriate since equation (1) is very similar to a regression of $\ln S_t$ on its own lagged value. Durbin's *h*-statistic reveals however that the

residuals are serially uncorrelated at conventional confidence levels.

5. This test was recently applied by Obstfeld (1978) to the analysis of the foreign exchange market during the 1970s and by Frenkel (1980a, 1980b) to the analysis of the foreign exchange markets during the 1920s.

6. The efficiency of the foreign exchange market can also be analysed from a different angle as in Frenkel (1980b). Consider the equation:

$$x_t = \alpha_0 + \alpha_1 t + \sum_{i=1}^{n} \beta_i x_{t-i} + \gamma \pi_{t-1} + w_t$$

where x_t denotes the percentage change of the spot exchange rate $(\ln S_t - \ln S_{t-1})$, π_{t-1} denotes the forward premium on foreign exchange $(\ln F_{t-1} - \ln S_{t-1})$, t denotes time, n denotes the number of lags, and w denotes an error term. If π_{t-1} summarises all available information concerning the future evolution of the exchange rate, then *given* the value of the forward premium π_{t-1}, the past history of the percentage change of the exchange rate should not 'help' the prediction (i.e. the past history should not be viewed as Granger-causing future changes), and the joint hypotheses that α_0, α_1 and β_i are zero and that γ is unity should not be rejected. The results of applying these tests to the three exchange rates for various numbers of lags as well as to the pooled data base of the three exchange rates show that the null-hypothesis cannot be rejected at the 95 per cent confidence level since the values of the various F-statistics fall well below the corresponding critical values. It is noteworthy, however, that the power of this test is low and that the joint hypothesis that $\alpha_0, \alpha_1, \beta_i$ and γ are zero could also not be rejected. The difficulties in 'explaining' the percentage change of the exchange rate in terms of past values of various variables reflect the fact that like the prices of other assets which are traded in organised markets, changes in exchange rates are dominated by 'news' which by definition could not have been incorporated in past changes or in the lagged forward premium. For a further elaboration see the following section.

7. The analysis of the role of 'news' in determining current exchange rates and in explaining forecast errors from the forward rate has been made forcefully by Mussa (1976a, 1976b, 1977, 1979a) and Dornbusch (1978). The large degree of volatility is also analysed by McKinnon (1976) who attributes it to insufficient speculation.

8. These and the following empirical regularities are analysed in detail in Mussa (1979a). See also Frenkel and Mussa (1980).

9. For an analysis of the relationship between the variances of series of predictions and series of realisations see Shiller (1979) and Singleton (1980).

10. The following paragraph draws on Frenkel and Mussa (1980).

11. See, for example, the comprehensive econometric model of Fair (1979).

12. A result of this general form is derived in Mussa (1976a). The unique role of expectations is also emphasised by Black (1973), Dornbusch (1976c, 1978), Kouri (1976) and Bilson (1978). In general the value of b may be viewed as the relevant parameter for determining whether or not a specific commodity (whose pricing rule is described in terms of equations like (6)–(7)) may be viewed as an asset. The higher the value of b for a given commodity, the larger its asset attribute.

13. New information might be 'permanent' when the relevant horizon is one month while it might be transitory when the relevant horizon is a year. In that case the correlation between the spot exchange rate and the contemporaneous one-month forward rate is likely to be high while the correlation between the spot rate and the 12-month forward rate is likely to be low. The perceived permanence of the new information can be inferred from the correlation between the spot and the various maturities of the forward rate. As expected it is generally found that this correlation diminishes with the maturity of the forward contract.

14. The normalised values of the spot rate, $\ln S_t^N$, and of the forward premium, $\ln(F_t/S_t)^N$, which are plotted in Figures 2.7–2.9 are defined as $\ln S_t^N \equiv (\ln S_t - \overline{\ln S})/\sigma_{\ln S}$ and $\ln(F_t/S_t)^N \equiv [\ln(F_t/S_t) - \overline{\ln(F/S)}]/\sigma_{\ln(F/S)}$ where a bar over a variable indicates its sample mean and where σ denotes the sample standard deviation of the subscripted variable.

15. It is noteworthy that since the forward premium (like the rate of interest) and the exchange rate are dimensionally incommensurate, their association raises questions that are familiar from the discussions of the Gibson Paradox. In a separate paper I intend to examine the relationship between exchange rates and the forward premium (or the interest differential) in light of the various explanations of the Gibson Paradox.

16. For theoretical developments and applications of the approach see, for example, Dornbusch (1976a, 1976b), Kouri (1976), Mussa (1976a), Frenkel (1976), Frenkel and Johnson (1978), Frenkel and Clements (1981), Clements and Frenkel (1980), Bilson (1978), Hodrick (1978), and Frenkel (1979).

17. It should be emphasised that this explanation of the positive association between the rate of interest and the exchange rate *does not* rely on a rigid form of the purchasing power parity theory. It only requires that domestic and foreign price levels, when expressed in terms of the same currency, are positively correlated. The evidence from the 1970s is consistent with this requirement: see Frenkel (1981).

18. The traditional prediction of a negative relationship between interest rates and the exchange rate could in principle be rationalised under the assumption that it concentrates on the short-run liquidity effects of monetary changes. It should be emphasised, however, that in an inflationary environment, like the one prevailing in the US, the applicability of this rationalisation is very limited. The short-run liquidity effect is emphasised in Dornbusch (1976b). The role of inflationary expectations in dominating exchange rate developments is emphasised in Frenkel (1976). Frankel (1979) and Edwards (1979) attempt to integrate these two factors.

19. For evidence on the robustness of the interest parity relationship see Frenkel and Levich (1977).

20. See, for example, Barro (1977) and Fischer (1980).

21. See also Bilson (1978), Frenkel and Mussa (1980), Isard (1980) and Longworth (1980).

22. In general, of course, the sign of the coefficient α depends on the source of the variation in the interest rate.

23. In all cases the lagged forward exchange rate was included as an instrument in order to obtain consistent estimates; see Nelson (1975). Adding lagged values of the percentage changes of the domestic and the foreign money

supplies as determinants of the expected interest differential and adding the current values of the percentage change of the money supplies as instruments for the unexpected interest differential did not affect the results in any material way. In order to obtain consistent estimates the assumption that is being made in the regressions reported in Tables 2.3–2.6 is that in forming expectations concerning the interest differential, individuals look only at the lagged forward premium and at past values of the differential. An alternative way to compute the expected differential would use data on the term structure of interest rates. Since data on the differential of two-month rates are not readily available, this computation would require interpolations.

24. The difficulties in obtaining instruments for data that are innovations are obvious since, by virtue of being 'news' it is unlikely that variables which characterise the history can serve as good instruments. The difficulties are acute in cases where a variable and its expected value appear in the same regression in which case consistent estimates require the use of an instrument that is contemporaneous with the innovation and is exogenous (see McCallum, 1979). Thus, in addition to a constant and the lagged forward exchange rate, Durbin's rank variable was used as an instrument for estimating the innovations in the interest rate differential.

25. To allow for the possibility that the exchange rate equation includes both the short- and the long-term interest rates where, as suggested by Frankel (1979) the former captures liquidity effects and the latter captures expectations effects, equation (9) was also estimated using the innovations in both the one-month and the twelve-month interest differential on the right-hand side. Since the two sets of innovations are highly collinear, none of the coefficients differed significantly from zero. In this context it is also noteworthy that the twelve-month interest rate contains elements of the one-month rates due to the characteristics of the term structure of interest rates. As a result, coefficient estimates from regressions which use both rates, like those in Frankel (1979), must be interpreted with great care.

26. For a further elaboration on the relationship between exchange rates and the current account see Kouri (1976), Branson (1977), Branson, Halttunen and Masson (1977), Dornbusch and Fischer (1980) and Rodriguez (1980). For a special emphasis on the role of innovations in the trade balance see Mussa (1979c) and for empirical evidence see Hakkio (1980) and Dornbusch (1980). It should be noted that the empirical work on the association between exchange rates and current account innovations faces some difficulties since, in contrast with data on financial variables like interest rates, data on the current account are not available at short intervals. Furthermore, findings on the association between exchange rates and current account innovations should be interpreted with care since rather than reflecting the sensitivity of exchange rates to 'news' they might just reflect invoicing practices according to which US exports are invoiced in terms of US dollars while imports are invoiced in terms of foreign currencies.

27. The failure of the regression of the franc/DM exchange rate on the ratio of the wholesale price indices is explained in terms of the large changes in the French intersectoral relative prices; for an elaboration see Frenkel (1981).

28. For evidence see Frenkel (1976, 1978, 1980a) and Krugman (1978).

29. On this see Mussa (1979a). It is noteworthy that the emphasis in the text has been on the words 'large *fluctuations*;' this should be contrasted with periods during which there are large *secular* changes in the exchange rate (like the changes which occurred during the German hyperinflation). During such periods the secular changes do not stem necessarily from 'news' and need not be associated with deviations from purchasing power parities.

30. If the deviations follow a random walk process then they do not entail (*ex ante*) unexploited profit opportunities. For a study of the deviations from purchasing power parities see Roll (1979). For an analysis of equilibrium deviations from purchasing power parities see Saidi (1977). It may be noted that the main difference between accepting the AR(1) rather than the random walk hypothesis relates to the economic interpretation of the two alternative processes. The random walk process implies that deviations from purchasing power parities do not tend to diminish with the passage of time while the stable AR(1) process implies that there are mechanisms which operate to ensure that in the long run purchasing power parities are satisfied. For the purpose of forecasting the near future, however, there is very little difference between using the AR(1) process with an autoregressive coefficient of 0.9 and using the random walk process.

31. It is interesting to note that this phenomenon was recognised by Gustav Cassel – the most recognised proponent of the purchasing power parity doctrine – according to whom:

> The international valuation of the currency will then generally show a tendency to anticipate events, so to speak, and become more an expression of the internal value that the currency is expected to possess in a few months, or perhaps in a year's time. (Cassel (1930), pp. 149–50)

REFERENCES

Barro, Robert J. (1977). 'Unanticipated Money Growth and Unemployment in the United States', *American Economic Review*, 67 (March), 101–15.

Bilson, John F. O. (1978). 'Rational Expectations and the Exchange Rate', in *The Economics of Exchange Rates: Selected Studies*, Jacob A. Frenkel and Harry G. Johnson (eds) (Reading, Mass.: Addison-Wesley).

—— (1979). 'The "Speculative Efficiency" Hypothesis', unpublished manuscript, University of Chicago.

Black, Stanley W. (1973). 'International Money Markets and Flexible Exchange Rates', Princeton Studies in International Finance, no. 32, Princeton University, March.

Branson, William H. (1977). 'Asset Markets and Relative Prices in Exchange Rate Determination', *Sozialwissenschaftliche Annalen*, 1, 69–89.

Branson, William H., Halttunen, Hannu and Masson, Paul (1977). 'Exchange Rates in the Short Run: The Dollar-Deutschemark Rate', *European Economic Review*, 10 (December), 303–24.

Cassel, Gustav (1930). *Money and Foreign Exchange After 1914* (London: Macmillan).

Clements, Kenneth W. and Frenkel, Jacob A. (1980). 'Exchange Rates, Money, and Relative Prices: The Dollar-Pound in the 1920s', *Journal of International Economics*, 10 (May), 249–62.

Dornbusch, Rudiger (1976a). 'Capital Mobility, Flexible Exchange Rates and Macroeconomic Equilibrium', in *Recent Issues in International Monetary Economics*, Emil Claassen and Pascal Salin (eds) (Amsterdam: North-Holland).

—— (1976b). 'The Theory of Flexible Exchange Rate Regimes and Macroeconomic Policy', *Scandinavian Journal of Economics*, 78 (May), 255–75. Reprinted in *The Economics of Exchange Rates: Selected Studies*, Jacob A. Frenkel and Harry G. Johnson (eds) (Reading, Mass.: Addison-Wesley, 1978).

Dornbusch, Rudiger (1976c). 'Expectations and Exchange Rate Dynamics', *Journal of Political Economy*, 84 (December), 1161–76.

—— (1978). 'Monetary Policy Under Exchange Rate Flexibility', in *Managed Exchange-Rate Flexibility: The Recent Experience*, Federal Reserve Bank of Boston Conference Series, no. 20.

—— (1980). 'Exchange Rate Economics: Where do we Stand?', *Brookings Papers on Economic Activity*, 1, 143–85.

Dornbusch, Rudiger and Fischer, Stanley (1980). 'Exchange Rates and the Current Account', *American Economic Review*, 70 (December), 960–71.

Edwards, Sebastian (1979). 'A Simple Monetary Model of Exchange Rate Determination in the Short Run – Some Preliminary Results for the Peruvian Experience 1950–1954', unpublished manuscript, University of Chicago.

Fair, Ray C. (1979). 'A Multicountry Econometric Model', National Bureau of Economic Research Working Paper Series, no. 414.

Fischer, Stanley (ed.) (1980). *Rational Expectations and Economic Policy* (Chicago: University of Chicago Press).

Frankel, Jeffrey A. (1979). 'On the Mark: The Theory of Floating Exchange Rates Based on Real Interest Differentials', *American Economic Review*, 69 (September), 610–22.

Frenkel, Jacob A. (1976). 'A Monetary Approach to the Exchange Rate: Doctrinal Aspects and Empirical Evidence', *Scandinavian Journal of Economics*, 78 (May), 200–24. Reprinted in *The Economics of Exchange Rates: Selected Studies*, Jacob A. Frenkel and Harry G. Johnson (eds) (Reading, Mass.: Addison-Wesley, 1978).

Frenkel, Jacob A. (1977). 'The Forward Exchange Rate, Expectations and the Demand for Money: The German Hyperinflation', *American Economic Review*, 67 (September), 653–70.

—— (1978). 'Purchasing Power Parity: Doctrinal Perspective and Evidence from the 1920s', *Journal of International Economics*, 8 (May), 169–91.

—— (1979). 'Further Evidence on Expectations and the Demand for Money During the German Hyperinflation', *Journal of Monetary Economics*, 5 (February), 81–96.

—— (1980a). 'Exchange Rates, Prices and Money: Lessons from the 1920s', *American Economic Review*, 70 (May), 235–42.

—— (1980b). 'The Forward Premium on Foreign Exchange and Currency Depreciation During the German Hyperinflation', *American Economic Review*, 70 (September), 771–5.

Frenkel, Jacob A. (1981). 'The Collapse of Purchasing Power Parities During the 1970s', *European Economic Review*.

Frenkel, Jacob A. and Clements, Kenneth W. (1981). 'Exchange Rates in the 1920s: A Monetary Approach', in *Development in an Inflationary World*, M. June Flanders and Assaf Razin (eds) (New York: Academic Press).

Frenkel, Jacob A. and Johnson, Harry G. (eds.) (1978). *The Economics of Exchange Rates: Selected Studies* (Reading, Mass.: Addison-Wesley).

Frenkel, Jacob A. and Levich, Richard M. (1977). 'Transaction Costs and Interest Arbitrage: Tranquil Versus Turbulent Periods', *Journal of Political Economy*, 85 (December), 1209–26.

Frenkel, Jacob A. and Mussa, Michael L. (1980). 'The Efficiency of Foreign Exchange Markets and Measures of Turbulence', *American Economic Review*, 70 (May), 374–81.

Frenkel, Jacob A. and Razin, Assaf (1981). 'Stochastic Prices and Tests of Efficiency of Foreign Exchange Markets', unpublished manuscript, University of Chicago.

Hakkio, Craig S. (1979). 'Expectations and the Foreign Exchange Market', unpublished PhD Dissertation, University of Chicago.

—— (1980). 'Exchange Rates and the Balance of Trade', unpublished manuscript, Northwestern University.

Hansen, Lars P. and Hodrick, Robert J. (1980). 'Forward Exchange Rates as Optimal Predictors of Future Spot Rates: An Econometric Analysis', *Journal of Political Economy*, 88 (October), 829–53.

Hausman, Jerry A. (1978). 'Specification Tests in Econometrics', *Econometrica*, 46 (November), 1251–72.

Hodrick, Robert J. (1978). 'An Empirical Analysis of the Monetary Approach to the Determination of the Exchange Rate', in *The Economics of Exchange Rates: Selected Studies*, Jacob A. Frenkel and Harry G. Johnson (eds) (Reading, Mass.: Addison-Wesley).

Isard, Peter (1980). 'Expected and Unexpected Changes in Exchange Rates: The Role of Relative Price Levels, Balance-of-Payments Factors, Interest Rates and Risk', Federal Reserve Board, International Finance Discussion Papers, no. 156 (April).

Kouri, Pentti J. K. (1976). 'The Exchange Rate and the Balance of Payments in the Short Run and in the Long Run: A Monetary Approach', *Scandinavian Journal of Economics*, 78 (May), 280–304.

Krugman, Paul (1977). 'The Efficiency of the Forward Exchange Market: Evidence from the Twenties and the Seventies', unpublished manuscript, Yale University.

—— (1978). 'Purchasing Power Parity and Exchange Rates: Another Look at the Evidence', *Journal of International Economics*, 8 (August), 397–407.

Levich, Richard M. (1978). 'Further Results on the Efficiency of Markets for Foreign Exchange', in *Managed Exchange Rate Flexibility: The Recent Experience*, Federal Reserve Bank of Boston, Conference Series, no. 20.

—— (1979). 'The Efficiency of Markets for Foreign Exchange', in *International Economic Policy: Theory and Evidence*, Rudiger Dornbusch and Jacob A. Frenkel (eds) (Baltimore: Johns Hopkins University Press).

Longworth, David (1980). 'An Empirical Efficient-Markets Model of Exchange Rate Determination', unpublished manuscript, Bank of Canada, March.

McCallum, Bennett T. (1979). 'Topics Concerning the Formulation, Estimation, and Use of Macroeconometric Models with Rational Expectations', unpublished manuscript, University of Virginia.

McKinnon, Ronald I. (1976). 'Floating Foreign Exchange Rates 1973–74: The Emperor's New Clothes', in *Institutional Arrangements and the Inflation Problem*, Karl Brunner and Allan Meltzer (eds), Vol. 3 of the Carnegie-Rochester Conference Series on Public Policy, a Supplementary Series to the *Journal of Monetary Economics*.

Mudd, Douglas R. (1979). 'Do Rising U.S. Interest Rates Imply a Stronger Dollar?', *Federal Reserve Bank of St. Louis Review*, 61 (June), 9–13.

Mussa, Michael (1976a). 'The Exchange Rate, the Balance of Payments and Monetary and Fiscal Policy under a Regime of Controlled Floating', *Scandinavian Journal of Economics*, 78 (May), 229–48. Reprinted in *The Economics of Exchange Rates: Selected Studies*, Jacob A. Frenkel and Harry G. Johnson (eds) (Reading, Mass.: Addison-Wesley).

—— (1976b). 'Our Recent Experience with Fixed and Flexible Exchange Rates: A Comment', in *Institutional Arrangements and the Inflation Problem*, Karl Brunner and Allan Meltzer (eds), Vol. 3 of the Carnegie-Rochester Conference Series on Public Policy, a Supplementary Series to the *Journal of Monetary Economics*.

Mussa, Michael (1977). 'Exchange Rate Uncertainty: Causes, Consequences, and Policy Implications', unpublished manuscript, University of Chicago.

—— (1979a). 'Empirical Regularities in the Behavior of Exchange Rates and Theories of the Foreign Exchange Market', in *Policies for Employment, Prices, and Exchange Rates*, Karl Brunner and Allan Meltzer (eds), Vol. 11 of the Carnegie-Rochester Conference Series on Public Policy, a Supplementary Series to the *Journal of Monetary Economics*.

—— (1979b). 'Anticipatory Adjustment of a Floating Exchange Rate', unpublished manuscript, University of Chicago.

—— (1979c). 'The Role of the Trade Balance in Exchange Rate Dynamics', unpublished manuscript.

Nelson, Charles R. (1975). 'Rational Expectations and the Estimation of Econometric Models', *International Economic Review*, 16 (October), 555–61.

Obstfeld, Maurice (1978). 'Expectations and Efficiency in the Foreign Exchange Market', unpublished manuscript, MIT.

Rodriguez, Carlos A. (1980). 'The Role of Trade Flows in Exchange Rate Determination: A Rational Expectations Approach', *Journal of Political Economy*, 88 (December), 1148–58.

Roll, Richard (1979). 'Violations of Purchasing Power Parity and Their Implications for Efficient International Commodity Markets', in *International Finance and Trade*, vol. 1, Marshall Sarnat and Gikorgio P. Szego (eds) (Cambridge, Mass.: Ballinger).

Saidi, Nasser (1977). 'Rational Expectations, Purchasing Power Parity and the Business Cycle', unpublished manuscript, University of Chicago.

Shiller, Robert J. (1979). 'Do Stock Prices Move Too Much to be Justified by Subsequent Changes in Dividends?', unpublished manuscript, University of Pennsylvania.

Singleton, Kenneth J. (1980). 'Expectations Models of the Term Structure and Implied Variance Bounds', *Journal of Political Economy*, 88 (December), 1159–76.

DATA APPENDIX

1. Exchange Rates

The spot exchange rates are end-of-month rates obtained from the IMF tape (May 1979 version, updated to July 1979 using the November 1979 issue of the *International Financial Statistics*) obtained from the International Monetary Fund.

The forward exchange rates are end-of-month rates for one month maturity. The forward rates for the UK pound and the DM for the period June 1973–June 1978 are bid prices obtained from the International Money Market (IMM). For the period July 1978–July 1979 they are sell prices obtained from the *Wall Street Journal*. The forward rates for the French Franc for the period June 1973–July 1974 are bid prices calculated from the *Weekly Review* publication of the Harris Bank which reports the spot rate and the forward premium; in each case the closest Friday to the end of the month was chosen. For the period August 1974–June 1978 the rates are bid rates obtained from the IMM and for the period July 1978–July 1979 they are sell prices obtained from the *Wall Street Journal*.

2. Prices

The wholesale and cost of living price indices are period averages obtained from the IMF tape, lines 63 and 64, respectively.

3. Rates of Interest

All interest rates are one-month Eurocurrency rates obtained from the *Weekly Review* of the Harris Bank. In all cases the figures used correspond to the last Friday of each month.

4. Stock Markets

The stock market indices correspond to the last trading day of the month. The sources are *Capital International Perspective*, Geneva, Switzerland, monthly issues.

Lessons from 1970s Experience with Flexible Exchange Rates: A Comment

Allan H. Meltzer

Jacob Frenkel's paper assesses the operation of the international monetary system, after almost a decade of floating. Frenkel studies the performance of three exchange rates – the dollar/pound, dollar/French franc, and dollar/DM rates – in the years of turbulence that followed the closing of the US gold window. The period includes the two oil shocks and ends with the institutionalisation of chaos in Iran.

Frenkel considers three main topics. First, he looks at the relation of spot to forward exchange rates. This leads him to the second topic, the relation of actual to anticipated exchange rates. Frenkel ends his paper with a brief discussion of purchasing power parity, the third topic.

The paper is a well-done, careful summary of our knowledge and ignorance about exchange rates. The reader gains from the investment of time. Hypotheses are clearly stated, and they are allowed to stand, or fall, according to their consistency with the 'facts'. Unlike many discussions of the instability of fluctuating rates, Frenkel's paper makes the reader aware that stability, or variability, of prices and exchange rates is a relative matter.

The world we inhabit is subject to changes that are unforeseen and unpredictable as to timing and magnitude. Weather and technical innovation are examples. Superimposed on these changes, or shocks, are political events – wars, revolutions, and more peaceful changes in political power, in the relative size of government, in the risks to private ownership and in the extent of market freedom. Changes in the relative growth of money in different countries are far less climatic but, at times, no more predictable than the more dramatic political events.

Exchange rates reflect all the events affecting the relative position of countries. A study of exchange rate volatility, therefore, must consider the influence of events that are not – or were not – predicted accurately. And this is why Frenkel's concern with what he calls 'news' is the appropriate place to start.

MAIN IMPLICATIONS

The paper makes several points, and makes them effectively. Two implications, or conclusions, are of particular interest for evaluating the operation of floating exchange rates. In this section, I comment on what I take to be the main implications and offer some criticisms. In the following section, I make some suggestions for further work.

One main implication is that an exchange rate is the relative price of two assets. This statement can be looked at as a truism; exchanges of domestic for foreign money are made at the exchange rate for the two monies. More is intended by the statement, however. Frenkel wants to convey that asset adjustment dominates the movement of exchange rates and that a reliable explanation of exchange rates can be developed without reference to the trade account. This is, generally, a correct statement, and Frenkel's paper shows, as others have shown, that most changes in exchange rates can be accounted for in this way.[1]

Our distinguished intellectual ancestor, David Ricardo, might have objected that Frenkel has neglected some important influences. England, he would say, produces cloth, and Portugal produces wine. When England spends more on wine than Portugal spends on cloth, gold or foreign exchange flows toward Portugal; prices in Portugal rise, with exchange rates fixed, and the escudo appreciates if exchange rates are variable. The price-specie flow mechanism is a more precise statement of the basic truth that exchange rates respond to asset movements and, later, commodity prices adjust.

But, Ricardo might add, suppose there are changes in relative technology. As an example, suppose the number of gallons of wine produced per man hour of labour falls. Then, Ricardo would say, the exchange rate must respond. Analysis of asset movements will miss the initial impact of the change in Portuguese productivity on spot and forward rates of exchange.

The example discusses a one-time change in the level of productivity that might be difficult to sort out of the purely random influences, or 'white noise', affecting exchange rates. A one-time change in the *growth* of productivity in Portugal, however, will have a persistent or permanent effect on the exchange rate. If changes in relative productivity growth occur frequently, Frenkel's hypothesis will miss a systematic influence on exchange rates.

An important implication of his tests is that they suggest that changes in relative productivity growth are small and/or infrequent. Or, the influence of relative productivity growth is small compared to the factors considered – principally the forward rate at the start of the period and the error in forming expectations of differences in interest rates for the two countries. Either of these interpretations would, if correct, provide strong evidence for the asset market approach.

The point is most relevant for the tests of purchasing power parity. Price levels reflect both differences in productivity and in productivity growth. Frenkel's evidence on purchasing power parity (PPP) gives relatively weak support to PPP. Productivity change – and its influence on the trade account – is one of the omitted factors that is capable of reconciling the evidence from asset markets with the less satisfactory evidence for, or against, PPP. If I am correct, the influence of productivity growth has not been dismissed by Frenkel's tests.

Frenkel's careful tests of market efficiency provide considerable evidence on the presence or absence of unused information. The tests are not complete, however. There is no test showing that the intercept terms are constant. Permanent changes in exchange rates can change the spot rate without affecting the relation of forward to spot exchange rates. If people cannot distinguish permanent and transitory changes as they occur, the intercept would adjust to the revised beliefs about the spot rate.[2] Techniques for implementing a test of this kind are available.

The second main implication of Frenkel's paper is related to the first. The variability of exchange rates, during the period of floating, is often described by market participants and governments as 'large' or even 'excessive'. Statements of this kind lack a standard of comparison. Frenkel shows that the variability of exchange rates arises mainly from the arrival of new information. To reduce the variability of exchange rates, we must reduce the variability induced by nature and policy arrangements.

The cost of 'natural' variability borne by people can be reduced by such well-known devices as pooling of risk and diversification. Under the Bretton Woods system, international reserves were mainly in dollar assets. Once the Bretton Woods system ended, the benefits of diversification increased. Highly variable policies and rising inflation in the US and Britain added to the benefits of diversification. Governments, and people, sold dollars and pounds and bought marks, yen and Swiss francs.

Attempts by central banks, governments and people to diversify depreciated the dollar and appreciated the currencies which were purchased with the dollars sold from portfolios. The US policy of refusing to reduce the stock of dollars meant that the dollar exchange for the mark, yen, and Swiss franc appreciated, but the nominal stock of dollars held by foreigners, including central banks and governments, did not fall. Countries that chose to slow the appreciation of their exchange rates bought the dollars that were offered on the market.

One way to analyse portfolio diversification of this kind is to treat some of the adjustments in the dollar exchange rates as a result of intermittent reductions in the demand for dollars and increases in the demand for the specific foreign currencies into which holders diversified. As the anticipated rate of inflation in the US rose, from year to year, further reduction of desired dollar balances became appropriate.

Looked at in this way, the series of adjustments, often described as speculative 'attacks' on the dollar (and the pound), is a sequence of one-time, permanent changes in desired portfolios. The attempt to diversify, to lower the cost of exchange rate changes to asset owners, produced the result that it was intended to avoid. The one-time adjustment gave a trend or drift away from purchasing power parity, particularly for bilateral exchange rates involving the so-called weak, reserve currencies – the dollar and the pound – and the stronger, emerging reserve currencies – the mark, the Swiss franc, the yen and, of course, the currencies that peg to the mark.

If my argument is correct, one should find that exchange rates for currencies that did not participate in the diversification remain closer to purchasing power parity, during the turbulent seventies, than the five currencies most subject to the one-time *permanent* shifts in the demand for money. By neglecting permanent shifts in demand, Frenkel has omitted a relevant part of the history of the period.

My argument supplements Frenkel's. He points out that fluctuations in exchange rates absorb uncertainty. A shift from fixed to floating exchange rates is a policy change that shifts some of the burden of adjusting to new information, 'news', from the output and labour markets to asset markets. Floating rates do not leave desired portfolios unchanged. To reduce the cost of increased fluctuations in asset price, more asset holders diversify. For a time, this increases the amount by which some key exchange rates change.

SUGGESTED EXTENSIONS

Some extensions of the analysis seem desirable. In this section, I discuss three ways in which Frenkel's paper can be extended and, I believe, strengthened.

I have discussed the first of the extensions in the previous section. I believe a more appropriate error structure for Frenkel's equation is

$$S_t = a_t + bF_{t-1} + u_t$$

with

$$a_t = a_{t-1} + v_t.$$

S_t is the current spot rate, F_{t-1} the forward rate at the start of the period and u_t, v_t are the usual normally distributed random variables. The shift in the constant, a_t, permits permanent changes. This change permits portfolio diversification, relative productivity growth and other permanent shocks to change exchange rates. Estimation by adaptive regression provides the necessary information on the relative size of permanent and transitory change.

The second proposed extension would introduce the term structure of interest rates in some of the tests of market efficiency. If one country has a rising term structure of interest rates and another has a declining term structure, there is relevant information that cannot be read from the forward exchange rate and the difference in home and foreign interest rates for a single maturity. Frenkel, and many other current students of exchange rates, neglect this information.

Changes in taxes are a third, commonly neglected influence on exchange rates. Border tax adjustments, changes in relative tariffs, and shifts from income taxes to value added taxes change relevant after-tax returns and costs. The fiscal change in Britain that reduced income taxes and raised valued added taxes reduced taxes on saving and strengthened the pound relative to other currencies. The introduction of VAT in Britain, earlier, not only affected exchange rates but drove a wedge between recorded prices and purchasing power parities. A reader of most of the empirical literature on exchange rates finds few references to influences of this kind.

These suggestions for extensions, like the comments that precede them, are a request for 'more'. My high regard for the paper and the author's contribution to our understanding of exchange rates encourages me to believe that we can look forward to his future work with anticipation that we will continue to receive 'news' about the operation of foreign exchange markets.

NOTES

1. An excellent survey is M. Mussa, 'Empirical Regularities in the Behavior of Exchange Rates and Theories of the Foreign Market' in K. Brunner and A. H. Meltzer (eds), *Policies for Employment, Prices and Exchange Rates*, V, 11 Carnegie-Rochester Conference Series, JME (suppl.) 1979.
2. On the distinction between permanent and transitory changes, see K. Brunner, A. Cukierman and A. H. Meltzer, 'Stagflation, Persistent Unemployment and the Permanence of Economic Shocks,' *JME*, 6, October 1980.

Flexible Exchange Rates in the 1970s: A Comment

André Farber

Professor Frenkel has presented an analysis of the behaviour of foreign exchange markets during the 1970s. His principal conclusions are that the behaviour 'has been broadly consistent with the general implications of the efficient market hypothesis and that the forward exchange rate summarises the relevant available information concerning the future evolution of the rate'.

I have been asked to discuss Professor Frenkel's paper from the viewpoint of the theory of finance. Efficiency of capital markets is a very central topic in the modern theory of finance. It means that prices of securities observed at any time fully reflect all available information (Fama, 1977). The implication is that, in an efficient market, it is impossible to realise profit by using the information reflected in the prices. The efficient market hypothesis has been extensively tested on various equity markets and is sustained by most studies.

The shift in the international monetary system from pegged to flexible exchange rates has triggered researches on exchange market efficiency using methodologies developed for stock markets. Early tests enquire on whether exchange rate's behaviour could be described by a random walk model (Dooley and Shafer 1976, Cornell and Dietrich, 1978). The results obtained are mixed: efficiency seems to dominate but some evidence of inefficiency is present. A second set of tests is concerned with the forecasting efficiency of forward rates. Professor Frenkel's results confirm those obtained previously by Cornell (1977), Levich (1978) and Papadia (1978) who have shown that forward rates are unbiased estimates of future spot rates. One should, however, be careful not to consider that efficiency implies the absence of a premium on the forward rate. The difference between the forward and the expected spot rate depends on the correlation between purchasing power and real world wealth. The empirical analyses performed are perhaps too crude to detect such a premium.

The analysis of how 'news' are incorporated in the exchange rate is an another issue. Professor Frenkel's presentation raises some difficulties in this respect. In his paper, the theoretical framework used is not explicit. The author mentions that exchange rates are viewed as the prices of assets that are traded on organised markets. However, nothing more explicit is provided.

This is unfortunate since the clarification of the exact theoretical framework is of some importance in a paper devoted to market efficiency. It is known that any test of efficiency is a joint test of the efficient market hypothesis and of some market equilibrium model. The interpretation of the test thus requires an understanding of the analytical framework used.

Fortunately, Professor Frenkel is a productive author and has previously presented various versions of a model of the exchange market. Known as the monetary approach to the exchange rate, the model is a macroeconomic model built upon the idea that, in a perfect competitive framework (where all arbitrage conditions hold, namely purchasing power parity, interest rate parity, Fischer condition and rational expectations), money is an asset which has to be held. The equilibrium exchange rate is such that the demand for money by individuals in their portfolio decisions is equal to the money supply. Presenting exchange rates as prices of assets is, in fact, a short-cut: exchange rates are ratios of the various prices of the national monies or, more generally, of national financial assets.

Whereas the monetary approach may be a relevant framework for analysing monetary issues, it is too crude and too aggregated to handle the main issue raised by flexible exchange rates: the uncertainty of the future spot rates and the exchange risk that this possibly creates.

REFERENCES

Cornell, B. (1977). 'Spot Rates, Forward Rates and Exchange Market', *Journal of Financial Economics*, 5, no. 1 (August), pp. 55–65.
Cornell, B. and Dietrich, K. (1978). 'The Efficiency of the Market for Foreign Exchange under Floating Exchange Rates', *The Review of* Economics and Statistics, 60, no. 1 (February), pp. 111–20.
Dooley, M. P. and Shafer, J. R. (1976). 'Analysis of Short Run Exchange Rate Behaviour – March 1973 to September 1975', International Finance Discussion Paper no. 76, February.
Fama, E. F. (1977). *Foundations of Finance* (Basic Books, New York).
Levich, Richard M. (1978). 'Further Results on the Efficiency of Markets for Foreign Exchange' in *Managed Exchange Rate Flexibility: The Recent Experience*, Federal Reserve Bank of Boston, Conference Series, no. 20.
Papadia, F. (1978). 'Forward Exchange Rates as Predictors of Future Spot Rates and the Efficiency of the Foreign Exchange Market', mimeo.

3 Alternative Intervention Rules in the Exchange Markets of the European Monetary System

Paul de Grauwe and Paul van den Bergh

1 INTRODUCTION

In this paper some aspects of the functioning of the European monetary system (EMS) are investigated. Three issues will be analysed. First, the choice of the currency in the intervention policies is studied. In particular the question will be asked what difference it makes to choose between an EMS currency or an external currency (the dollar) for the adjustment mechanism in the national money markets.

A second issue which will be addressed concerns the ECU as a target for intervention within the EMS. We will assume that interventions are carried out using national currencies (either the dollar or EC currencies). The only role of the ECU is to function as an indicator triggering off interventions in the foreign exchange markets. It should be mentioned that at this time the ECU fulfils this role to a limited extent within the EMS.

Finally, the issue of the enlargement of the original EMS will be studied. In particular, we will analyse how and to what extent the addition of another country (the UK) affects the monetary transmission processes within the EMS.

In order to analyse these issues we use an econometric model of the money markets of the EC countries.[1] In Section 2 the model is outlined briefly. In Sections 3, 4 and 5 the results of the simulations of the model are reported.

2 THE MODEL

The model consists of national models of the monetary sectors. These national models have essentially the same structure and the equations, whenever possible, take on the same econometric specification.

The national models are composed of three blocks: first, a monetary block, second, a price block, third, a policy reactions block. The models are essentially short-term in nature. They determine, among other things, the spot exchange rate, the interest rate, the stock of international reserves. All 'real' variables, for example the trade balance, national income in real terms, are assumed to be exogenous.

The first two blocks of the model are described in greater detail in the Appendix. Here we concentrate on the policy reactions block. The policy reactions in the foreign exchange market determine the exchange rate regime. Several alternative exchange rate regimes are studied here.[2]

2.1 A Currency Union (EMS)

The monetary authorities of the member countries of the currency union intervene to keep their cross-rates within specified margins. We now have that:

$$\Delta R_{it}^j = \theta(S_{jit} - S_{jit}^*) \tag{1}$$

where S_{jit} = the price of currency j in terms of currency i in period t;
S_{jit}^* = the parity exchange rate of j in terms of i;
R_{it}^j = the holdings of currency j by country i in period t.

Thus, country i sells (buys) currency j whenever S_{jit} tends to increase (decrease) beyond a certain limit. In the simulations the parameter θ is varied such that the observed spot rates always remain within the specified margins of fluctuations (2.25 per cent for the EMS countries, except for Italy).

Note that we must have the following triangular arbitrage conditions:

$$S_{jit} = S_{it}/S_{jt} \tag{2}$$

In addition we must have that:

$$S_{jit} = \frac{1}{S_{ijt}} \tag{3}$$

and

$$S_{jit}^* = \frac{1}{S_{ijt}^*} \tag{4}$$

and

$$S_{iit} = S_{iit}^* = 1 \tag{5}$$

It is important to note that the interventions within the currency union have implications for the money supply process in the member countries.

We now have that:

$$\Delta B_{it} = \Delta R_{it} + \Delta D_{it} \tag{6}$$

and

$$\Delta R_{it} = \Delta R_{it}^{\$} + \sum_{j \neq i} \Delta R_{it}^{j} - \sum_{j \neq i} \Delta R_{jt}^{i} \tag{7}$$

where $R_{it}^{\$}$ = the dollar holdings of country i, expressed in units of domestic currency;

R_{it}^{j} = the amount of currency j held by country i, expressed in units of domestic currency;

R_{jt}^{i} = the amount of currency i held by country j.

Thus when the authorities of country i buy or sell the currency of country j (ΔR_{i}^{j}), they raise (reduce) the money base of country i and reduce (increase) the money base of country j, in the absence of sterilisation policies.

Another way to intervene is to buy and sell dollars (the outside currency).[3] In that case we have to translate the target cross-rates S_{ji}^{*} in terms of dollar rates. The intervention function then becomes:

$$\Delta R_{it}^{\$} = \theta' \, (S_{\$it} - S_{\$it}^{*}) \tag{8}$$

where $S_{\$it}^{*} = S_{jit}^{*} S_{\$jt}$

and S_{jit}^{*} is, as before, the 'snake' parity rate between currency i and j, and is exogenous.

Note that $\theta' = \theta / S_{jt}$.

It can easily be seen that a dollar-intervention system is equivalent to intervention in snake currencies (as far as its monetary effects are concerned) when we impose the condition that all dollars sold (bought) by country i are bought (sold) by country j. In that case the monetary contraction (expansion) in country i is exactly offset by a monetary expansion (contraction) in country j.

2.2 A Currency Union (EMS) with an ECU as Intervention Target

The ECU is defined as follows

$$E_i = \sum_{j=1}^{n} a_j S_{ji} \qquad \text{for } i = 1, \ldots, n \tag{9}$$

where E_i = the price of the ECU in terms of currency i;

$\quad a_j$ = the amount of currency j in the ECU-basket;

$\quad S_{ji}$ = the price of currency j in terms of currency i.

Note that E_i and S_{ji} relate to observed market prices. The official ECU price of currency i (the ECU parity) can be written as

$$E_i^* = \sum_{j=1}^{n} a_j S_{ji}^* \qquad \text{for } i = 1, \ldots, n \tag{10}$$

where E_i^* = the official price of the ECU in terms of currency i;

$\quad S_{ji}^*$ = the official price of currency j in terms of currency i.

The matrix of S_{ji}^* forms the so-called parity grid.

In the ECU-intervention system considered here the monetary authorities buy and sell foreign exchange (dollars or European currencies) so as to maintain the ECU rate of their currency within a predetermined margin. This can be formalised as follows

$$\Delta R_{it} = \gamma_i (E_{it} - E_{it}^*) \tag{11}$$

where γ_i = the intervention parameter of country i. In the simulations of the model the numerical values of γ_i are chosen such that the ECU rate cannot diverge from the ECU parity by more than the margin.

As in the previous intervention system actual intervention can be carried out using dollars or European currencies. Therefore, in the following, the intervention both in dollars and in European currencies will be analysed.

If the authorities choose to intervene in dollars it is convenient to rewrite (11) as follows

$$\Delta R_{it}^{\$} = \gamma_i E_{\$t} \left(S_{\$it} - \frac{E_{it}^*}{E_{\$t}} \right) \tag{12}$$

where $E_{\$t} = \dfrac{E_{it}}{S_{\$it}}$ the price of the ECU in terms of dollars in period t;

$\quad S_{\$it}$ = the price of the dollar in terms of currency i in period t.

Note that (12) is an equivalent expression for (11) where we have made use of the triangular arbitrage condition $E_i = E_{\$} S_{\$i}$, and $E_i = E_{\$} S_{\$i}^*$. (Note that there is no official price of the ECU in terms of dollars, so that $E_{\$}^* = E_{\$}$.) The intervention function (12) will be used when the authorities intervene in dollars.

In a similar way we can rewrite (11) so as to obtain the cross-rates in the intervention function

$$\Delta R_{it}^{j} = \gamma_i (E_{jt} S_{jit} - E_{jt}^* S_{jit}^*) \tag{13}$$

Note that we have used the triangular arbitrage condition $E_i = E_j S_{ji}$ and $E_i^* = E_j^* S_{ji}^*$, and that contrary to the intervention function (12) we have to introduce E_j and E_j^* separately.

3 SIMULATION RESULTS: THE CURRENCY UNION

In this section the results of the simulations of the currency union are reported. Here we concentrate on the first version of the intervention mechanism where the authorities intervene to maintain the cross-rates within the margin. We will call this the 'snake' intervention system in contrast to the ECU-intervention system where the authorities use ECU rates as their intervention targets.

Two currency unions were studied. In the first union Belgium, Germany, the Netherlands and France form a mini-EMS. In the second union the UK is added (enlarged EMS). The purpose of this two-step simulation strategy is to find out how the extension of the original EMS agreement to more countries may affect the monetary interdependencies among the initial members of the EMS agreement.

The general simulation strategy has been to perform dynamic simulations of the model using the observed values of the exogenous variables. These simulations are then used as control solutions in the policy simulations. The multipliers of the exogenous (or policy) variables are then obtained by computing the deviation between the endogenous variables obtained in the policy simulations and their values in the control solution.

3.1 The Mini-EMS

As was pointed out earlier the authorities have the choice of intervening either in dollars or in European currencies. Here we compare two such choices. In the first one Belgium, the Netherlands and France buy and sell DM to keep the BF/DM, guilder/DM and FF/DM rates within the margin of 2.25 per cent around the parities. In the second one Belgium, the Netherlands and France buy and sell dollars to keep their parities with the DM within the limits. The results of the simulation of the different shocks are now discussed consecutively.

(a) An increase in the Euro-dollar interest rate

The dynamic multipliers of a one percentage point increase in the Euro-dollar interest rate are presented in Table 3.1. It can be seen that the effects on the DM/BF, DM/guilder and BF/FF rates are almost nil under both the intervention systems. In addition, the interest rates in the four countries move very little and the size of the intervention in either DMs or dollars is very little. Thus an exogenous increase in the US interest rate puts very little strain on the intra-snake movements of reserves and exchange rates. The underlying assumption, here, is that the expected DM/BF, DM/guilder and DM/FF rates are not influenced by the increased US interest rate.

TABLE 3.1 Effect of a 1 Percentage Point Increase in the US Interest Rate (73 I–73 II)

	On dollar spot rates (in %)	On DM spot rates (in %)	On interest rate (in % points)	On reserve flows (in billion nat-ional currencies)
Dollar intervention				
Belgium	0.253	+ 0.002	0.004	− 0.105
Germany	0.251	−	0.003	0.0
France	0.251	0.0	0.001	− 0.018
Netherlands	0.253	0.0	0.006	− 0.003
DM intervention				
Belgium	0.252	− 0.002	0.004	− 0.070
Germany	0.250	−	0.001	+ 0.012
France	0.251	−	0.001	− 0.008
Netherlands	0.253	0.003	0.005	− 0.003

(b) An expansion of domestic credit in the EMS countries

We discuss the effects of a 10 per cent expansion of the domestic component of the money base in Germany. These are shown in Table 3.2. One now finds significant differences according to whether the intervention is in dollars or in DMs. In a dollar-intervention system the effects of the German credit expansion on the interest rates of Belgium, the Netherlands and France are substantially higher than in a DM-intervention system.

The reason is that, in the absence of sterilisation policies, the purchase of DMs by Belgium, the Netherlands and France tends to reduce the money supply in Germany, and thereby diminishes the expansionary effects exerted by the German credit expansion. This is not the case in a dollar-intervention system: the dollars purchased by Belgium, the Netherlands and France have no monetary repercussion in Germany.

TABLE 3.2 Effect of an Expansion of Domestic Credit in Germany (10 per cent)[a] (73 I–73 II)

	On dollar spot rates (in %)	*On DM spot rates (in %)*	*On interest rates (in % points)*	*On reserve flows (in billions of national currencies)*
Dollar intervention				
Belgium	0.031	− 0.020	− 0.138	+ 8.3
Germany	0.051	–	− 0.186	0.0
France	0.033	− 0.018	− 0.100	5.1
Netherlands	0.079	+ 0.028	− 0.254	0.191
DM intervention				
Belgium	0.009	− 0.034	− 0.036	+ 1.80
Germany	0.043	–	− 0.172	− 0.15
France	0.005	− 0.019	− 0.016	+ 0.72
Netherlands	0.013	− 0.030	− 0.047	+ 0.034

[a] This corresponds to an initial increase of the money base of 1.2 per cent.

The difference in the two intervention systems is also apparent from the size of the intervention. In a dollar-intervention system Belgium, the Netherlands and France have to buy substantially more dollars (expressed in national currencies) than they have to buy DMs in a DM-intervention system. The reason for this difference is again due to the asymmetries of the dollar-intervention system. In this system Belgium, the Netherlands and France have to absorb more of the German credit expansion. Whereas in a DM-intervention system the Belgian, Dutch and French interventions are helped by the contractionary effects they produce in Germany, this is not the case in a dollar-intervention system. As a result the Belgian, Dutch and French authorities have to intervene more in the dollar-intervention system. Another way of putting this result is that intervening in dollars is less effective from the point of view of Belgium, the Netherlands and France than intervening in DM.

It should be noted that the use of sterilisation policies tends to reduce the difference in the monetary effects of the two intervention systems. This issue was analysed in P. de Grauwe and P. van den Bergh (1980).

(c) Exogenous speculative movements

First, the effects of an expected appreciation of the DM are analysed. This expectational change was assumed to take the following form: the expected appreciation of the DM produces a decline in the forward rate of the DM of 1 per cent (versus the dollar and the other snake currencies), compared to its exogenous value during three consecutive quarters, after which the forward rate comes back to its exogenous value. Thus during the first quarter the forward rate declines by 1 per cent, during the second quarter by 2 per cent (relative to the exogenous value), during the third quarter by 3 per cent, during the fourth quarter by 2 per cent, during the fifth quarter by 1 per cent. During the sixth quarter the forward rate returns to its exogenous value. The results of this speculative run are shown in Figure 3.1.

The results in a dollar-intervention system again illustrate the essential asymmetry of this system. The expected appreciation of the DM leads to equal appreciations of the spot DM versus the dollar. The German interest rate is unaffected. In order to keep the DM/BF, DM/guilder and DM/FF rates within the permissible band the Belgian, Dutch and French authorities are forced to sell dollars in substantial amount. This puts a strong upward pressure on the other countries' interest rates.

These asymmetries are reduced in a DM-intervention system because the sale of DMs by Belgium, the Netherlands and France reduces the German interest rate. As a result, the upward pressure on the Belgian, Dutch and French interest rates is lessened. Another implication of a DM-intervention system is that the appreciation of the DM vis-à-vis the dollar is reduced.

In a second simulation of a speculative movement it was assumed that the Belgian franc is expected to *depreciate* vis-à-vis all the other currencies. The set-up of this speculative run was similar to the previous speculative run. Note that we now have that the forward rate of the Belgian franc increases relative to its exogenous value. The results are shown in Figure 3.2. In the dollar-intervention system Belgium has to bear the full burden of the adjustment, mainly by an increase in the Belgian interest rate. The other countries are completely insulated from the effects of the expected depreciation of the BF. Note also that the spot BF depreciates vis-à-vis the dollar and vis-à-vis the DM in the same proportion.

In the DM-intervention system the upward pressure on the Belgian interest rate is lessened, because the other countries' interest rates move downwards. Note that an asymmetry remains in that the upward movement of the Belgian interest rate is larger than the downward movement of the Dutch, German and French interest rates. This asymmetry has to do with the small size of Belgium.

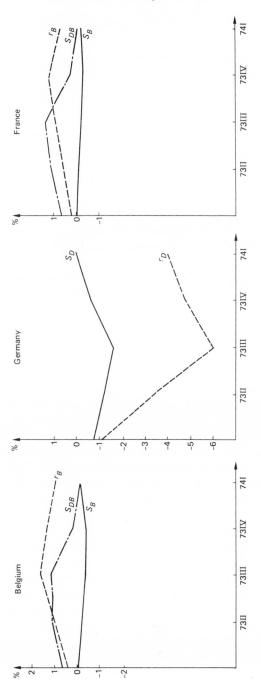

FIGURE 3.1 Expected appreciation of the DM (DM-intervention)

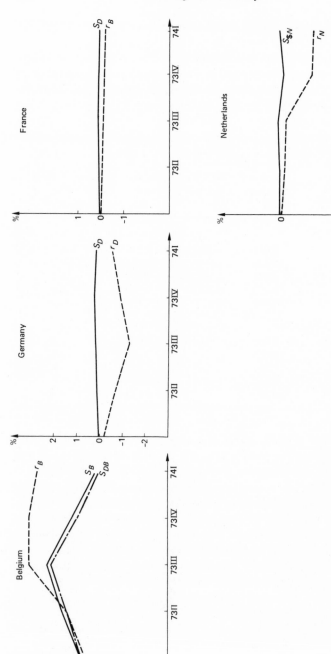

FIGURE 3.2 Expected depreciation of the BF (DM-intervention)

3.2 The Enlargement of the EMS

In this section the results of enlarging the currency union by including the UK are reported. We report the simulation of a credit expansion in Germany. The results are shown in Table 3.3. These results should be compared with those of the mini-EMS in Table 3.2.

TABLE 3.3 Effect of an Expansion of Domestic Credit in Germany (10 per cent) (73 I–73 II)

	Dollar spot rate	*DM spot rate*	*Interest rate*	*Reserve flows (in billions of national currencies)*
Dollar intervention				
Belgium	0.031	− 0.020	− 0.138	+ 8.3
Germany	0.051	–	− 0.186	0.0
Netherlands	0.079	0.028	− 0.254	0.191
France	0.033	− 0.018	− 0.100	5.1
UK	0.069	–	− 0.115	0.442
DM intervention				
Belgium	0.008	− 0.016	− 0.024	1.25
Germany	0.024	–	− 0.088	− 0.83
Netherlands	0.011	− 0.013	− 0.033	0.022
France	0.005	− 0.019	− 0.014	0.67
UK	0.009	–	− 0.035	0.050

A first striking result is that in a dollar-intervention system, with Germany playing the passive role, the addition of the UK does not influence the transmission mechanism of a credit expansion in Germany. Thus as in the mini-snake German monetary policies continue to influence the money markets of Belgium and the Netherlands in the same way. The reason has to do with the asymmetrical intervention system analysed here. The money markets of France, Belgium and the Netherlands are mere extensions of the German money market, without feedback effects going from these countries to Germany. The addition of the UK, therefore, does not affect the transmission of monetary shocks from Germany to Belgium, the Netherlands and France.

The situation is changed in the DM-intervention system (without sterilisation). Here we observe that the addition of the UK affects the transmission of a German monetary shock to Belgium, the Netherlands and France. These three countries are now less affected by a credit expansion in Germany. Part of the German credit expansion is absorbed by the UK. This in turn has a feedback effect on Germany, which reduces the effects of the initial credit expansion on the other countries.

In addition, the initial EMS countries have to intervene less when the UK is in the union, because the UK is now doing a part of the intervention. The counterpart is that the total official purchase of DM in the foreign exchange market of the union is higher when the UK is in the union than in its absence (830 million DM instead of 540 million DM). This also implies that the effect of the German credit expansion on the German interest rate is lower when the UK is in the union. Instead of declining with 117 basis points the German interest rate declines with only 88 basis points when the UK is in the union.

Another way to put this result is to state that the 'offset' of the German monetary expansion by a capital outflow from Germany to the other union members is larger when the UK belongs to the union. The 'offset coefficient'[4] of a domestic credit expansion in Germany implicit in the foregoing simulations is equal to -0.43 in the mini-EMS and -0.69 in the union with the UK. This means that in the mini-EMS a DM 1 expansion of credit in Germany is offset by a DM 0.43 reduction of net international reserves in Germany (in fact a purchase of DM 0.43 by Belgium, the Netherlands and France) and by a DM 0.69 reduction of net international reserves of Germany in the union with the UK (i.e. a purchase of DM 0.69 by Belgium, France, the Netherlands and the UK). Thus the size of the offset coefficient crucially depends on the size of the currency union.

4 SIMULATION RESULTS: ECU INTERVENTION

In this section the results of the simulation of the ECU-intervention system are reported. These are then compared to the same simulations under a 'snake'-intervention system (as reported in the previous section).

4.1 Domestic Monetary Shock

We analyse the results of a domestic monetary shock in Germany which takes the form of a 10 per cent increase of the domestic component of the money base above its observed values in Germany (Table 3.4). In these simulations the UK is assumed to be part of the EMS.

The results of Table 3.4 suggest the following. First, in a ECU-intervention system the choice of the currency to do the intervention in

TABLE 3.4 Effect of an Expansion of Domestic Credit in Germany (10 per cent*)
(73 I–73 II) (partial sterilisation policies, 50 per cent)

A. ECU is indicator

	Spot rate	DM	Interest rate	Reserves (in billions of national currencies)
Intervention in dollars				
Belgium	0.002	− 0.034	− 0.006	0.58
Germany	0.036	–	− 0.145	− 0.169
France	0.001	− 0.035	− 0.003	0.30
Netherlands	0.002	− 0.034	− 0.008	0.011
UK	0.001	− 0.035	− 0.002	0.004
ECU/$	− 0.012			
Intervention in DM				
Belgium	0.002	− 0.033	− 0.007	0.63
Germany	0.035	–	− 0.145	− 0.47
France	0.001	− 0.034	− 0.004	0.33
Netherlands	0.003	− 0.032	− 0.009	0.012
UK	0.001	− 0.034	− 0.002	0.005
ECU/$	− 0.016			

B. Cross-rates are indicators ('Snake' mechanism)
Intervention in dollars

	Spot rate	DM	Interest rate	Reserves (in billions of national currencies)
Belgium	0.020	− 0.031	− 0.085	8.6
Germany	0.051	–	− 0.186	0.0
France	0.017	− 0.034	− 0.057	5.3
Netherlands	0.040	− 0.011	− 0.156	0.208
UK	0.069	+ 0.018	− 0.115	0.442
Invervention in DM				
Belgium	0.004	− 0.033	− 0.015	1.4
Germany	0.037	–	− 0.135	− 0.93
France	0.002	− 0.035	− 0.009	0.75
Netherlands	0.005	− 0.032	− 0.021	0.037
UK	0.009	− 0.028	− 0.022	0.056

* This corresponds to an initial increase of the money base of 1.2 per cent.

the exchange market seems to matter little. In both cases of intervention in dollars and DM the results are very similar. Second, the ECU system allows a certain degree of symmetry in that the expansionary country will have to sell foreign exchange in the foreign exchange market, whereas all the other countries buy foreign exchange. This then tends to contract the money supply in the expansionary country and to expand it in the other countries. This expansionary effect in the other EMS countries remains relatively small because in the simulation run the authorities use sterilisation policies[5] and the cross-rates move within the permissible margin of fluctuation.

These results of the ECU-intervention system should be compared with the results obtained when the 'snake' mechanism is operative. The latter are shown in the bottom halves of Table 3.3. The comparison of these results allows one to draw the following conclusions.

A snake mechanism can be made to operate under similar symmetry conditions as an ECU system. In order to obtain symmetry in the snake mechanism it is sufficient that the central banks participating in the arrangement intervene in each others' currencies.

Asymmetries in the adjustment mechanism will be obtained in the snake mechanism if the intervention is in dollars and if one country follows a 'benign neglect' policy as far as its dollar exchange rate is concerned. In the simulations reported here we assumed that Germany was this country. In that particular set-up Germany will determine the monetary conditions in the other countries. This means, for example, that if it expands the domestic money base and reduces the interest rate, the other countries will have to follow suit. The opposite will be true if there is a contraction in Germany.

We conclude that an ECU-intervention system has similar (and symmetric) effects on the adjustment mechanism in the money markets to the 'snake'-intervention system provided intervention occurs in EMS currencies.

4.2 Changes in Expectations

In this section the simulations of expectational changes are reported. We assume a speculative cycle involving the DM. In the simulation runs reported here we assume that the DM is expected to appreciate against all currencies during three quarters, whereafter it returns to its initial value. The forward rate increases by 1 per cent each quarter during three quarters, and returns to its observed value afterwards.

The results are shown in Figures 3.3 and 3.4. Figure 3.3 represents the time path of the endogenous variables under a '*snake*' *system*, Figure 3.4 under an *ECU system*. In both cases the authorities buy and sell *dollars*. In the snake system all EMS countries have to adjust by increasing their domestic interest rate (because they sell dollars so as to raise their currency value vis-à-vis the dollar). Germany can insulate its domestic money market from the effects of the expectational change by letting the dollar/DM($S_{\$D}$) rate decline.

The ECU system changes this picture considerably. The expected

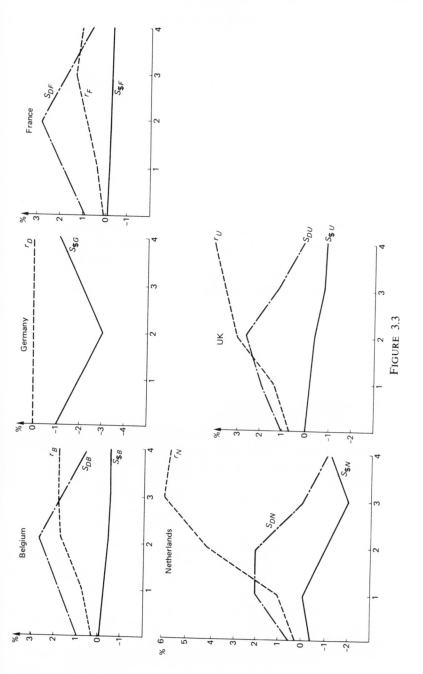

FIGURE 3.3

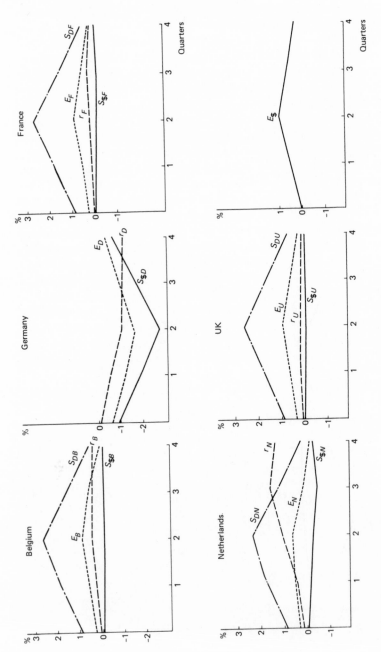

Figure 3.4

appreciation of the DM reduces the ECU/DM rate thereby forcing the German authorities to buy dollars. This leads to reductions in the German interest rate.[6] As a result the effects on the other countries' money markets are substantially reduced. Thus, the ECU adds substantial symmetry forcing Germany, in this case, to do much of the adjustment by letting its domestic interest rate drop. This reduces the burden of the adjustment for all countries.

In a second set of simulations we assumed that the intervention takes place using DMs instead of dollars. The format of the simulations is identical to the previous case. Two results of this simulation stand out. First, in the snake system (Figure 3.5) Germany is doing most of the adjustment, that is the German interest rate declines substantially.[7] This allows the other countries' interest rates to increase to a limited amount only. Second, in the ECU system (Figure 3.6) the adjustment burden imposed on Germany is somewhat reduced. At the same time the upward pressure on the other countries' interest rates is reduced even further. This may seem paradoxical. The rationale for this result is that in an ECU system the other countries intervene very little, because their ECU rates move very little. The DM accounts for 'only' 30 per cent in the ECU basket. As a result, most of the adjustment is taken care of by movements of the cross-exchange rates within the EMS. As can be seen, the cross-rates (S_{DB}, S_{DF}, S_{DM} and S_{DU}) increase substantially more in the ECU system than in the snake system. This then reduces the need to adjust interest rates.

This brings us to a problem of the ECU system as simulated here. When intra-EMS exchange rates move in opposite directions (e.g. the DM appreciates vis-à-vis the FF and the latter appreciates vis-à-vis the BF) third countries' ECU rates may move very little. As a result little or no intervention will occur even if the cross-rates move substantially. Put differently, setting fixed margins around ECU parities is compatible with a great number of variations of cross-rates.[8] If one wants to avoid large variations of intra-EMS exchange rates fixed ECU margins must be supplemented by fixed margins on bilateral exchange rates. One then returns, *de facto*, to a 'snake'-type arrangement.

5 CONCLUSION

In this paper we have studied the monetary transmission process in a currency union, and the implications of such a system on the exchange rates. First, we noted the importance of the choice of the intervention

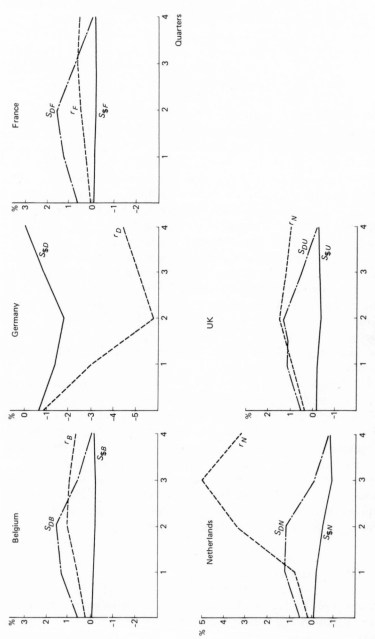

FIGURE 3.5 Snake expected appreciation DM, STER = 0.5, DM intervention

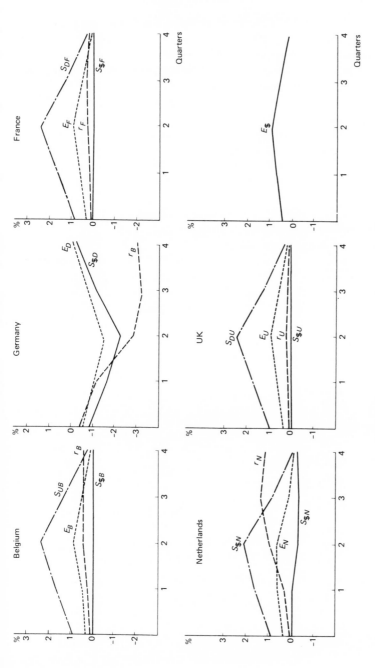

FIGURE 3.6 ECU expected appreciation, STER = 0.5, DM intervention

currency within the union. In particular it was found that the use of an external currency (e.g. the dollar in the EMS) may substantially reduce the effectiveness of control over intra-union exchange rates. Second, some implications for the European monetary system of an enlargement including the UK were analysed. Finally, the use of an ECU as an indicator for foreign exchange market interventions within the EMS was analysed. It was shown that such a system introduces some symmetry in the monetary adjustment mechanism, compared to a 'snake'-intervention system in which countries buy and sell dollars to maintain their cross-exchange rates within the margins. The ECU, however, does not add more symmetry in the adjustment mechanism when the EMS participants intervene in European currencies. Other simulations reported in this paper suggest that, without being harmful, the ECU does not stand out as a particularly attractive instrument in the intervention mechanism within the EMS.

In concluding, it is important to stress the limitations of the present study. The major limitation is the short-term nature of the model, which led us to assume that expectations are exogenous. Further work should go into the problem of endogenising expectations. This is especially important as one expects that the intervention rules used by the monetary authorities affect the expectations about the future spot rate.

APPENDIX A.1: THE THEORETICAL MODEL: MONEY MARKET BLOCK

The money demand equation:

$$\ln M_{it}^d = a_{1i} + a_{2i} \ln Y_{it} + a_{3i} \ln r_{it} + \ln P_{it} \qquad (A1)$$

where M_{it}^d = the money demand in country i in quarter t;
   Y_{it} = real GNP in country i in quarter t;
   r_{it} = the nominal interest rate in country i in quarter t;
   P_{it} = the price level in country i in quarter t.

The money supply equation is a definition

$$M_{it}^S = m_{it} B_{it} \qquad (A2)$$

where M_{it}^S = the money supply in country i in quarter t;
   m_{it} = the money base multiplier in country i in quarter t;
   B_{it} = the money base in country i in quarter t.

The money base   (in changes) is defined as:

$$\Delta B_{it} = \Delta R_{it} + \Delta D_{it} \tag{A3}$$

where R_{it} = the foreign component of the money base in country i in period t;

   D_{it} = the domestic component of the money base in country i in period t.

The *interest parity relationship* takes the following form

$$r_{it} - r_{Et} = x_{it} \tag{A4}$$

where r_{Et} = the Eurodollar interest rate;

   x_{it} = the forward discount on currency i, i.e.

$$x_{it} = \frac{F_{it} - S_{it}}{S_{it}} \times 400;$$

   $F_{\mathfrak{s}it}$ = the (three-month) forward exchange rate of currency i in quarter t;

   $S_{\mathfrak{s}it}$ = the spot exchange rate of currency i in period t.

All exchange rates are defined as prices of the *dollar* in terms of domestic currency.

The use of the interest parity equation implies that there is absence of transaction costs. The existence of capital controls and of political risk, however, leads to deviations from the interest parity condition.[A1]

Equilibrium in the money market of country i implies:

$$M_{it}^d = M_{it}^S \tag{A5}$$

APPENDIX A.2: THE THEORETICAL MODEL: WAGE PRICE BLOCK

The price and wage equations are specified as follows:

$$\ln P_{it} = b_{1i} + b_{2i} \ln PM_{it} + b_{3i} \ln W_{it} + b_{4i} \ln P_{it-1} \tag{A6}$$

and

$$\ln W_{it} = c_{1i} + c_{2i} \ln PR_{it} + c_{3i} \ln U_{it} + c_{4i} \ln P_{it} + c_{5i} \ln W_{it-1} \tag{A7}$$

where PM_{it} = the import price index, in domestic currency i;

   W_{it} = the index of the wage rate in country i;

   PR_{it} = the index of average labour productivity in country i;

   U_{it} = the unemployment rate in country i.

The import price index PM_{it} is defined as:

$$PM_{it} = \frac{S_{\$it}}{S_{\$i0}} \sum \gamma_j^i PX_{jt} \Big/ \left(\frac{S_{\$jt}}{S_{\$j0}}\right) \tag{A8}$$

where
$\qquad PX_{jt}$ = the export price index of country j expressed in currency j;

$\qquad \gamma_j^i$ = the share of imports from country j in country i's total imports;

$PX_{jt} \Big/ \left(\dfrac{S_{\$jt}}{S_{\$j0}}\right)$ = the export price index of country j expressed in dollars.

From the preceding it follows that by affecting the import price index exchange rate changes have an influence on the wage price mechanism. This feeds back into the demand for money.

APPENDIX A.3: THE ESTIMATED EQUATIONS

The money demand equations are presented in Table 3 A.1, the price equations in Table 3 A.2, the wage equations in Table 3 A.3.
The data sources were:

Data	*Source*
Spot rates	IFS: line AE
Forward rates	IFS except for Italy (EEC)
Interest rates	Morgan Guaranty, World Financial Markets
Money stock	IFS: line 34–5
Money base	IFS: line 14
International reserves	IFS: line 11–line 16c
National income	IFS: quarterly data calculated with industrial production indices
Consumer prices	IFS: line 64
Wages	IRES–
Productivity	IRES–
Unemployment rate	OECD
Par rates snake	Nationale Bank van Belgie

TABLE 3A.1 M-demand Functions – Log Linear Specifications

Country	Var.	CTE	P	Y	r	lagged var.	R^2	DW	Average lag
Belgium	M1	-0.419 (0.43)	0.566 (0.12)	0.203 (0.09)	-0.057 (0.02)	0.433 (0.12)	0.98	2.6	1.76
Germany	M1[a]	7.954 (0.29)	1.00	1.224 (0.04)	-0.077 (0.01)	–	0.94	2.24	–
France	M1	-0.279 (0.29)	1.182 (0.04)	0.120 (0.06)	-0.03 (0.02)	–	0.98	1.02	–
Italy	M2	-12.79 (1.9)	1.193 (0.07)	1.625 (0.18)	-0.048 (0.04)	–	0.98	1.28	–
The Netherlands	M1[a]	-4.89 (0.31)	1.09 (0.06)	0.719 (0.11)	-0.918 (0.01)	–	0.99	1.99	–
United Kingdom	M1	3.52 (0.31)	0.785 (0.028)	0.818 (0.13)	-0.044 (0.02)	–	0.99	0.73	–

[a] Estimated in real terms
Figures between brackets are standard deviation.

TABLE 3A.2 Price Functions – Log Linear Specification – '66 I – '77 IV

Country	CTE	Wages	Import prices	Lagged prices	R^2	DW	Average lag (in quarters)	Long-run import price elasticity
Belgium	0.0936	0.057	0.0569	0.87	0.99	1.8365	7.69	0.437
	(0.0699)	(0.015)	(0.0126)	(0.025)				
Germany	0.319	0.089	0.039	0.80	0.99	1.6575	5.0	0.195
	(0.085)	(0.019)	(0.018)	(0.0517)				
France	0.425	0.1378	0.052	0.72	0.99	1.579	3.57	0.186
	(0.069)	(0.0198)	(0.0084)	(0.0386)				
Italy	0.278	0.0621	0.0718	0.81	0.99	2.007	5.26	0.378
	(0.059)	(0.0128)	(0.0113)	(0.03)				
The Netherlands	0.27	0.1205	0.0147	0.81	0.99	2.519	5.26	0.077
	(0.076)	(0.0286)	(0.016)	(0.048)				
United Kingdom	0.076	0.0898	0.0533	0.84	0.99	1.5615	6.25	0.333
	(0.039)	(0.0407)	(0.031)	(0.036)				

Figures between brackets are standard deviations.

TABLE 3A.3 Wage Functions – Log Linear Specifications – '66 I – '77 IV

Country	CTE	Prices	Productivity	Unemployment rate	Lagged wages	R^2	DW
Belgium	-1.747	0.5915	0.1107	-0.014	0.70	0.99	2.92
	(0.498)	(0.183)	(0.064)	(0.003)	(0.10)		
Germany	-0.599	0.169	0.0603	-0.0091	0.911	0.99	1.98
	(0.262)	(0.114)	(0.0641)	(0.0027)	(0.05)		
France	-1.069	0.401	0.094	-0.00108	0.743	0.99	1.76
	(0.499)	(0.20)	(0.0629)	(0.0063)	(0.141)		
Italy	-1.158	0.106	0.264	0.0005	0.888	0.99	1.63
	(0.39)	(0.085)	(0.089)	(0.004)	(0.064)		
The Netherlands	-0.519	0.156	0.187	0.0083	0.763	0.99	2.29
	(0.34)	(0.176)	(0.065)	(0.0064)	(0.123)		
United Kingdom	-0.773	0.146	0.165	-0.00965	0.87	0.99	1.81
	(0.388)	(0.131)	(0.0879)	(0.0047)	(0.126)		

Figures between brackets are standard deviations.

NOTES

1. The detail of the model is explained in P. de Grauwe and P. van den Bergh (1980).
2. In another paper we analysed managed floating systems whereby the monetary authorities use 'leaning against the wind' strategies. See P. de Grauwe and P. van den Bergh (1980).
3. The EMS agreement provides that intervention in the exchange market should be carried out using European currencies. In practice, however, EMS participants have used dollars also.
4. This is defined as the ratio of the change in (net) international reserves and the change in the domestic component of the money base.
5. These were assumed to be partial (50 per cent).
6. Note that we assume sterilisation policies to be 'partial', that is, 50 per cent.
7. In another paper we showed that with an extension of the currency union to more members, the currency which is expected to depreciate or appreciate is forced to do more of the adjustment (See P. de Grauwe and P. van den Bergh, op. cit.).
8. This is essentially due to the underdeterminancy of the ECU system.
A1. Aliber (1973) has introduced the idea of political risk as a factor leading to observed deviations from interest parity. See also Dooley (1976) on this issue. Dooley's paper contains interesting information on the effects of the German capital controls programme during 1973–5, suggesting that these controls explain the large covered differential observed between the Euro-dollar interest rate and the Frankfurt DM interbank rate. The absence of capital controls within the Euro-currency markets also explains why the interest parity holds almost exactly in this market. For evidence see Marston (1976) and Frenkel and Levich (1975) and (1977).

REFERENCES

Aliber, R. Z. (1973). 'The Interest Rate Parity Theorem: A Reinterpretation', *Journal of Political Economy*.
de Grauwe, P. and van den Bergh, P. (1980). 'Exchange Rates and Monetary Policies in the E.C. Countries', *European Economic Review*.
Dooley, M. P. (1976). 'Note on Interest Parity, Eurocurrencies and Capital Controls', *International Finance Discussion Paper*, no. 80, Federal Reserve.
Frenkel, J. and Levich, R. (1975). 'Covered Interest Arbitrage: Unexploited Profits?', *Journal of Political Economy*.
Frenkel, J. and Levich, R. (1977). 'Transaction Costs and Interest Arbitrage: Tranquil versus Turbulent Periods', *Journal of Political Economy*.
Marston, R. C. (1976). 'Interest Arbitrage in the Euro-Currency Markets', *European Economic Review*.

Comments on the Paper by de Grauwe and van den Bergh

Michael Beenstock

I would like to divide my comments into three parts. First I shall discuss the conclusion that GB reach from their model simulations. Secondly, I shall comment on the model itself. Finally I shall consider in broader terms the role of the interest parity condition in models of this type.

POLICY CONCLUSIONS

GB reach three main conclusions:

(i)   Dollar intervention is less effective than DM intervention;
(ii) EMS enlargement increases the 'offset' coefficients;
(iii) ECU intervention generates more symmetry than dollar intervention but not more than European-currency intervention.

These conclusions are quite valid but one wonders whether it was necessary to establish them in such a laborious manner. Clearly, in order to stabilise the BF/DM rate it makes more sense to intervene in BF and DM than through a third currency such as the dollar. If DM and dollars are perfect substitutes then dollar and DM intervention would be equivalent. However, this condition is not generally satisfied. Therefore, the first conclusion seem transparent.

So does the second conclusion because the UK under enlargement becomes a receptacle for German credit expansion. The 'offset' coefficient must increase because there is greater scope for leakage.

To establish maximum symmetry each country should intervene in all markets. For example the German authorities should intervene with DM in the markets for BF, FF, etc. depending on whether the bilateral DM exchange rate has deviated from EMS rates. Likewise the Belgian authorities should intervene with BF in the markets for FF, DM, etc., depending on whether the bilateral BF exchange rate has deviated from EMS rates. And so on for all the EMS members.

ECU intervention can obviously never create more symmetry than this. On the contrary the symmetry must be reduced to some extent since if DM is rising against ECU this could be associated with a rise in the DM/FF rate but a fall in the DM/BF rate. ECU may or may not be a useful administrative device to obtain some degree of symmetry but it is plain to see that it can never achieve the symmetry of bilateral intervention behaviour. It is equally plain to see that ECU intervention must imply more symmetry than dollar intervention since the DM/$ rate need not change at a time when DM/BF, etc. rates are changing. In this case Belgium, etc. would be required to intervene while the Germans would not be required to intervene.

Therefore all of these conclusions could have been reached analytically within say half an hour and the main puzzle is why GB did it all the hard way.

THE MODEL

Perhaps the answer to this question is that only an econometric model can show what the orders of magnitude are. In this case two empirical issues are involved. First, do we have confidence in the parameter estimates? Secondly, do we have confidence in the dynamic specification? It is the latter question that I find most disturbing. GB admit that they abstract from expectations not only about the exchange rate but also about inflation and monetary policy. This shortcoming is bound to affect the dynamics of the model. For example adaptive expectations may prolong the dynamics while the opposite may apply in the case of rational expectations.

In addition there are econometric problems since not only are there some doubtful looking DW statistics but it should be remembered that DW is biased towards 2 when there are lagged endogenous variables. The pattern of the error structure is often a useful guide to dynamic specification and it is not sufficient to stop diagnostic checks at first-order autocorrelation. Therefore, the estimated dynamics are most probably biased.

INTEREST PARITY

The interest parity condition is not tested yet its role in the model is crucial. The appeal is usually made that it is consistent with market efficiency but this is clearly not so (see Farber's discussion of Frenkel's paper) because risk will generally introduce additive and multiplicative terms into the parity condition. Market efficiency implies the $\alpha = 0$, $\beta = 1$ and $\{u_t\}$ is white noise in the following model:

$$\mathop{E}_t(S_{t+1}) = \alpha + \beta S_{t+1} + u_{t+1}$$

where $E_t(S_{t+1})$ is last period's expectation of the current spot rate. If the interest parity condition is valid we may solve it for the implied expected spot rate as

$$\hat{E}_t(S_{t+1}) = \frac{S_t(r_{Et} - r_t) + 1}{400}$$

$\hat{E}_t(S_{t+1})$ can then be regressed on S_{t+1}. In the case of $£/\$$ at the three-month maturity (1972 Q1–1980 Q2) this exercise implied

$$\hat{\alpha} = 0.057, \quad \hat{\beta} = 0.971, \quad DW = 1.7$$
$$(0.135) \qquad (0.073)$$

Since the parentheses indicate standard errors this exercise suggests, as Frenkel argues, that interest parity is consistent with market efficiency. However, a more careful look at the residual autocorrelogram shows spikes (larger than one standard error) at periods 3, 4, 9, 13 and 20. Lagrange multiplier and small sample Box–Pierce statistics indicate that $\{\hat{u}_t\}$ is not random.

This suggests that interest parity and market efficiency are not necessarily compatible and I would argue that in general they are not.

Alternative Intervention Rules in the Exchange Markets of the European Monetary System: A Comment

Ronald Shone

The authors set themselves the task of answering three very important questions with regard to the functioning of the EMS by means of a simulation model. These are:

(i)   Does it matter whether intervention is in terms of a member's currency (e.g DM) or in terms of the dollar?
(ii) What difference, if any, is there between intervening to maintain the ECU within certain limits or to maintain cross-rates within certain limits?
(iii) Are the effects of monetary policy different when Britain is a member of the EMS than when it is not?

Although not exactly put in this way by the authors, they do show what type of questions are being addressed. They are certainly vital questions. One may even say that some sort of answer to them ought to have been sought before the EMS was embarked upon. But in this regard, political will was ahead of the likely economic implications being known.

One important point worth stressing is the interrelated nature of these questions, a point not mentioned by the authors. For instance, does the choice of currency for intervention depend upon whether the ECU rates or cross-rates are being maintained? The conclusions surrounding the mini-EMS from the enlarged EMS will undoubtedly be different when dollars are used. rather than if DM are used. Clearly, then, to make a choice depends very much on whether we are or are not concerned with a mini-EMS in contrast to an enlarged version. The authors avoid such interconnections by taking each logical possibility and considering them in turn by means of simulations. This is a common procedure to employ with simulation models.

The simulation model rests crucially on a set of equations which are, in fact, *reaction functions*. However, these seem to be unclear in the article. As specified, they are (a) irregular with respect to the currency units, (b) imply a rather particular type of behaviour on the part of the intervening authorities, and (c) seem to deal with the parameter denoting the speed of response (θ) in a rather unsatisfactory, or at least unclear, way.

Consider just their first reaction equation (although the same applies to all others) given by:

$$\Delta R_{it}^{j} = \theta \left(S_{ijt} - S_{ijt}^{*} \right)$$

The authors define S_{ji} to be the price of currency j in terms of currency i, while R_i^j is the holdings of currency j by country i (the time subscript I ignore). Let us be concrete and let $j =$ France and $i =$ Germany, then ΔR_i^j has a monetary unit of (FF). The term in brackets has a monetary unit (DM/FF) so that to be consistent, θ has a monetary unit of (FF^2/DM)! It seems to me that the appropriate formulation, using the notation of the authors, is

$$\Delta R_{it}^j = \theta\,(S_{ijt} - S_{ijt}^*)$$

in which case θ has a monetary unit of (DM).

Of course, had the reaction function been written in terms of percentage deviations.then θ would automatically have a monetary unit (FF) regardless of the way the exchange rate is defined. In the text the authors refer to θ in such a way that we obtain the impression that this was done in the simulations, but it is not clear whether it was or not. It seems to me that the model is best expressed explicitly in terms of percentage deviations.

This leads me into another point regarding the way θ is dealt with in the simulations. The authors say, 'In the simulations the parameter θ is varied such that the observed spot rates always remain within the specified margins of fluctuation' (p. 102). Notice in this quotation the switch to percentages. Consider the situation in terms of Figure 3C.1 where d_{ji} denotes the percentage deviation of S_{ji} from the central rate S_{ji}^*. Now consider a point such as α. Does their analysis mean that θ is adjusted to the slope of 0β so as to bring it *to* (and not *within*) the upper limit? If *within* then what do they mean?

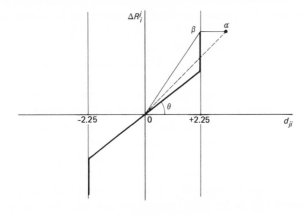

FIGURE 3C.1

Figure 3C.1 also illustrates the implied intervention behaviour assumed by the authors. Reserves are adjusted by some fraction, θ, of the discrepancy – here the percentage deviation rather than the absolute difference – until the margins are reached. Once the margins are reached or exceeded the reserves change by an amount necessary to keep such deviations at the margin. But by altering θ in this way it is no longer clear what reaction or behaviour is being posited.

A variety of interventions can be posed. For instance, it is possible to argue that intervention occurs only at the limits. In this case an alternative equation must be specified. Of course, some intervention formula has to be included if a simulation is to be undertaken. The one used by the authors assumes continuous intervention and takes a linear form. The question is whether this captures reality sufficiently well. Certainly, as formulated, it implies greater stability than is in fact the case, and secondly it probably implies greater reserve changes – since reserves change even when deviations lie within the band.

Let me now turn to some of the broader issues raised in the paper. The authors in considering the effect of a US interest rate change, in the form of a change in the Euro-dollar rate, on the mini-EMS, conclude that it has virtually a zero impact under either a DM or $ intervention system. But is this the best question to ask? If, as we would expect, the UK interest rate affected the mini-EMS and if the US rate affected the UK rate, then their conclusion may not be valid. The simulation considers only the *direct* impact of a change in the Euro-dollar rate on the countries of the mini-EMS, and not the *indirect* effects via the UK. If the authors' simulations were indicative of the real world, then the European countries need not have raised their interest rates in line with the rise in US interest rates, in what may be considered as an interest rate war. In one respect all I am pointing out is the interrelated nature of the questions I posed at the outset.

It is well recorded that one of the main reasons for the breakdown of the Bretton Woods system was the presence of asymmetries: an asymmetry in the adjustment burden and in the countries that could adjust (the *n*-Problem). The authors have paid particular attention to this question of symmetry. However, symmetry is a slippery concept. The simulations in regard of a 10 per cent expansion in the German domestic component of the money base differ depending upon whether intervention is in DM or in dollars. The authors therefore conclude that interventions are asymmetrical. But the assumed intervention is not quite the same under each alternative. In one Germany *actively* participates in the adjustment mechanism, while in the other she is *passive.* The asymmetry rests not so much on the currency of intervention, but rather on the active or passive behaviour assumed about Germany. This point is in fact recognised by the authors, both earlier (p. 107) and later when they state:

> Asymmetries in the adjustment mechanism will be obtained in the snake mechanism if the intervention is in dollars and *if one country follows a 'benign neglect' policy* as far as its dollar exchange rate is concerned. (p. 114) (My italics)

They in fact assume a system where Germany is pursuing a policy of 'benign neglect'.

But why assume a policy of 'benign neglect' on the part of Germany? Since Germany, by assumption, initiated the change then why should it be allowed to sit back and wait for the consequences? If this is in fact done then the EMS is a mini-Bretton Woods, with the same inherent built-in asymmetry. Given that this is now understood, surely we require to have a set of rules in which *all* EMS countries participate in the adjustment process. We can turn the problem around by asking the question, 'Is it *easier* to achieve symmetry in a dollar-intervention system than in a DM-intervention system?' This is a practical question, but an important one. If *de facto* intervention is in dollars it may be that notwithstanding the asymmetry alluded to, with real-world interventions a closer symmetry is achieved. If the same is true of a DM-intervention system, then we must ask, 'Which comes closest?' This places adjustment in the realm of second best. But given we have such difficulty in defining a truly symmetrical adjustment system, it would seem to me that this is inevitable.

In analysing the results of a monetary shock in Germany the authors conclude that it matters little in which currency intervention is done when it is the ECU rates which are being maintained. They also conclude that symmetry is more likely. I find this a little surprising. However, I cannot decide whether this is because the authors allow, for the first time, a 50 per cent sterilisation policy; or whether it is a result of their assumed reaction function, which I discussed earlier. I suspect that both are involved, each dampening the differences.

Finally, let me raise one last issue. Throughout their discussion there is a presumption that the only reason for the intervention is to keep something within a band, whether it be the spot rate, the cross-rate or the ECU rate. But this is not the only reason for intervention. If Europe is unconcerned about the level of the snake vis-à-vis the dollar, then all well and good. But the level of an exchange rate is by no means a matter of indifference to a country or a region – as is well testified by the $/£ rate at the present time. The implication from the simulations is that this question is not dealt with. There is nothing wrong with excluding it from analysis, but having done so we should not assume it is of no importance.

In conclusion, I would like to comment on the approach taken. So much loose talk is carried out concerning the EMS, most of which cannot be substantiated one way or another. In this respect it is a matter of belief, or even hope. The authors have undertaken one of the few approaches that can yield specific results, albeit within a specific model. For this they are to be commended. But this, and I think the authors would agree, is only a beginning; although a very important and fruitful beginning.

4 Exchange Rate and Monetary Policy in a World of Real Exchange Rate Variability

Pieter Korteweg

1 INTRODUCTION

In this paper we shall discuss in broad outline the main sources of exchange rate variability that characterised the 1970s. We shall try to distinguish between the sources of nominal exchange rate movements such as differential growth rates of money per unit of output, and the sources of real exchange rate movements such as the discovery and exploitation of North Sea oil and natural gas. Following that we shall consider the possible role of monetary policy in preventing such nominal and real exchange rate movements from occurring or affecting the spot rates of exchange. Specifically, we want to raise the question of what monetary policies should look like in order to obtain exchange rate and price level stability, whether pegged-parity arrangements like the current EMS are of any help in this respect, whether exchange rate stability is compatible with price level stability and, if not, what should come first, and whether exchange rate changes can be instrumental in changing a country's competitive position and equilibrating its balance of payments.

2 SOURCES OF EXCHANGE RATE VARIABILITY

Most economists seem to agree that the sources of change of the market (or spot) rate of exchange between two monies are both nominal and real.[1] Nominal changes in exchange rates arise when the rate of inflation differs between countries. For instance, if the rate of inflation in the United Kingdom is persistently above that of its trading partners and the German rate of inflation persistently below that of its trading partners, then the pound sterling will depreciate and the D-mark will appreciate against the currencies of these trading partners at a rate reflecting the relevant inflation differentials. The reason is that investors continuously reshuffle their portfolios by shifting out of assets denominated in currencies that are weak and into assets that are strong in terms of expected purchasing power. But even if inflation rates are the same everywhere, real changes in exchange rates between currencies may occur owing to specific diverging structural developments between countries such as international shifts in technology and trading patterns. For instance, if North Sea oil is discovered in the UK and natural gas in the Netherlands, which is subsequently exported abroad and replaces energy imports, then the pound and the guilder will tend to appreciate against all other currencies. And if, for instance, international demand for tradeables shifts away from exportables produced by the United Kingdom towards those of its trading partners, the pound sterling will depreciate against the other currencies. Finally, if productivity in the British tradeables sector grows more slowly than productivity in its non-tradeables sector, then the pound sterling will tend to depreciate against all other currencies.

Before proceeding, let us pause for a moment and look at the evidence on the nominal and real sources of exchange rate changes. Columns (1) to (3) of Table 4.1 tell the story. In column (1) it is shown at which speed the spot exchange rates of the major EC currencies and the dollar have changed against the D-mark on average over the period 1970–9. In part, the changes in these spot exchange rates are nominal and can be attributed to inflation differentials with respect to Germany. For another part, however, these changes are real and cannot be attributed to inflation differences with Germany. This part is shown in column (2). For each country, the difference between columns (1) and (2) equals that country's average inflation differential with Germany. Average inflation rates during the period 1970–9 are shown in column (3) of Table 4.1. As an example, let us look at the British-German inflation-exchange rate complex. The pound has been depreciating at an average rate of 9.4 per cent per annum, whereas the average British inflation rate exceeded the German inflation rate by 7.7 percentage points. The average rate of depreciation of the pound against the D-mark of 9.4 per cent per annum thus consisted of a *nominal* rate of *depreciation* of 7.7 per cent per annum and a *real* rate of *depreciation* of 1.7 per cent per annum. Due to real forces, the pound has depreciated against the D-mark at a faster rate than the inflation differential between the two countries would have led one to expect. From columns (1) to (3) of Table 4.1 a number of additional observations can be made:

(1) It appears that all currencies have depreciated in nominal terms on average during the 1970s, against the D-mark.

(2) Wide differences have existed in the speed at which currencies have been depreciating against the D-mark, with the Belgian franc, the Danish krone, and the guilder depreciating at low speed, and the French franc, the lira, the pound sterling, and the dollar depreciating at high speed.

(3) Whereas the spot exchange rates of the EC currencies against the D-mark have moved largely to accommodate inflation differences with Germany (nominal changes), the spot exchange rate of the dollar against the D-mark has moved largely in accommodation of structural shifts in productivity and trade patterns (real changes).

(4) Whereas all currencies have been depreciating against the D-mark in nominal terms, some currencies – notably those of Denmark and the Netherlands – have slightly appreciated against the D-mark in real terms.

(5) The dollar has been depreciating against the D-mark in real terms faster than any of the other currencies reviewed, implying that during the 1970s all EC currencies have appreciated on average against the dollar in real terms.

Let us summarise our findings. During the 1970s spot rate movements of most EC currencies against the D-mark have in large part been nominal, not real, whereas spot rate movements of most EC currencies against the dollar have for the most part been real, not nominal. Exchange rate stability against the D-mark thus would largely involve the turning off of the nominal sources of exchange rate changes, whereas exchange rate stability against the dollar would largely involve the turning off of the real sources of exchange rate changes. The policy question then is, whether this can be done at all, and if so what it would mean for policy and policy co-operation.

TABLE 4.1 Exchange Rate Movements, Inflation, Monetary Expansion, and Output Growth in Main EC Countries and the US 1970–9 Period Averages (percentage annual rates of change)

Country	Rate of appreciation (−) or depreciation (+) of currency against the D-Mark		Rate of consumer price inflation	Rate of growth of money supply (M1)	Rate of growth of gross real domestic product	Rate of growth of real demand for money because of real output growth[b]	Money growth in excess of real money demand growth	Inflation money ratio	Inflation consistent with stable spot exchange rates against the D-mark[c]	Money growth consistent with stable spot exchange rates against the D-mark
	spot exchange rate	real exchange rate[a]								
	(1)	(2)	(3)	(4)	(5)	(6)	$(7) = (4)-(6)$	$(8) = \frac{(3)}{(7)}$	(9)	$(10) = \frac{(9)}{(8)}$
	− %	− %								
Germany			4.9%	9.8%	3.2%	3.5%	6.3%	0.78	4.9%	9.8%
The Netherlands	1.8	−0.8	7.5	10.2	3.5	4.2	6.0	1.25	5.7	8.8
Belgium	2.3	0.1	7.1	7.9	3.8	2.8	5.1	1.39	4.8	6.3
Denmark	4.2	−0.2	9.3	10.1	2.6	2.9	7.2	1.29	5.1	6.8
France	5.9	1.9	8.9	10.2	4.0	3.6	6.6	1.35	3.0	5.8
Italy	11.2	3.8	12.3	19.6	3.1	7.4	12.2	1.01	1.1	8.5
United Kingdom	9.4	1.7	12.6	12.7	2.2	2.9	9.8	1.28	3.2	5.4
United States	8.1	5.9	7.1	5.9	2.9	1.5	4.4	1.61	−1.0	0.9

Sources: IMF: International Financial Statistics, August 1979–August 1980
   Commission of the EC: *Annual Economic Review* 1978/79
   Federal Reserve Bank of St. Louis: *International Economic Conditions*, June 1979.
   OECD *Quarterly National Account Bulletin* IV 1979 and *Economic Outlook* December 1979.

Notes

[a] The real rate of appreciation (−) or depreciation (+) of a country's currency against the D-mark is calculated by subtracting from the rate of change of that country's spot exchange rate against the D-mark its rate of inflation and adding to it the German rate of inflation.

[b] The figures in column (6) are calculated by multiplying the long-run real income elasticity of the country's demand for money (M1) by the average growth rate of that country's output. The values of the real income elasticities of the demand for money used are 1.10 for Germany, 1.20 for the Netherlands, 0.75 for Belgium, 1.10 for Denmark, 0.90 for France, 2.40 for Italy, 1.30 for the UK, and 0.50 for the US. These values are taken from various sources: own estimates; OECD: 'Demand for money in major OECD countries', OECD *Economic Outlook Occasional Studies*, January 1979, page 41; and M.M.G. Fase and J. B. Kuné: 'The demand for money in thirteen European and non-European countries: a tabular survey', *Kredit und Kapital*, 3, 1975.

[c] The rates of inflation consistent with exchange rate stability are calculated by subtracting from the German rate of inflation the rate of change of each country's real exchange rate against the D-mark as reported in column (2).

3 THE SOURCES OF NOMINAL EXCHANGE RATE CHANGES

Nominal exchange rate changes are those changes of the spot rate of exchange between the currencies of countries that occur in accommodation to the differences in inflation rates that exist between them. This raises the question of the causes of inflation. Wide agreement exists among economists that a country's rate of inflation mirrors the speed at which that country produces money relative to the speed at which it produces goods and services. Broadly speaking, if money is produced persistently faster than real output the result is inflation. More precisely, if the supply of money grows persistently faster than the real demand for money that arises from real output growth, the inevitable result is inflation.[2] This result is independent of the reasons why the monetary authorities produce money too fast. Whether money is produced to finance a war or the welfare state, to keep interest rates low or exchange rates fixed, or to prevent wage claims in excess of productivity from translating into unemployment, the unavoidable consequence of monetary growth persistently in excess of output growth is inflation.

Let us pause once again to look at the evidence. Columns (3) to (6) of Table 4.1 tell the story. The first three of these columns summarise the rate of inflation, the growth rate of money, and the growth rate of output that actually occurred in the EC economies and the US on average during the period 1970–9. Increases in production raise the demand for money balances. For each country, the speed at which its real demand for money has increased on average during the 1970s as a result of real output growth is given in column (6) of Table 4.1. Actual monetary growth in excess of growth of the real demand for money determines a country's *underlying* (or potential) rate of inflation.[3] As appears from column (7) of Table 4.1, in all countries reviewed money has grown much faster on average during the 1970s than has the real demand for money, thus giving scope for inflation. From comparing the *actual* average rate of increase of prices for each country during the 1970s in column (3) of Table 4.1 with the *potential* (or underlying) rate of inflation in column (7) of Table 4.1, two conclusions emerge. One is that, roughly speaking, a country's inflation rate in large part mirrors the excess of that country's money growth over its output growth. A second conclusion is that, again roughly speaking, inflation differentials between most countries are in large measure due to differences in the rates at which countries produce money relative to output.

4 TURNING OFF THE SOURCES OF NOMINAL EXCHANGE RATE VARIABILITY

To turn off nominal exchange rate changes as a major source of variability of the spot rates of exchange requires that inflation differentials between the EC countries and between these countries and the US should be wiped out. This raises a basic issue in monetary policy cooperation between these countries, which is to arrive at a *consensus* on what the common rate of inflation should be at which each country should aim in order to produce at least *nominal* exchange rate stability. Since a common rate of inflation of zero per cent would imply price level stability everywhere, such a rate would in our view be preferable to any other rate. But consensus on a zero inflation rate may be difficult to reach. The next best consensus rate of inflation for the current and prospective EMS members would then seem to be what Germany as the hegemonial currency country has frequently stated to be its maximum tolerable level of inflation of 2 per cent per annum.

The next policy issue then is how to reach such a low and common rate of inflation. Since, as we have seen, inflation is the result of too much money chasing too few goods, each country could bring its inflation rate under control by measures aimed at reducing the trend rate of monetary expansion and raising the trend rate of real output growth. To get some idea of the kind of monetary policy required it may be illustrative to calculate the growth rates of money that would have produced a common 2 per cent rate of inflation in the EC countries and the US as well as nominal exchange rate stability on average during the 1970s. Therefore we have to turn to columns (6)–(8) of Table 4.1. For a common average rate of inflation of 2 per cent, monetary expansion would have needed to exceed the rate of increase of the real demand for money because of real output growth by about 2.5 percentage points on average in Germany, 1.6 percentage points in the Netherlands, 1.4 percentage points in Belgium, 1.5 percentage points in Denmark, France and the United Kingdom, 2 percentage points in Italy, and 1.2 percentage points in the United States.[4] It follows that monetary growth rates would have needed to be much lower and much closer to one another, on average, than they have actually been, ranging from 4.2–6.0 per cent per annum for most EC countries except Italy, from 2–3 per cent per annum for the US, and from 9–10 per cent per annum for Italy.

The most promising way in which countries could reduce their inflation rates to a common level of 2 per cent and keep them there would seem to be that they adopt a *monetary rule*. Such a rule would imply a policy of stable and pre-announced rates of monetary expansion that would, for each country, be roughly equal in magnitude to the rate at which the real demand for their monies has increased as a result of normal output growth, plus the common 2 per cent rate of inflation.

At this stage it is important to stress the conditions for success of a policy of moderate and steady monetary expansion. A first condition is that such policies should be conducted by all countries. If, say, only Germany and the Netherlands practised monetary discipline and achieved low rates of inflation, the result might be a rising foreign demand for D-marks and guilders and appreciation of these currencies. This would leave insufficient monetary growth to satisfy the rising domestic demand for both monies that arises from a 2 per cent inflation target and a normal output growth target of, say, 3 per cent. The prospects of a recession in Germany and the Netherlands owing to the rising international demand for guilders and D-marks would greatly increase political pressure to raise the monetary growth targets or abandon them altogether, whereas the proper reaction would be to stick to one's monetary target by accommodating the increase in foreign demand for one's currency.[5] Indeed, it was this course of affairs that, in the course of 1978, made Germany and Switzerland temporarily abandon their monetary growth targets, which subsequently led to an unfortunate acceleration of their inflation rates in 1979.

A second condition for the success of monetary targets is that policy-makers be able to convince the public at large that they will persist in generating no more money than is compatible with their declared inflation-growth objectives. If policy-makers started out moderating monetary expansion whereas major market participants were convinced that the authorities would in the end validate any wage- and price-setting behaviour that occurred for fear of recession, a policy of monetary growth would indeed lead to recession.

5 THE SOURCES OF REAL EXCHANGE RATE CHANGES

The real exchange rate between the currencies of two countries is defined as the spot exchange rate between the own and foreign currency divided by the ratio of the own country's price level over the foreign country's price level.[6] Changes in the real exchange rate can therefore only occur in the case of developments that affect the spot exchange rate *differently* from the price level ratio between two countries. In other words, real exchange rate changes are those changes in the spot rate between the currencies of countries that cannot be attributed to inflation differentials between them but which occur in accommodation to specific structural differences in real economic performance between these countries. Let us try to trace the effects of a number of developments on the real exchange rate between the currencies of two countries, thereby assuming that spot rates of exchange rate between the currencies of two countries are free to fluctuate.[7]

We start with the real exchange rate effects of *monetary policy instability*. Sudden unforeseen accelerations or slowdowns in a country's rate of monetary expansion will affect that country's market exchange rate immediately but its rate of inflation only later on due to stickiness of wages and prices. A sudden monetary acceleration, by raising a country's spot market exchange rate faster than its inflation rate, will result in a temporary rise of its real exchange rate (i.e. a real currency depreciation). And a sudden monetary slowdown, by lowering a country's spot rate faster than its inflation rate, will produce a temporary fall of its real exchange rate (i.e. real currency appreciation).[8]

Let us trace next the real exchange rate effects of a *rise in the growth rate of a country's productivity in manufacturing tradeable goods* relative to the growth rate of its productivity in manufacturing non-tradeables. As a result, total output starts rising faster. This induces faster growth of the demand for real money balances. Given the country's rate of monetary expansion, this in turn means that output grows faster than demand for it. This results in less inflation and lower rates of increase of the prices of both tradeable and non-tradeable goods. Since competition in the world market tends to ensure that tradeables prices denominated in a common currency are the same everywhere, the country's currency starts to appreciate. The rate of appreciation must exceed the (falling) rate of inflation since, on the assumption that the same wages are paid in the tradeables and non-tradeables sectors, faster productivity growth in the tradeable goods sector implies that tradeable goods prices have to fall relative to non-tradeable goods prices. Rising productivity growth in a country's tradeables sector thus leads to real appreciation of its currency against all other currencies, a reaction known as the Balassa-effect.

Let us pursue now the real exchange rate effects of a *shift in international demand* towards a country's tradeable goods sector and away from its competitors. Such a shift does not affect the country's rate of monetary growth nor its growth rate of output, given full capacity. As a result, inflation remains unaffected. The increased international demand for the country's tradeables at given world market prices leads to a surplus on its current account and, consequently, to an accumulation of foreign assets for which there is no demand at the going exchange rate. To restore portfolio balance, the prices of these foreign assets expressed in the country's currency have to fall. By implication, the country's spot exchange rate starts to fall against all other currencies, thereby raising the value of its currency against all others. With the rate of inflation unaffected, a shift in international demand towards a country's tradeables thus results in a real appreciation of that country's currency.

Let us next pursue the real exchange rate effects of a rise in a *country's labour costs* relative to those of its competitors, owing to rapid growth of social security taxes. By lowering profits one result of faster rising labour costs will be a lower growth rate of the country's output of both tradeables and non-tradeables. With the rate of monetary expansion unchanged, lower output growth brings more inflation. More inflation implies that the domestic price of tradeables starts rising faster than the world market price of tradeables. Since competition tends to ensure that the price of tradeables expressed in a common currency will be the same everywhere, the second result of rising social security taxes and labour costs will be a tendency for the country's spot exchange rate to increase (currency depreciation). However, as long as the growth rates of output of tradeables and non-tradeables are affected equally negatively by rising social security taxes, nothing will happen to the country's real exchange rate. If, however, such taxes reduced the growth rate of output of non-tradeables more than that of tradeables, the result would be a real appreciation of the country's currency. Conversely, if such taxes reduced tradeables output growth more than non-tradeables output growth, a real depreciation of the country's currency would result.

Subsequently, let us trace the real exchange rate effects of the *discovery of new natural resources*, such as North Sea oil or natural gas, which attracts demand from abroad and leads to import substitution of energy. One effect of the discovery and exploitation of oil or gas is that a country's normal growth rate of output increases. With no change in the rate of monetary expansion this leads to a lower rate of inflation. A further effect of the discovery and exploitation of gas and oil is a balance of trade improvement due to increased exports and reduced imports of oil and/or gas. As a result, foreign assets are accumulated for which there is no demand at the going exchange rate. Consequently, the country's spot exchange rate has to fall against all other currencies, thereby raising the value of its currency against all others and lowering the prices of foreign assets expressed in that currency. A final effect of the discovery and exploitation of a new source of tradeables is that a country's tradeables prices have to fall *relative* to its non-tradeables prices. With a lower rate of inflation of the general price level this relative price change can only occur through appreciation of the country's currency that exceeds its (falling) rate of inflation. The discovery and exploitation of oil and natural gas thus tend to lead to lower inflation and real appreciation of a country's currency. This real appreciation of the currency helps to shift resources out of the tradeables sector towards the non-tradeables sector. And the less mobile these resources are the greater the real appreciation is likely to be.

Now, let us pause again and look at the evidence on real exchange rates once more. From column (2) of Table 4.1 it is clear that the real rates of exchange between the currencies of Belgium and Germany have remained virtually unchanged on average during the 1970s, that the Dutch guilder and the Danish krone have appreciated in real terms against all other EC currencies including the D-mark, and that the D-mark has appreciated in real terms against the French franc, the Italian lira, and the pound sterling. The rising real value of the guilder against all other EC currencies may safely be attributed in part to the coming up to steam of the exploitation and sales of Dutch natural gas resources during the first part of the 1970s. The rising real value of the D-mark against franc, lira and pound might well be attributed in part to the more rapid productivity growth of Germany's tradeables manufacturing sector, especially of capital goods, relative to that of France, Italy and the UK. And the rising real value of all EC currencies against the dollar must no doubt be partly attributed to the narrowing technological gap between Europe and the US.

6 THE SOURCES OF REAL EXCHANGE RATE VARIABILITY: CAN THEY BE TURNED OFF?

The sources of nominal exchange rate movements between currencies can be turned off if countries are prepared to close the inflation gaps between them by appropriate monetary policies. But can economic policy turn off the sources of real exchange rate movements? The – seemingly obvious – answer is a solid no except in the case of real exchange rate fluctuations that are the result of monetary policy instability. Such real exchange rate movements, which are transitory by nature, can easily be prevented by following a more predictable monetary policy of stable and pre-announced rates of monetary expansion. Real exchange rate movements that result from diverging structural economic developments between countries such as shifts in productivity and trade patterns cannot be prevented by economic policies. The reason is that such shifts are difficult to predict and their quantitative effects on real exchange rates virtually unknown.

If adjustment of real exchange rates to structural economic change cannot be prevented as long as the structure of economies changes at different speeds and in different directions, the next question is whether real exchange rate changes can be prevented from affecting the spot market exchange rates. The answer is: in principle probably yes, but in practice probably no. As argued in the preceding paragraphs, the rate of change of a country's spot exchange rate against another country's currency ($\hat{e}$) equals the sum of the rate of change of its real exchange rate against the other country's currency ($\hat{e}r$) and the inflation differential between them ($\hat{p} - \hat{p}^*$):

$$\hat{e} = \hat{e}r + (\hat{p} - \hat{p}^*)$$

It follows that changes in a country's real exchange rate can be prevented from affecting that country's spot exchange rate if it manages its inflation rate such that the inflation differential with the other country is the exact opposite of the real exchange rate change:

$$\hat{e} = 0 \quad \text{if} \quad \hat{e}r = -(\hat{p} - \hat{p}^*)$$

In general, those currencies that experience real currency appreciations against the D-mark would have to inflate faster than Germany, whereas those countries that experience real currency depreciations would have to inflate at a slower pace than Germany. For instance, the guilder's real appreciation of 0.8 per cent per annum against the D-mark during the period 1970–9 need not have changed the guilder/D-mark spot rate of exchange if the Dutch had kept their inflation rate 0.8 percentage points above the German rate of inflation. Conversely, the pound's real depreciation of 1.7 per cent per annum against the D-mark during the same period would have left the pound/D-mark spot exchange rate unchanged if the UK had kept its inflation rate 1.7 percentage points below the German inflation rate. In column (9) of Table 4.1 we summarise the rates of inflation in the EC countries and the US that would have been *consistent*, on average, with *stable* spot exchange rates during the period 1970–9, given the German rate of inflation and the movements in real exchange rates that actually occurred. And in column (10) of Table 4.1 the rates of monetary expansion are shown that would have generated these rates of inflation.[9]

From comparing the rates of inflation and monetary growth that would have been consistent with exchange rate stability during the 1970s with the rates of inflation and money growth that actually occurred, two striking observations can be made.

One is, of course, that exchange rate stability has apparently not been a first priority of the countries of Europe and the US. This follows from the fact that actual monetary policy in Europe and the US has been seriously inconsistent with stable exchange rates. Indeed, exchange rate instability in our part of the world during the 1970s has been due mainly to a fundamental mismatch of monetary policy preferences and a serious lack of monetary policy harmonisation between countries. Given the German rate of inflation of about 5 per cent per annum and given the real exchange rate movements that occurred, exchange rate stability would have required monetary policies substantially less expansive and less diverging from each other than they actually have been. Indeed, only Germany and the Netherlands have pursued monetary policies that have been more or less consistent with bilateral exchange rate stability. However, monetary growth rates in Belgium, Denmark and France should have been 2–4 percentage points less than they have actually been, whereas monetary growth rates in Italy, the UK and the US should have been less than half of what they actually have been.

A second observation is that monetary policies which are compatible with exchange rate stability are not normally compatible with price level stability. The reason is that there are real exchange rate movements. Stability of exchange rates implies that real exchange rate changes must be neutralised by appropriate inflation differences between countries. Consequently, even if Germany would prefer zero inflation, the aim of stable spot exchange rates would force those countries whose currencies appreciate against the D-mark in real terms to inflate their price levels, and those countries whose currencies depreciate in real terms to deflate their price levels.

But even if countries did declare exchange rate stability their first priority, stable spot exchange rates might prove difficult to obtain in practice. Stable spot exchange rates require monetary policies that produce inflation differences with Germany which exactly equal the real exchange rate movements against the D-mark. Given the lags in the effect of money on inflation, such policies require that real exchange rate movements are well-understood and well-predictable. The problem is that the causes of real exchange rate movements are numerous, difficult to predict and their quantitative impact not very well known. Given this state of affairs it would seem very difficult, if not impossible, for countries to chart the growth paths of their money stocks that would be consistent *ex-ante* with exchange rate stability.

7 PEGGED-PARITY ARRANGEMENTS: BRETTON WOODS, THE SNAKE AND THE EMS

The lack of monetary co-operation as exhibited by the fundamental mismatch of monetary policy preferences between countries and the unpredictability of real exchange rate movements have been the two major factors undermining all post-war fixed exchange rate arrangements. Both factors caused the collapse of the fixed-parity gold-dollar standard of Bretton Woods in March 1973, after a series of serious exchange rate crises. And the same factors have caused the snake arrangement of pegged parities between the currencies of Belgium, Denmark, France, Germany, Italy, Luxembourg, the Netherlands, Norway, Sweden and the United Kingdom to rapidly lose most of its members and degenerate into a mini-snake involving only Germany and its small neighbouring countries. The chronological history of the snake is summarised in Table 4.2.[10]

It is this fate of previous fixed exchange rate regimes that raises the question whether the new European monetary system (EMS) will have a chance to survive and bring exchange rate stability in the 1980s. The answer depends on the willingness of the EMS member countries and the US substantially to reduce the sizeable inflation differentials that exist between them, on the size and predictability of real exchange rate movements between the EMS currencies and between them and the dollar, and on the willingness of Germany as the hegemonial currency country of the EMS to adjust its monetary-policy to that of its EMS partners and the US.

As regards the inflation differentials between the EMS partners and between them and the US, nothing points to their disappearance yet. Indeed, as Table 4.3 indicates, since 1978 inflation and inflation differentials between Belgium, Germany and the Netherlands on the one hand, and the other EMS members and the US on the other hand, are on the rise again, thereby increasing the need for further parity adjustments within the EMS and keeping up the downward pressure on the dollar.

As regards real exchange rate changes between the currencies of the EMS on the one hand and the US dollar on the other hand, one might consider the technological gap between Europe and the US to have by and large disappeared by now, implying that there might be much less

TABLE 4.2 Chronological History of the Snake and the EMS

1972	24 April	Basle Agreement enters into force for narrowing of the margins of fluctuation between EC currencies: the snake (margins of 2.25 per cent) in the tunnel (plus or minus 2.25 %). Participants: Belgium, France, Germany, Italy, Luxembourg, the Netherlands.
	1 May	The United Kingdom and Denmark join.
	23 May	Norway becomes associated.
	23 June	The United Kingdom withdraws.
	27 June	Denmark withdraws.
	10 Oct.	Denmark returns.
1973	13 Feb.	Italy withdraws.
	19 March	Transition to the joint float; interventions to maintain fixed margins against the dollar ('tunnel') are discontinued.
	19 March	Sweden becomes associated.
	19 March	The DM is revalued by 3 per cent.
	3 April	The establishment of a European Monetary Co-operation Fund is approved.
	29 June	The DM is revalued by 5.5 per cent.
	17 Sep.	The guilder is revalued by 5 per cent.
	16 Nov.	The Norwegian krone is revalued by 5 per cent.
1974	19 Jan.	France withdraws.
1975	10 July	France returns.
1976	15 March	France withdraws again.
	17 Oct.	Agreement of exchange rate adjustment ('Frankfurt realignment'): The Danish krone is devalued by 6 per cent, the guilder and Belgian franc by 2 per cent, and the Norwegian and Swedish krone by 3 per cent.
1977	1 April	The Swedish krone is devalued by 6 per cent and the Danish and Norwegian krone are devalued by 3 per cent each.
	28 Aug.	Sweden withdraws temporarily; the Danish and Norwegian krone are·devalued by 5 per cent each.
1978	13 Feb.	The Norwegian krone is devalued by 8 per cent.
	6, 7 July	European Council in Bremen: agreement on the main lines of a European Monetary System.
	17 Oct.	The DM is revalued by 4 per cent, the guilder and the Belgian franc by 2 per cent.
	12 Dec.	Norway announces decision to withdraw.
1979	12 March	European Council in Paris: announcement of the formal introduction of the EMS on 13 March 1979.
	13 March	EMS enters into force. Participants: Belgium, Denmark, France, Germany, Ireland, Luxembourg, the Netherlands (bilateral fluctuation margins 2.25 per cent), and Italy (bilateral fluctuation margins 6 per cent).
	23 Sep.	Realignment of central rates among EMS currencies: 2 per cent revaluation of the DM and 3 per cent devaluation of the Danish krone.
	29 Dec.	5 per cent devaluation of Danish krone

TABLE 4.3 Inflation Rates (percentage changes at annual rates).

Country	1974	1978	1979	1980 forecast
Germany	7.0%	2.8%	4.1%	5.5%
Netherlands	9.4	4.1	4.2	6.5
Belgium	12.7	4.5	4.4	6.3
Denmark	15.2	10.1	9.6	13.5
France	13.7	9.1	10.7	13.3
Italy	19.1	12.1	14.7	20.0
United Kingdom	16.0	8.3	13.4	18.0
United States	10.9	7.5	11.3	13.5
Whole group				
—average	13.0	7.3	9.1	12.1
—standard deviation	3.9	3.2	4.3	5.5
EMS Group (incl. UK)				
—average	13.3	7.3	8.7	11.9
—standard deviation	4.1	3.5	4.5	5.9

Sources: IMF *International Financial Statistics*, August 1980.
OECD *Economic Outlook*, July 1980 and Economic Surveys of various countries.

need in the 1980s for permanent real appreciations of the EMS currencies against the dollar than was the case in the 1970s. As regards real exchange rate movements between the EMS currencies, predictions are much more difficult to make. If the past is a reliable guide to real exchange rate behaviour then in the future one must expect a continued need for the real value of the currencies of the former mini-snake countries (Belgium, Denmark, Germany and the Netherlands) to rise relative to the currencies of the other current and prospective EMS members, although North Sea oil might halt and reverse the pound sterling's past record of real depreciation.[11]

The picture which thus emerges for the near future of the EMS is one of a continuous need for nominal and a lesser need for real dollar depreciation against the EMS currencies and, consequently, a somewhat lesser threat to its survival from the outside, but also one of a continued need for nominal appreciations of the currencies of Belgium, Germany and the Netherlands against the other EMS currencies and, consequently, a persistent threat to the survival of the EMS from the inside. If these inside pressures on the EMS are not to materialise, then the countries of Denmark, France, Italy and the United Kingdom will have to redress their long-existing and overly expansionary monetary policies towards a degree of monetary discipline far greater than they seem to prefer in view of the temporary contraction that such a redress might involve for their real economies. If these countries failed to make the necessary policy adjustments, then the monetary authorities of Belgium, Germany and the Netherlands would be forced – under the rules of the EMS – either to prevent their currencies from appreciating against the Danish krone, the French franc, the lira and possibly the pound sterling through continued purchases of these currencies in the exchange market or to adjust their parities. Continued interventions on the part of the strong currency countries to stabilise their exchange rates against the weak currencies would imply that the strong currency countries in the EMS *subordinate* their monetary policy to those of the weak currency countries and import their rates of inflation and monetary expansion. The strong currency countries would then be confronted with the choice between adhering to an exchange rate target or a money supply and inflation target. From the statements issued by the monetary authorities of the strong currency countries – especially those of Germany and the Netherlands – it seems clear that in such situations they would prefer to adjust parities, revalue their currencies and stick to their inflation and monetary targets.[12] As history teaches us, however, the prospects of such parity changes, which normally come too late and often are too small, will revive speculation. Massive speculative runs in or out of the currencies whose parities are to be adjusted will then visit us again. Large-scale market interventions, capital controls, and, eventually, abrupt parity changes will be tried but found wanting since they fail to solve one of the basic problems underlying exchange rate instability, which is inconsistent monetary policies between countries. If such policies remain, and nothing yet points to their disappearance, the prospects of survival of the EMS are dim indeed, and chances are that it will end up in a series of exchange rate crises and collapse.

8 THE CHOICE BETWEEN PRICE STABILITY AND EX-CHANGE RATE STABILITY

As argued above, if confronted with the choice between importing inflation and money growth from the weak currency countries or sticking to a target of low and stable rates of inflation and monetary growth, the strong countries will choose the latter and adjust their parities instead. We strongly endorse this choice. As a rule, stable prices or, for that matter, low and stable inflation rates are to be preferred to stable exchange rates. The reason is that in our countries many more contracts are affected by the purchasing power risk posed by price level variability than by the exchange rate risk posed by exchange rate variability. This follows from the fact that in most countries (except the very small ones like Luxembourg, Liechtenstein or Monaco) people's assets and liabilities are largely expressed in domestic currency and much less so in foreign currencies. Moreover, insurance against exchange rate risk is more readily available than insurance against inflation risk.

Like the monetary authorities of Germany and the Netherlands we prefer monetary and price level stability to exchange rate stability. But unlike our monetary authorities we do not think that the consequence of this preference is to accept the EMS as an adjustable-peg system rather than a genuinely fixed exchange rate system. Chances are that operating the EMS as an adjustable-peg system will revive currency speculation, cause exchange controls, and induce unnecessary exchange rate variability.

Indeed, our proposal would be to use the EMS not as an engine to produce exchange rate stability but, rather, as an instrument to equalise inflation rates in its area. Only those countries should be granted membership which agree to conduct their monetary policies for the sole purpose of stabilising their inflation rates at the lowest possible common level, preferably zero per cent. By preventing inflation differentials this way, a major source of exchange rate variability would be turned off. Real exchange rate movements then are the sole major source of exchange rate variability left. Since such movements can hardly be prevented by economic policy, spot market exchange rates would need to be flexible in order to be able to float smoothly to whatever level real exchange rate movements force them to, and in order not to provoke currency speculation. Under our kind of EMS, members would pursue their monetary policies with the sole aim of reducing, stabilising and equalising their inflation rates, and would not try to prevent real exchange rate changes from affecting their spot market exchange rates. Consequently, monetary policies would be much less demanding than under the current EMS, but would nevertheless substantially reduce exchange rate and purchasing power risks by reducing nominal exchange rate variability and inflation.

9 FLOATING AND INTERNATIONAL COMPETITIVENESS

From what has been said before it will be clear that we prefer a system of floating exchange rates to the current system of fixed – but adjustable – pegs, provided member countries conduct monetary policies aimed at a low, stable and common rate of inflation.

An opposing view exists which argues against a system of floating rates that leaves the determination of spot exchange rates to the exchange markets. In this view, exchange rates should not be market-determined but government-determined and used as an instrument of economic policy. Those holding this view are located mainly in strong currency countries such as Germany and the Netherlands. They seem to argue that in the recent past floating rates have induced the guilder and D-mark to rise rapidly in value against their partner currencies, thereby damaging the international competitive position and export-oriented industrial structure of the two economies. Consequently, the monetary authorities of these countries should take control over their exchange rates and raise them in order to devalue the guilder and D-mark and restore competitiveness.

The view that it has been the floating rate system that has permitted a deterioration of Dutch and German international competitiveness is at odds with the broad facts. From a macroeconomic point of view a country's competitive position may be thought of as being determined by the value of its currency in terms of a trade-weighted basket of its competitors' currencies (the *effective* spot exchange rate) as well as by the country's tradeable goods price level relative to a trade-weighted average of its competitors' tradeable goods prices (the *effective* price ratio). If the effective value of a country's spot exchange rate rises at the same speed at which its tradeable goods prices fall relative to those of its trading partners, or vice versa, nothing happens to its competitive position (the *effective* real exchange rate) vis-à-vis its trading partners. In Table 4.4 the competitive positions of sixteen countries are given for 1978 and 1979 and are compared to the situation of March 1973. As is shown in column (3) of Table 4.4, between 1973 and 1979 Germany's competitive position deteriorated by a mere 4.2 per cent and Dutch competitiveness by a trifling 0.2 per cent. As appears from Table 4.4, during the years of floating rates the effective spot exchange rates of the D-mark and the guilder, and of most other currencies including the dollar, for that matter, have largely moved so as to maintain international competitiveness of the countries involved. Competition, it seems, tends to ensure that the prices of tradeables expressed in a

TABLE 4.4 Exchange Rates and Inflation (index numbers, March 1973 = 100)

Country	1979-indexes Using bilateral exchange weights			1978-index of effective real exchange rate	Standard deviation of effective real exchange rate March 1973– December 1978
	Effective spot rate of exchange	Effective foreign price ratio	Effective real exchange rate		
	(1)	(2)	(3) = (1):(2)	(4)	(5)
USA	97.6	102.5	95.2	95.5	2.83
Canada	84.2	90.7	92.8	92.0	5.60
Japan	115.4	118.5	97.4	108.8	8.37
UK	72.9	61.4	118.7	106.3	4.58
Germany	136.5	131.0	104.2	103.2	2.96
France	89.9	91.1	98.7	97.1	2.58
Italy	55.1	59.0	93.4	93.8	4.52
Belgium	110.6	114.1	96.9	99.5	2.11
Netherlands	118.5	118.3	100.2	103.6	2.03
Switzerland	166.7	143.4	116.2	119.7	9.46
Austria	118.2	109.6	107.8	109.9	3.89
Denmark	99.7	98.1	101.6	104.4	3.30
Norway	101.8	112.9	90.2	98.4	2.52
Sweden	87.9	88.6	99.2	96.1	4.91
Australia	74.2	86.7	85.6	86.9	6.58
Spain	76.5	73.5	109.4	97.0	5.70

Source: Morgan Guaranty *World Financial Markets*, April and December 1979 and February 1980.

The index of the effective exchange rate for a currency is a measure of that currency's trade-weighted average appreciation or depreciation vis-à-vis the currencies of 15 other major countries. An index above 100 implies that a currency has appreciated against these 15 other currencies, and vice versa for a depreciation. The exchange rates used are the averages of daily noon spot exchange rates in New York for the months shown. Column (2) shows the ratio of trade-weighted foreign to domestic wholesale prices of non-food manufactured goods. The trade weights used are based on 1976 bilateral trade in manufactures.

common basket of currencies will be the same everywhere. By implication, inconsistent rates of inflation of tradeables prices tend to be largely accommodated by changes in effective spot rates of exchange. Of course, exceptions exist. As can be seen from Table 4.4, the pound sterling and the Swiss franc have both experienced rather sizeable effective real appreciations against trading partner currencies during the period 1973–9, whereas over that same period the Australian dollar has experienced a rather strong effective real depreciation against trading partner currencies. As can be seen, however, from comparing columns (3) and (4) of Table 4.4, the effective real appreciation of the pound sterling occurred largely after 1978, probably in connection with increased North Sea oil production.

10 THE USE OF EXCHANGE RATES AS AN INSTRUMENT OF POLICY

The conclusion suggested by Table 4.4 seems to be that, if free, spot exchange rates automatically move so as to maintain a country's competitive position in the world market. This raises the question whether spot exchange rates can be used as a policy instrument to bring about improvements in a country's competitive position. Let us answer this question by way of an example.

Assume that the North Sea oil is found by the United Kingdom, that natural gas is discovered in the Netherlands, and that these countries start to exploit these resources and to export. As argued in Section 5 above, these shifts in productivity and trade patterns would cause the spot exchange rates of the pound sterling and the guilder as well as their real exchange rates to fall against all other currencies. The rising real value of the pound and the guilder which results from increased productivity of and/or demand for *specific* exportables (oil and gas) would damage the competitive position of all other exportables produced by the UK and the Netherlands. Would this damage be prevented by keeping spot exchange rates fixed? Or could the damage be undone by discretely devaluing the pound and the guilder in order to restore their initial spot exchange rates? The answer to both questions is most probably no. Following the shifts in productivity and trade patterns indicated, the pound and the guilder would have to appreciate in real terms, no matter whether their spot rates are fixed or flexible. With fixed spot rates, the required real appreciation of the pound and the guilder would eventually take place via rising rates of inflation in the UK and the Netherlands relative to inflation elsewhere. Nor could the monetary authorities of the two countries undo the real appreciation of the pound and the guilder, and restore competitiveness of their other tradeables, by discretely devaluing both currencies in order to restore the spot exchange rates to their initial level. Such action would raise the cost of production which would – in a world where money illusion is scarce – be promptly passed into higher domestic prices, thereby raising domestic inflation relative to inflation elsewhere.

There are better ways than currency devaluation by which the governments of the UK and the Netherlands could help to prevent the competitive position of their 'veteran' tradeables industries from being damaged by the real appreciations of the pound and the guilder that accompany the rapid development of their 'infant' tradeables like oil and gas. One way to do so would be to use the proceeds of oil and gas to subsidise capital investment and wages by lowering taxes on profits and wages and social security taxes instead of using them to finance major increases in social security payments, as was done in the Netherlands.

At this point it needs to be stressed that discretionary re- or devaluations of a country's currency fail to affect that country's real rate of exchange and competitive position *only* if such actions cause the spot exchange rate to move away from its equilibrium level. However, if such discretionary re- or devaluations are aimed at restoring the real exchange rate to its equilibrium level, then such actions would affect a country's real exchange rate and competitive position, albeit in a special sense. For example, if certain shifts in productivity and trade patterns require the real value of a country's currency to rise relative to all other currencies, but spot exchange rates are fixed, then that country's inflation rate would have to increase relative to inflation elsewhere to bring about the required real appreciation of the currency involved. However, if inflation adjusts slowly, the country's real exchange rate would temporarily be away from its equilibrium value, the real exchange rate being higher, and the real value of the currency lower, than required. In theory, the temporary effects of such disequilibrium real exchange rates on a country's competitive position could be prevented by a discretionary revaluation of the country's currency (i.e. a decrease of its spot rate) of a size equal to the required appreciation of the currency. In practice, however, policy-makers may find it impossible to fine-tune their spot exchange rates this way, given the lack of knowledge of what the equilibrium level of their real exchange rates is.

11 SUMMARY, AND THE LESSONS TO BE LEARNT

Let us summarise by briefly repeating the major points we have made. *First*, we have argued that pegged-parity systems like the EMS can only be successful in bringing exchange rate stability in the 1980s and in preventing exchange rate crises if nominal and real exchange rate movements are transitory and small. *Second*, we have defined nominal exchange rate movements to be equal to the inflation differentials between countries. Inflation is the result of too much money chasing too few goods. Inflation and inflation differentials can be reduced if countries are prepared to achieve stable and pre-announced monetary growth targets aimed at a low, stable, and common rate of inflation. This raises a basic issue in monetary policy co-operation between the members of any pegged-parity system, the issue being how to arrive at a consensus on what this 'common' inflation rate should be. *Third*, we have defined real exchange rate changes as those changes in spot exchange rates that cannot be attributed to inflation differentials between countries. We have argued that most such real exchange rate changes are due to international shifts in productivity and trading patterns and cannot be prevented by economic policy. *Fourth*, we have argued that as long as real exchange rates change, fixed spot exchange rates are incompatible with a stable and common rate of inflation. *Fifth*, we have argued that stable prices or, for that matter, low and stable inflation rates, are to be preferred to stable spot rates, the reason being that many more people are affected by purchasing power risk than by exchange rate risk, given the fact that most of their assets and liabilities are expressed in domestic currency. *Sixth*, we have argued that, if the past is a reliable guide to the future, nominal and real exchange rate movements between the currencies of the EMS member countries will be of a magnitude that will threaten the survival of the EMS from the inside. *Seventh*, we have argued that, if free, spot exchange rates tend to move so as to maintain a country's competitive position in the world market. A corollary of this argument is that exchange rate changes cannot be used as an instrument to bring about changes in a country's competitive position.

From our analysis of the aims and scope of monetary and exchange rate policy three important lessons can be learnt. *One* is that fixed spot exchange rates may retard but can never prevent the adjustments of a country's real exchange rate which become necessary when productivity and trade patterns shift.

A *second* lesson is that fixed spot exchange rates, since they cannot adjust, shift the burden of adjustment that arises from disturbances to those variables that are left to adjust: prices, output, unemployment, real exchange rates, international competitiveness, etc. Fluctuations in these variables need to be larger the less scope there is for spot rate fluctuations.

A *final* lesson is that in a world with little or no money illusion left, discretionary changes in a country's spot exchange rate cannot be expected to affect its real exchange rate and competitive position. Over the past twenty years we have learnt the hard way that the rate of inflation cannot be used as an instrument to lower real wages and unemployment. By the same token, spot exchange rates cannot be used to devalue a currency in real terms in order to improve a country's competitive position. With money illusion absent, higher prices will be passed on promptly into higher nominal wages, thus leaving the real wage rate unchanged. Likewise, discretionary increases of a currency's spot exchange rate away from its equilibrium value will increase import prices and the costs of production, which will be passed on promptly into higher domestic wages and prices, thus leaving the real exchange rate unchanged. It took a decade of accelerating inflation and continued stagnation to learn that the Phillips Curve is dead, that no relation exists between the rate of inflation and real wages that can be systematically exploited by inflationary policies aimed at lowering unemployment. It is to be hoped that it will not take us another decade of stagflation to learn also that no relation exists between the spot exchange rate and the real exchange rate that can be systematically exploited by exchange rate policy to reduce the real value of the currency, improve competitiveness, and raise output and employment.

NOTES

1. We prefer not to follow the common terminological practice of calling the spot (or market) rate of exchange the nominal exchange rate. We shall instead separate changes in the spot (or market) rate of exchange into a nominal and a real component. Changes in the spot rate of exchange between the currencies of two countries are called nominal if they reflect nominal sources: diverging inflation rates between countries. Changes in the spot rate of exchange are called real if they reflect real sources: diverging developments in technology, resources, institutions and trading patterns between countries. With e the spot (or market) rate of exchange (defined as the number of domestic currency units per unit of foreign currency), p the domestic price level, p^* the foreign country's price level, er the real exchange rate defined as $er = e/(p/p^*)$, and with hats ($\hat{}$) indicating percentage rates of change, it follows that $\hat{e} = \hat{er} + (\hat{p} - \hat{p}^*)$, where $\hat{er}$ reflects the real sources and $(\hat{p} - \hat{p}^*)$ the nominal sources of change of the spot (or market) rate of exchange.

2. The exchange rate effects of differential growth rates of domestic and foreign money and domestic and foreign output are further investigated in Bomhoff and Korteweg (1980).

3. The assumption being that changes in interest rates and their effects on velocity can be disregarded in the long run.

4. In calculating these numbers use is made of the inflation-money ratios in column (8) of Table 4.1. This involves the assumption that the ratios of $\hat{V}$ to $\hat{M} - \eta\hat{y}$ that actually existed in the countries mentioned during the period 1970–9 would have also existed if these countries had produced the rates of

monetary expansion that would have generated a common average rate of inflation of 2 per cent during 1970–9. (Here, $\hat{V}$ is the growth rate of velocity, $\hat{M}$ the growth rate of money, $\hat{y}$ the growth rate of output and η the real income elasticity of the demand for money.) From what we know empirically about the determinants of the demand for money this assumption does not seem too heroic, although it comes close to violating the hypothesis of rational expectations.

5. The common practice in Europe being that monetary targets are formulated in terms of monetary aggregates that do *not* include non-resident money holdings.

6. For the formula, see note 1.

7. For some empirical results on the determinants of real exchange rate movements, see Bomhoff and Korteweg (1980).

8. Money demand instability has real exchange rate effects analogous to monetary policy instability. Sudden unexpected declines (increases) in the demand for a country's money will result in a temporary rise (fall) of its real exchange rate against the other currencies.

9. In calculating the structure of growth rates of money that would have been consistent with stable exchange rates on average during the period 1970–9, use is made of the inflation-money ratios in column (8) of Table 4.1. As stressed in note 4 above, this involves the assumption that the ratio of $\hat{V}$ to $\hat{M} - \eta\hat{y}$ that actually existed in the countries reviewed during the period 1970–9 would have also existed if these countries had produced the rates of money growth that would have generated those international inflation differences that would have been consistent with stable exchange rates during 1970–9.

10. Table 4.2 is an updated version of a table published in a recent essay in the Princeton series of Essays in International Finance by Thygesen (1979, p. 13, table 3).

11. Indeed, since 1977, along with the continuing benefits of North Sea oil, the trend rate of real depreciation of the pound sterling against the dollar and most EMS currencies has been halted and reversed into a trend real appreciation. For further evidence, see Terry Burns *et al.* (1977, pp. 13–20).

12. This has been made particularly clear by the former President of the Bundesbank, Otmar Emminger, in an article in *Handelsblatt* of 26 March 1979 and an article in *Lloyds Bank Review* of July 1979.

REFERENCES

Bomhoff, Eduard J. and Korteweg, Pieter (1980). 'Exchange Rate Variability and Monetary Policy under Rational Expectations: Some Euro-American Experience, 1973–1979', paper presented at the Konstanzer Seminar on Monetary Theory and Monetary Policy, June.

Burns, Terry *et al.* (1977). 'Forecasting the Real Exchange Rate', *Economic Outlook*, October.

Emminger, Otmar (1979). 'Das Europäische Währungs System und die Deutsche Geldpolitik', *Handelsblatt*, 16 March.

Emminger, Otmar (1979). 'The Exchange Rate as an Instrument of Policy', *Lloyds Bank Review*, July.

Thygesen, Niels (1979). 'Exchange-rate Experiences and Policies of Small Countries: Some European Examples of the 1970s', *Princeton Essays in International Finance*, no. 136, December.

Exchange Rate Policy, Monetary Policy and Real Exchange Rate Variability: Comments on Professor Korteweg's Paper

Mica Panić

Pieter Korteweg has produced a stimulating paper. Its main purpose is to discover some of the lessons for economic policy that can be learned from the experience of industrial countries over the past decade.

My comments will concentrate on two important policy issues raised in the paper, both of which are of considerable interest and relevance at this moment. The first of these deals with the pressure which differences in underlying *real* economic performance are likely to exert on exchange rates in a system of fixed parities; and the second concerns the long-term effectiveness, or lack of it, of exchange rate policies.

There is nothing, it seems, like a period of 'floating' to produce a widespread yearning for fixed or stable exchange rates. The Bretton Woods system was a reaction to the experience in the inter-war period; and, similarly, though on a much smaller scale, the EMS represents a reaction to disappointments of the 1970s.

At the same time, there is a tendency, even among the most ardent advocates of fixed or stable exchange rates, to neglect the extent to which the long-term viability of such a system depends on the members' ability to reconcile more than simply their monetary policies. The way that they pursue their monetary policies is obviously important. But, as Pieter Korteweg reminds us, it is not the only condition that has to be satisfied in the long run. The reason for this is, of course, that, even if countries manage to harmonise their monetary policies, serious stresses will appear in a regime of fixed rates if there are growing disparities in their levels of productivity and incomes.

The long-run viability of such a system – and this is an important point which is not mentioned in the paper – will depend to a great extent, therefore, on the ability and willingness of the dominant member country, or countries, to take on the role performed by Britain before 1914 and the United States after 1945, including large-scale exports of its excess savings in the form of long-term capital. This eases the upward pressure on the strong, surplus countries' exchange rates; and allows them to pursue, as Britain and the United States did, monetary and other policies which ensure that they have low rates of inflation – without threatening the viability of the whole system.

An important reason for this is that imports of long-term capital enable the 'weak', deficit, countries to catch up, in the long run, in terms of structural changes and improvements in productivity and income. The transfer of resources, which they need in order to ease internal policy conflicts, should also make it possible for these countries to adjust their monetary policies more in line with those followed by the dominant members of the system. In the absence of such transfers, internal policy conflicts and dilemmas in the 'weak' countries are likely to be reflected either in strong inflationary pressures or in even greater relative economic decline, or both. Whatever the exact form that the pressure takes, developments of this kind are bound eventually to cause the breakdown of a system of fixed exchange rates.

The second policy issue is, probably, of even greater importance at the moment. Korteweg argues, correctly in my opinion, that 'exchange rate policy' cannot 'reduce the real value of the currency, improve competitiveness and raise output and employment' in the long run. The reasons given for this are the absence of money illusion and the stickiness of real wages and prices.

Many economists would probably now agree with this conclusion. The experience of the 1970s has demonstrated clearly that depreciation gives no more than a temporary improvement in relative costs and profitability. The gains disappear quickly, as higher import prices push up costs: first, directly, through higher costs of raw materials and energy; and then, indirectly, through their effect on prices of competing goods and wages. What is more, the longer the period of depreciation, the more likely it is that increases in incomes and prices will incorporate not only past but also expected rates of inflation. In the absence of strong counter-inflationary policies, depreciation will tend to lead, therefore, to an acceleration in the rate of inflation – which, inevitably, requires further depreciation in order to maintain gains in competitiveness. Developments of this kind are bound to create a good deal of uncertainty and, in this way, adversely affect investment and, thus, long-term output and employment.

There is, of course, an additional reason why it is difficult to achieve, in the long run, the original objectives of devaluation in a world of highly imperfect markets, that is the world in which economic policies have to be applicable in practice. In such an environment price elasticities in international trade will be insufficiently high to produce the required balance of payments adjustments in the short run. Hence, as the experience has shown, depreciation has to be accompanied by cuts in absorption even in cases where there is excess capacity. The more serious and persistent the external imbalances are the greater and more prolonged the cuts have to be. This will inevitably adversely affect investment and the pace of structural adjustment and, therefore, long-term output and employment.

At the same time, one should be extremely careful not to under-estimate the problems inherent in policies which rely, among other things, on exchange rate appreciation to combat inflation. This is essential because exchange rate changes appear to produce, at least in the short to medium term, asymmetric effects not only, as some economists have suggested, in the world economy as a whole but also in individual economies. Depreciation will tend to cause a much greater increase in the rate of inflation, and with a shorter lag, than the reduction in the rate of price increase that can be achieved by appreciation. In addition, unemployment levels created by appreciation are likely to be much more serious than improvements in employment created by depreciation.

Although the short- (or even medium-) term behaviour of exchange rates is often difficult to explain, it is reasonable to assume that nominal appreciation will indicate that, *ceteris paribus*, a country is pursuing stricter, more deflationary monetary and other policies than the rest of the world. If it normally also inflates at a lower rate than other countries, nominal appreciation may produce little or no real appreciation so that the required adjustment, in terms of resource reallocation, will be relatively small.

However, if a country which persistently inflates faster than the rest of the world adopts such policies the adjustment problem may well be very serious. The sectors which are involved (both directly and indirectly) in external trade will find it difficult now to pass on increases in costs in higher prices. There will be a squeeze on profits and a reduction in both output and employment. The size of these reductions will depend on the scale of the original problem and the vigour with which the policy of 'squeezing inflation out of the system' is pursued.

Whatever the exact severity of the policy stance adopted and the period over which it is applied, alternative sources of employment will have to be found for labour made redundant in the process. This is, of course, bound to take time. Resources are never perfectly mobile, particularly in industrial countries where a good deal of both occupational and regional specialisation has taken place. Furthermore, a deflationary environment is not exactly conducive to the development of new industries and enterprises in a market economy. It is impossible to predict, therefore, the time that the process of structural adjustment and resource reallocation might take. However, it is worth remembering that when Britain adopted the policies needed to pave the way for its return to the gold standard the rate of unemployment jumped to over 10 per cent. That was at the beginning of the 1920s; and the unemployment rate never fell below the 10 per cent level until 1940 – when the sharp improvement could hardly be attributed to the self-adjusting properties of the economy.

It is very doubtful, therefore, that a country which tends to inflate persistently faster than the rest of the world could realistically adopt Pieter Korteweg's policy objective of a zero rate of inflation – desirable though this may be – except in the long run. A more ambitious period of transition could easily involve, in this case, serious economic and social costs and thus carry also considerable political risks.

In conclusion, the acceptance of a 'high' exchange rate (as part of monetary and fiscal packages) in order to achieve certain policy objectives is bound to create – in a world of highly imperfect markets – adjustment problems which ought to be considered very carefully before such policies are adopted. Even the proposition that 'things will work themselves out in the long run' is not necessarily true under these conditions. How exactly is the adjustment to take place? How long is 'the long run'? or, perhaps more appropriately, how long is 'the short run'?

These are some of the crucial questions for economic policy to which we economists have failed to give coherent, let alone convincing, answers.

Comments on Exchange Rate Policy, Monetary Policy and Real Exchange Rate Variability

Alan Budd

I find myself in more or less complete agreement with the contents of Pieter Korteweg's paper. The approach he uses – the monetary approach modified by the Balassa distinction between traded and non-traded goods – is the one we have used at the London Business School and we have used it in a similar way. We have, for example, used it to derive approximate rules for the required relative growth of the money supply to maintain stable exchange rates (Budd *et al.*, 1978). We have also used it to consider the viability of the European monetary system though I must admit that – so far – the system has proved more robust than we would have expected (Budd and Burns, 1978).

I have some minor quibbles about the paper which I shall mention briefly and then I shall develop three more general points arising from the paper. My first quibble refers to Pieter Korteweg's suggested terminology for exchange rate changes. He proposes that the expression 'change in the nominal rate' be used to define changes in exchange rates which simply compensate for differences in inflation rates. While this is a perfectly sensible suggestion, I am afraid it is too late. The expression 'nominal exchange rate' has become firmly established as equivalent to the spot rate or the market rate, just as 'nominal interest rate' means the market rate of interest. It would only confuse the issue to try to introduce another usage at this stage. (It is hard enough to remember that, in the rest of the world, a rise in the exchange rate is what we would call a fall in the exchange rate.)

My second quibble concerns his account of the adjustment process following a balance of trade shock, as for example, when there is a shift in international demand towards a country's traded goods sector and away from its competitors. The shift results in a current account surplus and an unwanted accumulation of foreign assets. The exchange rate then rises to validate the holding of foreign assets. Although this process is not a necessary part of the paper's argument, I do not completely understand how it works. In the first place there is no need for an accumulation of foreign assets to take place since the exchange rate could rise to maintain equilibrium in the trade balance. Second, if the accumulation does take place it is not clear why equilibrium will be restored by a rise in the exchange rate. The attractiveness of a foreign financial asset is unaffected by changes in the exchange rate. If the exchange rate rises (in the UK sense) the sterling price of a foreign asset falls but so does the sterling value of the income from the asset; demand is unchanged. It is true that if the exchange rate rises, those who hold overseas assets will find that their sterling value has fallen but that will not necessarily restore portfolio equilibrium.

My third quibble relates to the table in which Pieter Korteweg demonstrates the stability of real exchange rates since 1973 (Table 4.4). I have two points. The first is that it would be interesting to know whether there has been more variability in real exchange rates since the collapse of the Bretton Woods system than there was before. If there has been it would not, of course, establish that the move to flexible exchange rates had caused the greater variability of real exchange rates. There might have been more real shocks to the world's economies. But since there is a general suspicion that, under flexible exchange rates, nominal shocks have tended to have short-term real effects it would at least be worth knowing whether there is a case to answer. The second point is that the observation that some real exchange rates ended at a similar level in 1978 or 1979 to where they started in 1973 does not by itself establish stability. According to our calculations, the real exchange rate of the guilder rose by 6 per cent from its 1973 level before it ended close to where it started. The Norwegian real exchange rate rose by over 20 per cent from its 1973 level before it ended with a real depreciation of 10 per cent. There were other large movements in real rates during this period. The figures for the standard deviation provide a reasonable indication of variability but it cannot distinguish between trend movements consistent with Balassa effects and erratic fluctuations.

So much for the quibbles. I have three points I would like to develop at greater length. The first is to add to Pieter Korteweg's list of events which can change the exchange rate. The second is to add a UK view of the effects of North Sea oil on the exchange rate. The third is to comment on Pieter Korteweg's view that it is easier (and better) to conduct policies for price stability than for exchange rate stability.

First the question of changes in the exchange rate. One case that could be added to Pieter Korteweg's list, and it is particularly relevant for the UK, is the effect of a change in VAT (Budd and Burns, 1979). We can consider the case in which an increase in VAT of 5 per cent is applied to traded and non-traded goods sold domestically (I abstract from the fact that not all goods bear VAT). We assume that there is no change in monetary policy and that the world price of traded goods is unchanged. The conditions of the problem are therefore as follows:

(1) The world price of traded goods is unchanged. If we assume perfect competition in markets for traded goods it must follow that the foreign currency price of UK traded goods is unchanged. (That is, of course, an oversimplification but it is in the spirit of Pieter Korteweg's paper.)
(2) The price level in the UK is unchanged, *ceteris paribus*. This follows from the assumption that monetary policy is unchanged.
(3) Goods and services bear an extra 5 per cent VAT.

Conditions (2) and (3) can only be met if *factor cost* prices fall by 5 per cent, leaving market prices unchanged. But the relevant price for international competition is factor cost prices (since imports bear VAT and exports do not). How, then, is condition (1) to be met, since the sterling price of traded goods has fallen by 5 per cent? The answer is that the sterling exchange rate must rise by 5 per cent to preserve price equilibrium in foreign markets. Therefore an increase in VAT raises the exchange rate. One might ask whether the *real* exchange rate has risen. In terms of market prices the real exchange does appear to have risen since market prices are unchanged while the nominal exchange rate has risen. However, this result is illusory since imports must also pay VAT and it is factor cost prices which are relevant rather than market prices. In terms of factor cost prices the real exchange rate is unchanged.

My second point relates to the question of the effect of oil or natural gas on the real exchange rate. Since we at the London Business School have persistently failed to forecast the exchange rate correctly this is a matter which concerns us greatly. It is fairly clear that our attempt to forecast exchange rate movements solely on the basis of relative monetary growth has proved inadequate. It is possible (and I believe this is Patrick Minford's view) that the current level of the exchange rate can be explained by relative money supply provided that expectations are modelled correctly. In other words the real rate will fall back as UK prices come into line with announced monetary policy. But we have also investigated the possible role of interest rates and North Sea oil (Beenstock *et al.*, 1981). Our results so far suggest that the role of interest rates in the determination of the real exchange rate is a temporary one. However, the role of North Sea oil, especially with regard to its effect on the current account, appears to have a significant and permanent effect. In theory North Sea oil may also have capital account effects as agents anticipate the effects of discoveries on the future current account.

Discoveries of oil or increases in the price of oil thus have an immediate impact on the exchange rate. It is also possible that there will be capital account effects which arise from the increased confidence in sterling as an investment currency. For example, the North Sea oil revenues may provide a 'painless' source of income for the government. It will therefore be easier for the government to achieve the fiscal and monetary targets set out in the medium -term Financial Strategy. This in turn could reduce the variance of inflation and could thus reduce the risk of changes in the nominal exchange rate. A reduction in risk could in turn raise the real exchange rate.

In general, our attempts to model the sterling exchange rate lend support to Pieter Korteweg's comment that it is extremely difficult to understand (and even more difficult to predict) changes in the real exchange rate.

My third point relates to the question of whether it is better to aim for exchange rate stability or price stability. Pieter Korteweg argues that, on welfare grounds, it is better to aim for price stability than for exchange rate stability. He also argues that it is much more difficult to achieve exchange rate stability and it is the latter point which particularly interests me. I have been puzzling about it off and on since Pieter Korteweg raised it at a conference in Madrid.

It would appear to be an empirical rather than a theoretical matter. I cannot think of any *a priori* reason for deducing that exchange rate stability is easier to achieve. Pieter Korteweg emphasises the difficulty of forecasting changes in the real exchange rate. He asserts, and I agree with him, that external shocks of the type that result in real exchange rate changes are likely to be less predictable than real shocks to the domestic economy. (Under this classification the discovery of North Sea oil would qualify as an external shock.) Although I agree that this is likely to be true as an empirical matter it does not necessarily follow that exchange rate stabilisation will be more difficult than price stabilisation. Suppose there is a shock which raises the real exchange rate. If there is a nominal exchange rate target, equilibrium will require that domestic prices rise which will in turn require a rise in the money supply. But if the authorities intervene to hold the nominal exchange rate constant, the monetary expansion can occur automatically through the inflow of reserves. Thus there could in principle be an automatic response. In practice the adjustment could be far less smooth. I agree that, on grounds of practicality, a policy of price stability with flexible exchange rates is both better and easier than a policy of exchange rate stability. In other words it is better to let changes in the real exchange rate be brought about by changes in the nominal rate rather than through changes in the domestic price level.

Finally I should say that I completely agree with the paper's general conclusions about the role of exchange rate policy. The government cannot in the long run change the real exchange rate by manipulating the nominal rate and it should not attempt to manipulate the exchange rate in the short term.

REFERENCES

A. Budd, T. Burns, R. Davis and G. Dicks (1978). 'Monetary Targets and the World Economy', London Business School *Economic Outlook*, 2, No 5, February.
A. Budd and T. Burns (1978). 'Should we join the European Monetary System', London Business School *Economic Outlook*, 3, No 1, October.
A. Budd and T. Burns (1979). 'Price Shocks and the Economy', London Business School *Economic Outlook*, 3, Nos 9 and 10, July.
M. Beenstock, A. Budd and P. Warburton (1981). 'Monetary Policy, Expectations and Real Exchange Rate Dynamics', *Oxford Economic Papers*.

5 Is an Exchange Rate Policy Possible?

Patrick Minford

In this paper[1] I wish to approach the foreign exchange market within the framework of an overall macroeconomic model. The paper deals with the UK specifically, though the approach is intended to be of general applicability. I assume throughout a floating exchange rate regime (not necessarily 'clean').

After some introductory remarks and an indication of the conclusions, there is a theoretical account of the model; this is illustrated with a diagram of the long-run equilibrium. The second part considers simulations of the effects of some exogenous shocks (including North Sea oil) and particular policies bearing on the exchange rate (including monetary and fiscal and social security policies).

The exchange rate can most conveniently be considered in two parts, the 'real' and the 'nominal' exchange rate. Let S be $\$/\pounds$, P be the domestic price level, P_F the foreign ('US') one. Then

$$\frac{S.P}{P_F} \equiv e$$

where e is the 'real' exchange rate (the ratio of prices in one currency or 'competitiveness'). Therefore:

$$\log S \equiv \log e + \log (P_F/P)$$

which reveals that the real exchange rate and foreign prices constant, a doubling, for example, of domestic prices, will halve the nominal exchange rate.

Concerns about the exchange rate are similarly divided into a real part and a nominal part. Much popular economic commentary would like policies to deliver high competitiveness (low *e*) so as to 'encourage manufacturing' and zero inflation (stable *P*) implying a rising *S* if there is world inflation. At the same time, the same commentary fears that these two aims are incompatible. It is often said for example that monetary targets low enough to deliver stable prices necessarily will cause low competitiveness. The mechanism popularly cited runs: tight money works by raising the nominal exchange rate, some of this rise shows up in a *P* lower than it would otherwise have been, but some shows up in a higher real exchange rate because money wages will not fully drop by the change in the nominal exchange rate. This thesis divides those who accept it into one camp which rates inflation control – so a 'high' nominal exchange rate – the highest priority and another camp which rates the health of manufacturing – and so a low exchange rate – the highest one. The first accordingly favours 'tight' money, the second attacks it.

Another example of these concerns is provided by North Sea oil. This is widely perceived as raising both the nominal and the real exchange rate. The same camps regard this respectively as blessing or curse.

I shall argue that these perceptions are confused and in general wrong. Monetary growth provided it contains no 'surprises' will not show up in the real exchange rate at all. The determinants of the real exchange rate are real things – notably, the social security/taxation regime. North Sea oil probably implies some rise in the real exchange rate, but this rise has been highly exaggerated. Furthermore, the aggregate effect has been to benefit British industries, even though the distribution of these benefits could have caused actual contraction in some. Abrupt policy changes ('surprises') can cause jumps in the real exchange rate which subsequently are eliminated.

Policy conclusions will be that as much advance warning as possible should be given of monetary and fiscal changes; hence the desirability of medium-term targets. Secondly, social security benefits should be reduced relative to productivity per man. Thirdly, foreign exchange intervention as such is pointless in a regime of monetary targets since it will have to be exactly offset by changes in domestic credit. Fourthly, though one may conceive of money supply rules one of whose objectives is the minimisation of shocks to the real exchange rate, these are unlikely to be worthwhile, money supply targets should be reduced as rapidly as possible and should be adhered to as tightly as possible. The only worthwhile (real) exchange rate policy is therefore one for the labour market – reducing government intervention through benefits, reducing union intervention, and improving the workings of closely related markets (notably housing). But it should not be surprising that the only way to obtain lasting improvements in real performance is via the elimination of market distortions.

THE MODEL

Let us suppose, as in the 'Scandinavian' model (Aukrust (1970) and Edgren *et al.* (1969)), that there is a non-traded and a traded goods sector. The price of traded goods is given in competitive world markets as $P_T = P_{T,F/S}$.[2] There is mobility of labour between these two sectors at a nominal wage rate, W.

The supply of labour in total to the two sectors depends upon the wage, W, relative to the social security rate, B; it is assumed that under the social security system it is possible for men and women to obtain benefit when not working, regardless of whether there is a job they could do or not. The reason is that the criteria of the 'distance' of an available job for a claimant's 'qualifications' are applied generously; the job has to be reasonably 'close' in area (e.g. not in Manchester for a Liverpool worker) and in description (e.g. not a 'streetcleaner' for a welder). The system assumes, for better or worse, that society should compensate a man if a job rather like his previous one is not available. Therefore, in practice we argue men or women can choose relatively freely whether to take a job *unlike* their previous one or to take benefit. Such a choice implies that the ratio of the wage rate to the benefit will be a major determinant of labour supply. Notice in passing that this is quite different from the usual argument that the benefit/wage ratio affects *search* activity and so may raise the duration of unemployment; though it is not ruled out that a rise in benefit will raise the ratio and so also raise such search activity. Rather it predicts that *permanent* unemployment will be raised by higher benefits at any given level of wages. Evidence on this is provided by a variety of time-series work (e.g. Holden and Peel, 1979; Benjamin and Kochin, 1979), as well as by our own model.

We therefore write the level of labour supply,

$$L = \left(\frac{W}{B} \right)^{\lambda}$$

and unemployment,

$$U = \overline{L} - L$$

where $\overline{L}$ is the 'registered' labour force; that is, those working plus those registered for benefit.

For convenience, we assume that the non-traded sector (N) provides services so that output, $Q_{NT} = L_{NT}$, labour employed there and $P_{NT} = W$ and that technology in the traded goods sector is Cobb–Douglas with a specific factor, T (which we can regard as representing 'entrepreneurship' and 'land') or $Q_T = L_T{}^\alpha K_T{}^\beta T^{1-\alpha-\beta}$. If capital is freely available (internationally mobile) at a real cost of r, then we can write

$$Q_T = T\left(\frac{W}{\alpha P_T}\right)^{-\frac{\alpha}{1-\alpha-\beta}}\left(\frac{r}{\beta}\right)^{-\frac{\beta}{1-\alpha-\beta}} \equiv \left(\frac{W}{P_T}\right)^{-\alpha'} k$$

and

$$L_T = \alpha\left(\frac{W}{P_T}\right)^{-1} Q_T$$

Q_T is the supply of traded goods, all of which will be sold at P_T the international price. In so far as the domestic demand for traded goods, D_T, exceeds Q_T there will be a current account deficit and vice versa. Domestic demand for non-traded services D_{NT}, must be equal to the supply of these services, L_{NT}. This is achieved by driving up the wage, W, until the total supply of labour equals the total demand, that is

$$L_{NT} + L_T = L$$

If we write the demand as depending on real spending ('absorption') a, and relative prices of traded and non-traded goods, P_T/W, we have:

$$D_{NT} = \left(\frac{P_T}{W}\right)^\sigma a; \quad D_T = a - \frac{W}{P_T} D_{NT};$$

$a = A/P_T$, where A is nominal spending and we deflate by tradeables' prices. So the market clearing wage is given by:

$$\left(\frac{W}{P_T}\right)^{-\sigma} a + \alpha k \left(\frac{W}{P_T}\right)^{-1-\alpha'} = \left(\frac{W}{B}\right)^\lambda.$$

The current account supply deficit (deflated by P_T) is:

$$x\,\mathrm{val} = Q_T - D_T = \left(\frac{W}{P_T}\right)^{-\alpha'} k - a\left(1 + \left(\frac{W}{P_T}\right)^{1+\sigma}\right)$$

The particular functional forms are of little interest; they are supplied to illustrate the possibilities. The essence of the analysis can be captured in a simple diagram (Figure 5.1). In the right-hand quadrant are shown the demands for goods and the supply of traded goods (the supply of non-traded goods is identical to the demand; this is forced through the labour market clearing condition). At any given (market-clearing) wage

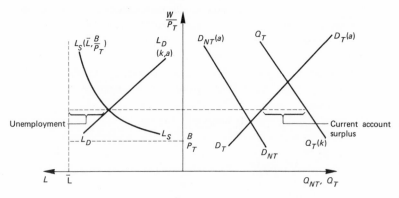

FIGURE 5.1

relative to traded prices, there is defined a demand for non-traded services and traded goods which both shift to the right with rising absorption, a, and a supply of traded goods, which shifts to the right with increases in specific factors, T, and falls in the cost of capital, r (summarised as k). Turning to the left-hand quadrant we see the total demand for labour, L_D, which is the sum of L_T (depending on Q_T) and D_{NT} and so shifts to the left with rises in a and k. The supply of labour is illustrated as being asymptotic to the total labour force, $\overline{L}$, at one extreme and the real benefit rate, B/P_T, at the other; this assumes we could get zero work at wages equal to real benefits and that there is some physical maximum labour supply at $\overline{L}$. Registered unemployment is shown as $\overline{L}$ minus equilibrium L.

To simplify matters, we have assumed that the unemployed man gets benefits only and does not work. But in practice he may choose to work part of the time in the 'shadow economy', that is, in undeclared activities. An overwhelming amount of (by definition) casual evidence suggests that this is a flourishing part of most western economies today; for the UK, the former chairman of the Inland Revenue (Pile, 1979) has estimated it at $7\frac{1}{2}$ per cent of GNP.

Allowing for the shadow economy would complicate but not alter the essentials of our analysis. It means that we have two labour markets and that the official labour market, for any given benefit rate, obtains a lesser labour supply than it would without the shadow economy. This increases registered unemployment. It also means that the registered unemployed are to some extent usefully occupied, so that the figures overstate the wasted resources. Whether the emergence of the shadow economy improves resource allocation overall or not is a problem of second-best which cannot be settled without detailed analysis. But for our purposes we simply need to note that our supply curve would become an aggregation over both the official and the shadow economy, and that $\overline{L} - L$ would be, not registered unemployed, but that proportion of their time not devoted to the shadow economy. Raising the benefit rate would reduce total labour supply, as before.

Reading then from the left-hand side the market-clearing real wage, we can derive the level of output, $y = D_T + D_{NT}$, and the current account balance, x val. We can see that both x val and y decrease with rising W/P_T. Notice that real wages W/P and the real exchange rate, $S \cdot P/P_F$ $= e$ are a simple transform of W/P_T. If $P = W^\pi P_T^{1-\pi}$ (π is the weight on non-traded services in the general price index, P), then W/P $= (W/P_T)^{1-\pi}$ and $e = (W/P_T)^\pi$. So Figure 5.1 illustrates that real wages (the real exchange rate) determine output and the current balance, technology and absorption constant; and that real benefits are a major determinant of real wages. If we suppose finally that absorption is forced over time to equal output so that there is zero net borrowing from abroad (x val $= 0$), then we can argue as follows. A rise in real benefits (technology constant) raises real wages and the real exchange rate, which cuts output and via the resulting current deficit forces a cut in absorption.

What we have been discussing is the 'supply side' of the economy, and in doing so we have abstracted from any 'short-run dynamics' such as would be provided by the assumption of adjustment costs, union labour contracts and information lags. These elements give rise to a wage equation of the form:

$$\Delta \log W = (E_{-1} \log P - \log P_{-1}) + \Delta \log w^* + \gamma (\log w^*_{-1} - \log w_{-1}) + \varepsilon$$

where $E_{-1} x_{+j}$ = expectation (formed at time $t - i$) of x at $t + j$, $w(w^*)$ = actual (equilibrium) real wage, and ε is an error term which may exhibit auto-correlation. The arguments of w^* are given by our 'supply side' analysis, as that level of real wages where there is current account balance, given the real benefit rate, technology and the labour force.

The derivation of this short-run equation is in Minford (1980). Its properties are that real wages and the real exhange rate converge on full equilibrium at the rate γ; 'shocks' to prices unanticipated at the time of contracting will cause shocks to real wages and the real exchange rate; along the converging path back to full equilibrium the labour market is clearing continuously as labour shed (acquired) by the union sector alters the market-clearing real wage in the non-union sector. It is worth noting that this real wage will probably not drop even in the short run below the 'floor' set by the real social security rate, which makes the social security system implicitly the 'employer of last resort'. If one wishes to explain 'real wage rigidity', one need look no further than such government intervention in the labour market.

To complete the model, we require a 'demand side' in the short run (in the long run as we have seen demand has to be equal to supply as set out in our previous analysis). This is described at length in Minford (1980) and Minford *et al.* (1980). In this model, financial markets are 'efficient', which is taken to mean that given publicly available information expected returns are equated on domestic and foreign securities at all maturities; this implies perfect international capital mobility at any point in time. Expectations are rational in the now familiar sense of Muth (1961); in the simulations here this implies that expectations and the forecasts of the model are constrained to be one and the same. Demand for money and goods is overwhelmingly determined by the desire of consumers and firms to achieve equilibrium in their portfolios between goods and financial assets and, within financial assets, between money and bonds; this 'portfolio balance' motive implies *inter alia* that, when financial assets fall unexpectedly, private demand for goods suffers an unexpected cut as private agents attempt to save in order to increase their holdings of financial assets.

Another corollary of portfolio balance is that the government cannot in the long run finance a deficit by issuing bonds and money in proportions different from those that the private sector would wish for at constant interest rates. This argument therefore underlines the medium-term link between the money supply growth rate and the public sector borrowing requirement or deficit.

SOME IMPLICATIONS OF THE MODEL

This model's simulation properties differ in quite a number of ways from those of the now-conventional 'neo-Keynesian' model. This can be illustrated by the effects of an unanticipated fall in the budget deficit (due to lower public spending) by 1 per cent of GDP, assuming that the money supply grows at a consistent rate (about 2 per cent per annum lower) shown in Figure 5.2.

This decrease lowers expected inflation when it occurs and with it nominal interest rates. The latter fall raises the real value of financial assets and this in turn causes private demands to rise by roughly as much

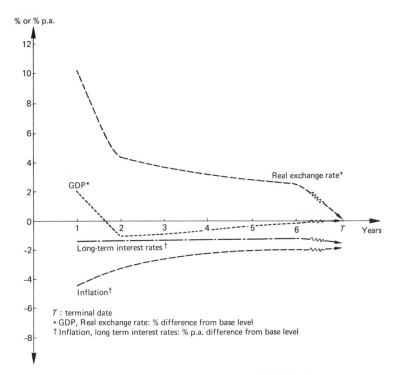

FIGURE 5.2 Budget deficit cut by 1 per cent of GDP (Money Supply Growth by 2 per cent per annum) – no pre-announcement

as (initially by more than) public demands have fallen; output consequently is little affected after initial 'bumpiness'. The fall in interest rates and the rise in the real value of financial assets both raise the demand for money; the supply of money having fallen, the incipient excess demand for money causes an incipient capital inflow which causes the (nominal) exchange rate to rise. As it rises, it lowers prices and this serves to equilibrate the money market. Thus inflation falls (the nominal exchange rises) immediately in response to this policy. A final twist is that since wages were fixed by contract before the policy change, real wages and so the real exchange rate also rise (so called 'overshooting'). When inflation falls unexpectedly this effect, the simulation suggests, could be substantial. As time passes real wages, real assets and real GDP are gradually adjusted back to an equilibrium in which all real variables are the same but inflation, interest rates and money supply growth are 2 per cent lower, the budget deficit 1 per cent (of GDP) lower.

This illustrates some general properties of the model worth remarking on.

(1) Any change in the expected future sequence of the exogenous variables causes plans to be revised (is a 'shock'), but the *further ahead* in the sequence the change is, the less the shock. It follows that *announcing* policy changes well in advance lessens the shock to the system; the economy moves more smoothly to the new equilibrium than if announcement and policy change coincide (Figure 5.3). Notice in passing that there can be no such thing as a 'fully' anticipated change; however, a change can be anticipated x periods before (at which point the shock would have occurred), and the implication of Figure 5.3 is that x should be made as large as possible – in fact as $x \to \infty$, the shock $\to 0$.

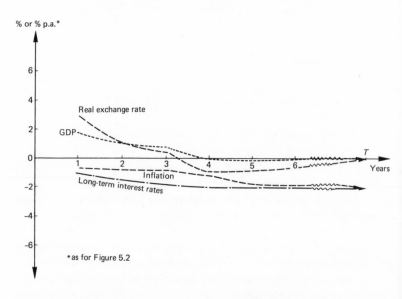

FIGURE 5.3 Budget deficit cut by 1 per cent of GDP (Money Supply Growth by 2 per cent per annum) from year 3 – announced in year 1

(2) Major shocks to real variables (such as consumption or investment, or relative prices) cause minor shocks to the important nominal variables, inflation and interest rates (though the price level may be substantially affected), major shocks to other real variables. Relevant real shocks are the discovery of North Sea oil

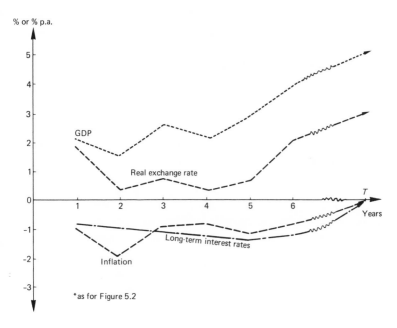

FIGURE 5.4 North Sea oil discovery

(Figure 5.4) (equally relative oil prices) and changes in real social security benefits (Figure 5.6).

(3) Major shocks to nominal variables will however cause major shocks to both real and nominal variables. Such a shock is the fall in public borrowing and money supply growth shown in Figure 5.2.

The reason for property (1) is that the early announcement allows adjustment to begin at once so forcing a smaller immediate adjustment. Formally, a rational expectations model solution for current endogenous variables is a weighted average of expected future and actual past values of the exogenous variables, where the weights decline both forwards and backwards, therefore an unexpected change in a distant future forecast event will have a smaller effect on current values than the same unexpected change in a current or nearby future forecast event.

Property (2) reflects the absence of money illusion that is an inherent feature of rational expectations models.

Property (3) is a characteristic of all rational expectations models in which information on general monetary conditions is available only with a lag or there are 'contracts'.[3] In this case the shock to nominal variables will respectively be misperceived (partly as a real shock) or be perceived too late for avoiding action to be taken.

We begin with the real shocks.

North Sea Oil (Figure 5.4)

We assume for illustration that North Sea oil was discovered in 1975 and that actual real revenues (net of foreign factor earnings) as a share of GDP were then (correctly) expected to be: 75:1 per cent, 76:2 per cent, 77:3 per cent, 78:3 per cent, 79:4 per cent, 80 and onwards: 5.5 per cent. The effect in steady state is shown in our diagram (Figure 5.5). The supply of traded goods shifts rightwards reflecting the additional productivity of UK factors. This extra income is spent on traded (D_T shifts to right) and non-traded goods (D_{NT} shifts to right) in proportions given by preferences and distribution of the North Sea oil income.[4] To the extent that it is spent on non-traded goods, $L_D L_D$ shifts outwards as the demand for labour rises; this raises real wages and the real exchange rate. In the new equilibrium total output and employment are higher, not just by the increase in oil output but also by the increased non-oil output induced by higher real wages. However, there is some reduction in non-oil traded goods production as a result of the real wage rise. In the more general model where there is imperfect competition between these and foreign traded goods, then there is not necessarily a net reduction in traded goods, for traded goods as for non-traded goods the income effects of the extra oil income may outweigh the substitution effects due

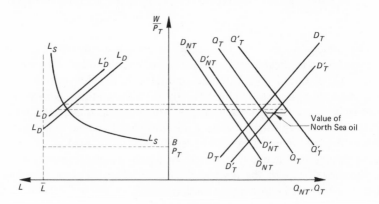

FIGURE 5.5

to the higher real exchange rate. Notice that in the two models the polar cases where the real exchange rate does not change are when all extra oil income is spent respectively on traded goods and on imported goods, in these cases output rises only by the extra oil income.

The path the economy takes when the North Sea oil discovery is announced is one of reasonably straightforward convergence to the steady state but some fluctuations in the early stages as the real exchange rate appreciation effects slightly outweigh the wealth effects. There are minimal effects on inflation and interest rates, as noted.

Social Security Benefit (Figure 5.6)

We assume a cut in real social security benefit by 10 per cent. It is not assumed to be announced in advance. The steady state effect is shown in

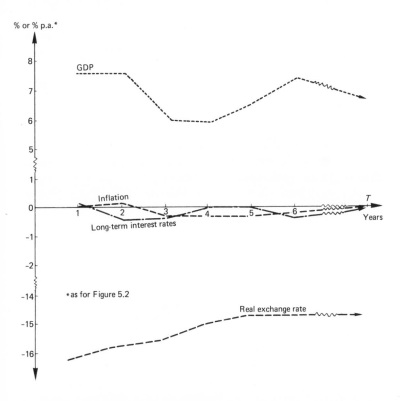

FIGURE 5.6 10 per cent reduction in real social security benefits

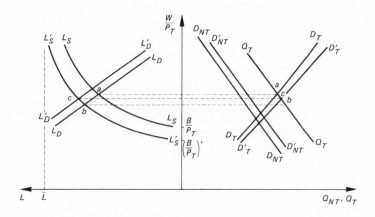

FIGURE 5.7

Figure 5.7: from initial equilibrium (a) the first effect is to shift $L_S L_S$ to the left as labour supply expands, thus lowering W/P_T. This causes a rise in traded and non-traded goods output. Demand for traded goods however falls. There is therefore a trade surplus with W/P_T at point b. This eventually causes absorption to rise so that trade balance is re-established, $D_T D_T$ and $D_{NT} D_{NT}$ shift rightwards moving $L_D L_D$ leftwards and raising W/P_T until a new equilibrium with trade balance is established at (c). We can see that employment is raised in two stages by the 'direct' effect on labour supply (a) to (b) and also by the 'indirect' effect as labour demand shifts ((b) to (c)).

By contrast with North Sea oil where the rise in non-oil output is caused by higher demand for UK goods, here it is caused by a lower supply price of UK goods. So there the real exchange rate rose, here it falls.

In response to this unexpected cut in benefit the economy moves rapidly to equilibrium as the change in real exchange rate is immediately discounted and acted upon.

Import Controls

Although our diagram considers traded goods in aggregate we can use it if we now think of P_T as a weighted average of import prices inclusive of tariffs, P_M and of export prices, P_X; let us for simplicity suppose that the exportables and the importables industries are of the same size and have the same supply/demand elasticities so that we can assign them equal weights. Now hold aggregate P_T and W constant and ask what alteration import controls would make in our equilibrium. P_T held constant implies that P_X goes down by as much as P_M goes up; so for example, a tariff of 10 per cent would imply a rise in the exchange rate of 5 per cent. Labour supply is unaltered; non-traded goods demand is unaltered. The supply of importables goes up, demand for importables goes down, and vice versa for exportables by our assumption on elasticities the net effect on supply of traded goods and on demand for them is zero. The equilibrium is completely unchanged in aggregate terms. However, due to the distortion introduced by the tariff-equivalent of the controls, there is a loss of consumer surplus, which can be evaluated (e.g. see Batchelor and Minford, 1976); welfare therefore drops even if measured output does not.

Of course we have chosen the weights conveniently so that exactly this occurs. In practice there will be small changes in W/P_T and in output and employment, up or down according to the detailed elasticities. The point remains that (*a*) welfare is reduced in *all* these cases (*b*) there is no presumption even that measured output and employment will rise with import controls.

Notice that implicitly in order to get a rise in output and employment the CEPG have assumed that real wage cuts via implicit tariffs are possible. They assume the tariff does not raise P_M as perceived by the worker. Hence in terms of our diagram they have Figure 5.8. In the above assume P_T is a weighted average of import prices exclusive of tariff, and of export prices. Now, when the tariff is imposed, for a given W/P_T there will be (according to the CEPG) no shift in $L_S L_S$, but $D_{NT} D_{NT}$, $Q_T Q_T$ shift to the right, $D_T D_T$ to the left as importables rise in market price.

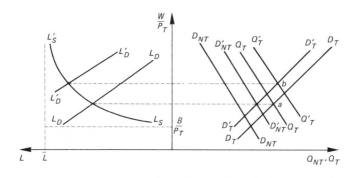

FIGURE 5.8

Hence $L_D L_D$ shifts to the left. The new equilibrium at (b) is one where output and 'real wages' (in terms of ex-tariff prices) are higher. Yet it is clear that is fallacious owing to the CEPG's failure to assume that workers care about wages relative to tariff-*inclusive* import prices (i.e. $L_S L_S$ would shift to the right). The CEPG assumption is inconsistent *even with their own wage equation.*

Nominal Shocks

We now turn to *nominal* shocks. The major ones that concern us are the two policy-induced shocks: (i) fiscal and monetary policy changes towards more or less 'expansion'; (ii) devaluation/revaluation which in the floating rate system is equivalent to a once-for-all unannounced money supply expansion/contraction.

We have already discussed the former in Figure 5.2. This showed that a shift to 'expansion' will in general lower the real exchange rate for a time since contracted wage earners are taken by surprise. However, it is unlikely to deliver a significant expansion in output even in the short term and in spite of this real depreciation. Inflation and interest rates rise immediately and the nominal exchange rate also depreciates immediately.

Can then the authorities engineer a real depreciation without worsening inflation? Figure 5.9 shows a once-for-all unanticipated rise in money supply by 2 per cent (i.e. in year 2 money supply maintains the higher year 1 level). It shows that indeed the real exchange rate is lowered for a time; but the operation yields only small temporary gains in output as well as serious temporary inflation. In the steady state there is no change in any real variable, as revealed by our diagram. Devaluations cannot change real wages.

Stabilisation of the Real Exchange Rate

An issue that worries many policy-makers is the gyration of the real exchange rate in response to shocks of the sort we have discussed. Central bankers frequently express the desire to stabilise these gyrations. Can this be done?

It is a by now familiar point (Fischer, 1977; Phelps and Taylor, 1977) that if there are contracts extending over some period of time, the Central Bank can react to shocks within a *shorter* period and so stabilise. We can simulate this within our annual model (with annual wage contracts) by assuming that the Bank reacts 'contemporaneously' to

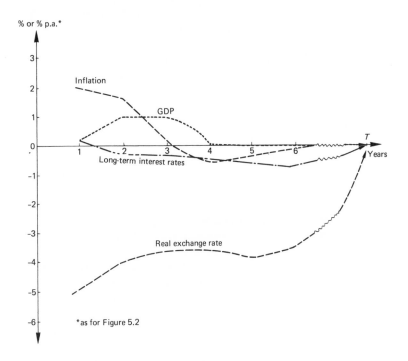

FIGURE 5.9 Rise in money supply by 2 per cent causing exchange rate depreciation

shocks – Figure 5.10.[5] The figure reveals that, given the parameters of this model, attempts to stabilise the real exchange rate by raising money supply growth as it appreciates (or equivalently in this model, selling sterling and buying foreign exchange) will not always dampen fluctuations in the real exchange rate. If the shock is a nominal foreign shock, it will worsen them substantially. This is a serious qualification since presumably many of the shocks to the exchange rate *are* foreign in origin.

Furthermore, this policy may worsen inflation and output fluctuations. For real foreign shocks both these are worsened, for real domestic and nominal foreign shocks inflation gets worse though output improves. In fact only when the shock is a domestic nominal one do all three variables improve.

There is therefore no *prima facie* case for this policy, unless one believes that the shocks of exclusive importance are domestic and monetary in origin. That belief has little foundation in general for an open economy; even though in recent years there has been major

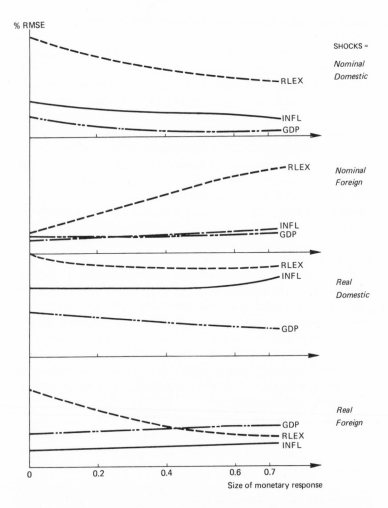

FIGURE 5.10 Effects of monetary 'stabilisation' of the exchange rate

Notes: Four separate shocks were applied to the 1980 model solution for one year: to inflation ('nominal domestic'), to foreign real interest rates ('nominal foreign'), to non-durable consumption ('real domestic'), and to exports ('real foreign'). The money supply growth rate was allowed to respond to the *unexpected* change in the real exchange rate, with progressively larger positive coefficients (e.g. '0.4' means that for every unexpected rise in the real exchange rate by 1 per cent of its equilibrium value money supply rises 0.4 per cent faster in the same year). The figure plots for each shock the Root Mean Square effect of the shock for inflation (INFL, per cent per annum), output (GDP, per cent of base level), and the real exchange (RLEX, per cent of equilibrium). Negative responses of the money supply to the exchange rate are not shown because they give uniformly much worse results than no response.

monetary instability in the UK, it is far from clear that this has arisen from the private sector rather than from the actions of the authorities themselves, and if the latter are the cause, then the appropriate remedy is to remove official monetary unpredictability.

This exercise has been carried out on the assumption that the model's parameters are unchanged, as is necessarily the case with all such exercises. The possibility that in particular contracting behaviour could change weakens further the case for this monetary intervention.

The real exchange rate could perfectly well be stabilised by the contracting parties themselves – for example by indexing nominal wages. Perhaps it is not because the transactions costs of indexation are too high. If this is so, and the government transactions costs are lower, then presumably private agents would happily accept government stabilisation. But it may also be that the non-indexed private reaction to shocks is *optimal*, transactions costs being very low; if so, the government rule will be overridden by the new contracts.

If this is so, then the government's contribution could be to minimise uncertainty about the nominal variables which it controls – namely the monetary base and the PSBR – because this would increase the information on which contracts could be based. In principle minimising the stochastic component of *any* rule (including complicated stabilisation rules) would do. But the difficulties for private agents of distinguishing 'stabilisation behaviour' from stochastic behaviour suggest that close adherence to pre-announced nominal targets offers the best prospect for minimising nominal uncertainty.

NOTES

1. This paper is a revised version of the one I gave to the City University Conference on Exchange Rate Policy, September, 1980. I am grateful for the comments of the conference participants, especially to my discussants Desmond Fitzgerald and Ivor Pearce, also to Christos Ioannides and Satwant Marwah who carried out the simulations.
2. This assumption of 'purchasing power parity' in tradeables can be dropped without altering any of the conclusions; but it is a convenient simplification to assume that the price elasticities of demand for exports and imports are infinite.
3. It is possible for contracts to be 'contingent' on, for example, nominal shocks. Indexed contracts are an example. Such contracts avoid property (3); but presumably there is some (transactions) cost attached to such indexing or contingent clauses which limits their adoption.
4. I am grateful to Harold Rose for discussions on this point.

REFERENCES

Aukrust, O. (1970). 'Prim I: A model of the Price and Income Distribution of an Open Economy', *Review of Income and Wealth*, 16.

Batchelor, R. A. and A. P. L. Minford (1976).'Import Controls and Devaluation as Medium-Term Policies' in *On How to Cope with Britain's Trade Position*, by H. Corbet, W. M. Corden, B. Hindley, R. Batchelor and P. Minford, (Thames Essays, Trade Policy Research Centre).

Benjamin, D. and L. Kochin (1979). 'Searching for an Explanation of Unemployment in inter-war Britain', *JPE*, 87, No. 3, 441–8.

Cambridge Economic Policy Group *Economic Policy Review*, annually 1975–80, Dept. of Applied Economics, Cambridge.

Edgren, G., K. O. Faxen and G. E. Ohdner (1969). 'Wages Growth and the Distribution of Income', *Swedish Journal of Economics*, 71(3), September, 133–60.

Fischer, S. (1977). 'Long-term contracts, Rational Expectations and the Optimal Money Supply Rule', *JPE*, 85, 191–206.

Holden, K. and D. A. Peel (1979). 'The Determinants of the Unemployment Rate: Some Empirical Evidence', *The Statistician*, 28, No. 2.

McCallum, Bennett T. (1976). 'Rational Expectations and the Natural Rate Hypothesis: some consistent estimates', *Econometrica*, 44, 43–52.

Minford, A. P. L. (1980). 'A Rational Expectation Model of the United Kingdom under Fixed and Floating Exchange Rates', in *The State of Macroeconomics*, Carnegie-Rochester Conference Series on Public Policy, 12, 293–355.

Minford, A. P. L., M. J. Brech and K. G. P. Matthews (1980). 'A Rational Expectations Model of the UK under Floating Exchange Rates', *European Economic Review*, 14, 189–219.

Muth, J. F. (1961). 'Rational Expectations and the Theory of Price Movements, *Econometrica* 29, 315–35.

Phelps, E. and J. Taylor (1977). 'Stabilising Powers of Monetary Policy under Rational Expectations', *JPE* 85, 163–90.

Pile, Sir Walter (1979). Evidence to House of Commons Public Accounts Committee, (London, HMSO), 26.3.79.

Discussion on the Paper by P. Minford: Is an Exchange Rate Policy Possible

Ivor Pearce

In the course of his talk Professor Minford remarked that 'he was much attached to his model'. I hope I may be forgiven for suspecting that it is not the model to which he is attached but the conclusion he draws from it. In fact it is usually the case that small models are developed as instruments of persuasion rather than tools of enquiry. Their primary purpose is to canvass preconceived ideas.

The conclusion to which Professor Minford is especially attached seems to be that there is no point in attempting to 'control' the 'real' exchange rate since it is impossible, in the long run, for any feasible policy to affect it. In order to produce this result all that is necessary is to construct a model with no exogenous real variable. With suitable time lags such a model will generate a wide variety of behaviour patterns all leading inexorably to the same real stationary state and hence to the same real exchange rate. *Ergo*, whatever you do you will not achieve your intended aim.

Of course all this is fine if the real world, over which we wish to exercise control, is properly represented by the model. But in the present case it would be hard to argue this.

In particular Professor Minford's model takes it for granted that, provided we preserve flexible money exchange rates, there can be no imbalance of payments. To be specific he assumes that 'absorption' will always be equal to production. But the world *I* live in seems not to have this property. Indeed I observe an accumulation of international debt amounting, presently, to a figure in dollars of the same order of magnitude as the entire USA gross national product. The existence of this debt seems to point to the fact that the *same* countries must have been persistently in balance of payments deficit long enough to accumulate such debt. Furthermore an annual growth rate of 25 per cent in the total seems to suggest that flexible exchange rates have done very little as yet to correct the malfunction.

Far from a world where absorption equals income for each country I seem to observe many countries living beyond their means, supporting their expenditure by borrowing in the international money market from countries in surplus. Accordingly I would not think it proper to construct a model which fails to show that widely different real exchange rates can persist, with goods markets cleared, each different real exchange rate corresponding to a different balance of payments situation. Indeed Professor Minford's model could be used to demonstrate this very point if only he would eliminate the equation which prohibits it.

Nor is this the worst of it. In the world in which I live, I observe huge stocks of international debt held in various currencies, all subject to uncertainties, a good proportion of which falls due for repayment each month. The resulting market in debt is entirely unrepresented in Professor Minford's model yet it must affect the real variables with which he is concerned. Not only would it seem possible to influence real exchange rates but, given the world as it is, one might count it desirable.

I am not in general in favour of governmental controls but I do believe that one form of control generates the need for another. This implies that, if *one* is to come off, *all* must come off. It implies also that controls cannot be removed, even *in toto*, in world full of institutions owing their very existence to the same controls that we are now seeking to remove, unless at the same time we repair the damage already done.

Comments on 'Is an Exchange Rate Policy Possible?' by Patrick Minford

Desmond Fitzgerald

Professor Minford's paper is somewhat difficult to assess. It presents a somewhat cursory survey of what is clearly a rather complex macroeconomic model, and then describes a series of simulations from the full model. No details are given of the econometric properties of the model, whether it is well-fitted or how successful it has proved in describing the behaviour of the UK economy. What I shall therefore attempt to do is draw attention to some perhaps unusual features of the economic model presented in the paper, give some general comments on macroeconomic models characterised by rational expectations, and finally give my intuitive impressions of the simulation results.

One of the central features of the model is the structure of the labour market. The supply of labour and consequently the unemployment rate is a direct function of the ratio of the nominal wage rate to the social security rate: however no mention is made of how the social security rate is to be measured. Yet the question of measurement of the social security rate and indeed of nominal wages is an important one, because it is not obvious that the distributions of expected social security benefits and expected nominal wages are identical or even similar. Moreover, casual observation would say that it is extremely difficult on the basis of this simple model of employment determination to explain the concentration of unemployment in particular employee sectors such as school-leavers and younger workers where the ratio of nominal wages to social security benefits is higher than the average. A more disaggregated model of the labour supply function would seem to be in order therefore.

Additionally we cannot really judge from the paper whether we are considering a single period or a multi-period framework. Presumably in the real world, individuals make employment decisions on the basis of comparisons of the present values of expected lifetime earnings from alternative sources utilising some appropriate risk-adjusted discount rate. Now it seems highly unlikely that the decision to supply or not to supply labour in one time period is independent of that in other future time periods. Again we observe from casual observation that the longer the period an individual is unemployed, the less likely that individual is to be able to find employment at some later date regardless of temporal movements in the nominal wage–social security benefits ratio. In other words single-period labour supply decisions will shift the probability distribution of expected obtainable nominal wages for the individual in future time periods. Labour supply in aggregate would then become not just a function of the current nominal wages–social security benefits ratio, but also of expected values of the ratio in all future periods and potential shifts in the future distributions of the two variables. Again the lesson seems to be that the form of the labour supply function is too simplistic.

The distinction between the traded and and non-traded goods sectors does appear to be useful. The model basically sets out two equations,

$$S \cdot P/P_F = e$$

$$S \cdot P_T/P_{T_F} = 1$$

where $S = \$/\pounds;$

P = overall domestic price level;

P_F = foreign price level;

P_T = domestic price of traded goods;

P_{T_F} = foreign price of traded goods;

e = 'real' exchange rate.

The second condition is merely the traditional purchasing power parity condition for traded goods – making appropriate assumptions about transactions costs it is difficult to raise substantive problems with this condition. The first condition merely says that there is no reason why you would expect purchasing power parity to hold if you do your calculations using composite price indices containing both traded and non-traded goods prices. Again this is hard to argue with. However it seems difficult to support a natural interpretation of e as the 'real exchange' rate, when it is basically a function of the purchasing power parity exchange rate, the ratio of non-traded prices to non-traded foreign prices, and the relative proportions of the traded and non-traded goods sectors in each country. To me what altering the real rate means is producing deviations from purchasing power parity in the traded goods market, which is the central argument put forward by manufacturing industry in the United Kingdom as having occurred. Now it seems clear that measured relative to historical indices, it is difficult to explain the current value of the pound on the basis of purchasing power parity. Various other explanations have been put forward. One possibility is a portfolio rebalancing effect; that is, the discovery of North Sea oil has altered the characteristics of sterling-denominated assets so that the desired proportion of sterling holdings in a diversified international portfolio has altered. An alternative explanation would be that we should define purchasing power parity in expectational terms – in that case you could get systematic departures from purchasing power parity for traded goods prices in any given time period, because of differential speeds of adjustment in financial markets and real goods markets. I may say that my intuitive feeling is that neither of these explanations nor the other arguments put forward in Professor Minford's paper seem to provide a convincing explanation for the current level of sterling in the foreign exchange markets.

Nonetheless the paper's stress on dividing exchange rate changes into real effects and those due to differences in monetary growth rates seems useful. We may note that it is the difference in monetary growth rates that matters, not inflation differentials, because in a particular sense it is the difference between money supply growth rates and price growth, assuming a constant velocity of circulation, that is a measure of the real effect.

At this point it seems appropriate to say something about rational expectations in general. All Professor Minford's conclusions, apart perhaps from that concerning the level of social security benefits, are traditional implications of the assumption of rational expectations. In simple terms only unanticipated policy variables impact upon the real variables in the economy – anticipated policy impacts on price variables. This holds true in external markets as well as domestic markets. Looking at the simulations therefore it is not too surprising that derived from a model based upon rational explanations, they should fit in with the general conclusions of such models. As I mentioned before, the more important point is how adequate is the underlying model of the UK economy, which this paper does not tell us.

Professor Minford also discusses whether the government is able to control the variance of the real exchange rate, even if they cannot control its average level. It is still a matter of some dispute in the rational expectations literature as to whether information lags and the existence of long-term contracts in the labour and real goods markets allow a stabilisation role for government policy. It is, for example, known that automatic fiscal stabilisers can reduce the variance of real output through time because they automatically offset any stochastic shocks to the system. As Professor Minford points out, an automatic and contemporaneous adjustment of monetary policy to shocks in the exchange market could perform a similar role. The paper tends to argue that from the point of view of the private markets, it would be simpler to reduce the size and frequency of the shocks directly by minimising deviations in the monetary base and the public sector borrowing requirement from announced targets. This seems a debatable point since the borrowing requirement is largely a function of the automatic fiscal stabiliser system mentioned above, and it is the type of funding of the borrowing that is the source of the domestic component of the base.

In any case there has been a good deal of discussion in recent years about the extreme information assumptions required for rational expectations models to operate fully. While one has little doubt that such information requirements are fulfilled in financial markets, because of the existence of financial intermediaries, the situation is nowhere near so clear-cut, it seems to me, in the real goods market, where the process of adjustment is likely to be much slower. In those circumstances the government would be able to affect the real exchange rate for a shorter or longer period.

To sum up, the conclusions of the paper are not surprising in view of the underlying rational expectations assumptions. In a world characterised by rational expectations and confidence in the stability of government policy, then I agree that attempts to influence the real exchange rate by traditional methods are inappropriate, and in the case of the UK I would, as I think Professor Minford does, expect the real goods markets to validate the previous adjustments in the exchange markets. I may also say that I don't think that is going to happen – I think agents in the foreign exchange markets have a very different distribution of expectations about the future evolution of government policy than do the agents in the domestic real goods markets including labour markets, and I see little chance of those expectations converging in the near future. In particular, I believe that agents in the foreign exchange markets are perhaps more irrational in these circumstances than domestic agents, because they appear to pay more attention to government policy statements than observed policy actions.

6 Exchange Rates, Interest Rates and the Mobility of Capital

Andrew Britton and Peter Spencer[1]

INTRODUCTION

In October last year, the UK Government announced the abolition of exchange controls. Before that date, there was one obvious reason why domestic capital at least was not perfectly mobile between UK and foreign assets. It is too early to say how profound an effect the abolition of exchange control has had on the integration of domestic and foreign capital markets, but the direction in which the system has moved is clear enough. This has stimulated special interest in this country in the implications of enhanced mobility. Within the Treasury, it has stimulated various pieces of analysis on which the present paper is based.

The first section derives a simple, and indeed a familiar,[2] algebraic model of the relationships which determine the real exchange rate and the real interest rate for an open economy in long-run equilibrium. This is a very simple and highly abstract analysis, but some conclusions can be drawn about the effects of shifts in these relationships which could represent the effects of changes in policy assumptions or changes in foreign interest rates. In this first section the emphasis is on the substitution effects of changes in relative prices; in the second section we discuss the complications which might arise if income, or wealth, effects are added to the model.

In the third section the timescale of the analysis is contracted and we consider what might be the nature of short-run adjustment. This requires the model to be changed in several ways. In long-run equilibrium, as we have defined it in the first two sections, the real economy can be discussed without reference to any nominal variables. It makes no difference to the equilibrium behaviour of the system whether the exchange rate or the money supply is assumed to be fixed. This dichotomy does not hold in the short run, so the behaviour of nominal variables has to be examined simultaneously with that of real variables. It is assumed that the authorities achieve a pre-set target for the growth of the money supply which is invariant to all the changes in exogenous variables or in other policy instruments. There is no intervention in the foreign exchange markets.

The move from the long run to the short run involves two kinds of disequilibrium. First, there is a disequilibrium in the adjustment of the price level: we assume that the goods market clears much more slowly than financial markets. In the short run it is convenient therefore to treat prices as given, with the implication that demand and supply in the goods market are not equal, in which case we assume that output is determined by demand. Secondly, there is a disequilibrium of expectations: in long-run equilibrium it may be assumed that expectations about the exchange rate and the price level are fulfilled, but for the short run some theory about the determination of expectations is required.

In Section 4 we use the algebra of the first three sections to consider some questions about the way an open economy works that are both topical and perennial. What happens when demand is cut, for goods that are internationally traded or for goods that are only produced at home? What happens when foreign interest rates change?

This final section also draws on the results of some simulations of the Treasury's macroeconomic model, which are described at greater length in the Appendix. The model is one possible representation of a sequence of dynamic adjustments which include elements of both the short-run and the long-run relationships set out, as algebra, in the first three sections of the paper. The quantitative results are extremely uncertain, but they may be regarded as illustrative of the implications of one way of interpreting such empirical evidence as we have – a modest claim, but the most a sober assessment will allow.

We interpret greater capital mobility, following the abolition of exchange control, as equivalent to a readier substitution between UK and foreign financial assets. This ease of substitution is represented as a parameter (or parameters) in the algebraic models, and also in the numerical model used for the simulations. By increasing the size of these parameters we can get some idea of the ways in which the new relationships may differ from the old. The extent of the difference is a much more difficult question, one indeed which cannot be answered until more time has elapsed since the abolition of exchange control and more data appear which would be germane to the issue.

1 A SIMPLE MODEL OF LONG-RUN EQUILIBRIUM

The long-run equilibrium for an open economy may be described in terms of two key relationships, which determine internal and external balance. These relationships suffice to determine two endogenous relative prices; any other relative prices must be assumed to be determined, outside the model, by world markets in which the demand of this particular country is insignificant. The characterisation of the goods and financial assets can be established in a variety of ways, all leading to essentially the same algebraic model. We start with the most familiar possible interpretation, and comment on some alternatives at the end of the section.

The condition of internal balance is that supply and demand for domestic output are equal. Supply (y) depends on methods of production and factor availability and will, for the moment, be taken as fixed. Demand depends on the relative price of the goods and foreign substitutes. It also depends on the level of interest rates, principally on the yield on domestic bonds, but perhaps also on the yield on foreign bonds as well (a complication to be introduced at a later stage). The equation also includes a shift parameter (A) to be used in subsequent analysis:

$$y = A - br - d\pi \qquad (1)$$

The parameter (d) must be positive if it is defined as a compensated price elasticity. The other parameter (b) is also positive if it too is interpreted as a compensated substitution term between present and future expenditure. Income and wealth effects will be discussed in Section 2 below, and they are assumed, for simplicity, to balance out at zero.

The second equation is the condition for external balance. Since the prices of both foreign goods and foreign bonds are exogenous, the two can be treated as if they were a composite good traded against domestic goods and bonds in a single market. The excess demand for this composite good can be written as:

$$B - e\pi + j(r - r_f) - ty = 0 \qquad (2)$$

The parameter (*e*) is assumed positive and refers to the current account of the balance of payments. The current account also responds to the level of domestic output if this is varied.

The other parameter (*j*) measures the international mobility of capital. The term refers to the capital account of the balance of payments, which is defined here in terms of a *flow* equilibrium rather than an equilibrium of *stocks*. It is worth pausing a moment to see what this implies. Abstracting as before from any wealth or income effects of changes in interest rates, we are referring here to the substitution between alternative financial assets when allocating a given flow of savings, whether that flow is generated in the domestic economy or in the outside world. In this long-run analysis, the composition of the underlying stocks of assets is assumed to be fully adjusted to the level of relative yields, but the overall size of the stock of wealth is growing. This is consistent with the assumption in the first equation that expenditure is sensitive to the level of interest rates.

In principle, indeed, one could add to the second equation a term in the average level of interest rates as well as the differential between rates at home and abroad. This term (which is left out here to keep the model simple) would represent the choice that determines the size of total savings, which may be (roughly) independent of its allocation between assets. On the other hand, a switch from saving to consumption might equally increase the demand for foreign exchange (i.e. for foreign goods plus foreign bonds) if the increment to expenditure had a high import content.

Equations (1) and (2) can readily be solved for the two endogenous variables:

$$(be + jd)r = e(A - y) + jdr_f - d(B - ty) \tag{3}$$

$$(be + jd)\pi = j(A - y) - jbr_f + b(B - ty) \tag{4}$$

We can now read off the effects on interest rates and relative prices of changes in the shift parameters (*A* and *B*) or the exogenous variables representing foreign interest rates and domestic production. These will be discussed in some detail in Section 4 below.

The model would be even simpler if, as some empirical work suggests, expenditure is not in fact very sensitive to the level of interest rates. In that case the relative price of domestic and foreign production (one definition of competitiveness, or the real exchange rate) would be determined by the first equation alone: the price would simply adjust to ensure that all that was produced would be sold.

This suggests a direction in which the model might well be extended. Is it really appropriate to assume that domestic output is fixed? If capital mobility includes the migration of capital, considered now as a factor of production, from country to country in pursuit of the most profitable location for production, there should be a response of supply as well as demand to the relative price term, π. The algebra need not change, but the parameter (d) would have a rather wider interpretation. Similarly, output may respond in the long run to the level of interest rates, since investment decisions determine the capital stock. Again the change can be made by a change in the definition of a parameter, (b) in this case, without actually rewriting the algebra.

As was suggested in the opening paragraph of this section, there are many further possibilities for the reinterpretation of these two simple equations.[3] Instead of classing goods as home and foreign production, they can be taken to mean traded and non-traded goods. In this case the relative price (π) refers to the price of the two goods in the domestic market, not to the competitiveness of home production as such. Indeed, one cannot speak meaningfully of price competitiveness if the 'law' of one price holds for traded goods. The important distinction for this model is between one good (whether exported or consumed at home) for which domestic production has a significant effect on the world price and a second good (whether it is produced at home or not) for which the economy in question is effectively a price-taker.

A very similar taxonomy can be applied to bonds. There would not need to be any change in the algebra if domestic residents were able to issue 'foreign' bonds – that is to issue bonds which were perfect substitutes on the world market for bonds issued in other countries. There could be two classes of bonds – tradeable bonds and non-tradeable bonds, with yields described by r_f and r respectively. The distinguishing feature is simply that the yield on tradeable bonds is determined in the world market, whilst the yield on non-tradeable bonds reflects the quantity issued within the domestic economy.

These taxonomic points are clearly important to the precise meaning one attaches to enhanced capital mobility. We shall be interpreting the parameter (j) as a measure of capital mobility in the analysis of subsequent sections. Strictly, however, it is a measure of the ease of substitution between what may be called tradeable and non-tradeable bonds. In terms of UK institutions, it may measure, not the ease of substitution between Euro-dollar deposits and local authority debt, but the ease of substitution between local authority debt or gilts on the one hand and building society deposits or national savings certificates on the other.

2 INCOME AND WEALTH EFFECTS

In the last section we treated changes in interest rates and prices as if they were compensated effects, or at least as if the substitution effects outweighed the income effects. In this section we investigate some of the income effects potentially at work and assess their importance.[4]

A rise in the price of any good (or asset) will benefit the holder of that good at the expense of non-holders. Consequently, real income and wealth effects usually depend upon distributional effects for their validity. For this paper the most important example is a transfer of real income or wealth from non-residents to residents, which may leave the world as a whole no better or worse off, but will nevertheless probably affect expenditure patterns. In particular, it is likely to increase expenditure on domestically produced assets and goods, raising their relative prices, and leading to a higher real exchange rate and a lower real interest rate.

The model could also be used to consider the effects of transfers of income or wealth between the public and private sectors of the domestic economy. An increase in the domestic bond yield for example will mean a cut in the value of the national debt, which can be described as a transfer of wealth from the private to the public sector. What happens next depends on the spending patterns of the private sector and the response of policy in the public sector. Is it reasonable to treat public spending and taxation as given in the context of such a transfer if we are considering long-run equilibrium? This is a rather tedious definitional question which can perhaps be by-passed by reference to the now familiar argument that the public sector is in principle nothing other than the private sector in a different guise. If this is generally recognised, then apparent transfers of wealth between the two sectors are really no different in kind from transfers within the private sector – which we all neglect with some degree of equanimity.

We revert then to transfers between domestic and foreign residents, which we assume do entail shifts in expenditure. The analysis of terms-of-trade changes associated with variations in the relative price (π) will not be pursued here. Instead we will treat, very briefly, the implications of a change in the foreign interest rate (r_f). Since it is the interest rate on foreign bonds, we might well assume that a rise in this rate will generate an inflow of income to the domestic economy from overseas residents on the invisible account of the balance of payments. (Of course if domestic residents are net borrowers at the foreign rate (r_f), then the effect on invisibles would go the other way.)

We suppose in this case that an invisible inflow can therefore be added to the equation for external balance, equation (2) above. It may, however, be compensated by an outflow on visible trade or on the capital account. This depends on the way that foreigners allocate their loss of real income as compared with the way domestic residents react to their increase in real income. We assume that tastes are such that the income flow on invisible account predominates. An additional term then appears in equation (2), offsetting the negative sign of the parameter for the foreign interest rate.

We have thus identified a possibility that a rise in foreign rates will eventually tend to *improve* the balance of payments rather than cause it to deteriorate and hence put *upward* rather than downward pressure on the real exchange rate. For this to be true the effect on invisible account must be greater than the effect on the capital account – income effects must predominate over substitution effects.

A shift in the stock of wealth underlying these flows on both capital and current account could lead to a lasting change in the balance of payments and hence to the equilibrium real exchange rate. Suppose, for example, that domestic residents decide to increase their (net) holdings of foreign assets – because exchange control is abolished. This will constitute a capital outflow whilst the adjustment is taking place, and during that transitional period it will tend to depress the real exchange rate. Once the adjustment is complete, however, its effect on the flow equilibrium in the balance of payments is not so clear. There will be presumably a continuing outflow as new savings in the domestic economy are allocated across all assets, including the newly-available overseas assets. On the other hand, there will be an income flow back from the stock of overseas assets already acquired. The net effect on the balance of payments, and hence on the equilibrium real exchange rate, could go either way.

3 DISEQUILIBRIUM

In the equilibrium model considered in Section 1, supply and demand for domestic output are equal. In the simplest case the supply is exogenous, and the demand adjusts, through changes in relative prices, until it matches the output which is available. We know, however, that this process of adjustment takes time to complete. This delay reflects some stickiness or resistance to change in the prices of goods (and underlying that resistance a stickness in wages). We cannot therefore continue to work with a strictly dichotomised system in which all real variables are determined independently of the absolute price level.

For the short run we shall assume instead that the price level in the domestic economy is fixed – fixed in the sense that it has not yet had time to adjust. Since the foreign price (in terms of foreign currency) is also assumed fixed, the real exchange rate and the nominal exchange rate amount to the same thing. The variable π can be regarded indifferently as referring to either. Similarly, with inflation exogenous, there is no operational distinction here between the real and the nominal interest rate.

The level of output in this short-run model becomes an endogenous variable, determined by demand rather than supply. This means, of course, that a third equation is needed. This must provide for equilibrium in the money market. (No equation for this market was required in the analysis of Section 1 since it would have demonstrated simply that the price level must respond proportionally to changes in the stock of money – or vice versa.) For the first time we must be explicit about the policy of the monetary authorities. We shall assume that the money supply is exogenous and the exchange rate is floating freely.

The result is a three-equation model, as follows:

$$y = A - br - d\pi \tag{5}$$

as before;

$$B - e\pi + j(r - r_f) - ty = 0 \tag{6}$$

as before

and

$$C = -lr + uy \tag{7}$$

where C is a shift parameter which could represent the (exogenous) level of real money balances.

If equation (5) is substituted into equations (6) and (7), we have a two-equation model involving the variables (r and π) comparable to that in Section 1:

$$-(e - td)\pi + (j + tb)r = tA + jr_f - B \tag{8}$$

$$ud\pi + (l + ub)r = uA - C \tag{9}$$

The first coefficient on the relative price term (π) is not really ambiguous in sign, since e must surely be greater than td – because t is the marginal elasticity of trade in response to an increase in total demand for domestic goods, and because e is a value elasticity, whilst d is a volume elasticity. Solving equations (8) and (9), we have some new 'reduced form' equations for the two endogenous variables:

$$\Delta r = udjr_f + uea - udB - (e - td)C \tag{10}$$

$$\Delta\pi = -(l + ub)jr_f + (l + ub)B + (ju - lt)A - (j + tb)C \tag{11}$$

where $\qquad \Delta = (e - td)(l + ub) + (j + tb)ud > 0$

The next stage in the progression from the long-run equilibrium to short-run adjustment must be the explicit treatment of expectations. In the long-run equilibrium it is certainly convenient (and surely appropriate) to assume that expectations are fulfilled, so there is no role for expectational variables at all. In the short run such an assumption is at least debatable. By way of extreme contrast, we shall assume here that expectations are simply exogenous and formed moreover in terms of levels rather than rates of change. Since the price level is fixed, we are concerned here only with expectations about the exchange rate. We shall assume that the expected rate of depreciation in the exchange rate varies directly with its actual level – the higher it rises, the further it is expected to fall. This is an extreme case of regressive expectations and represents a very stabilising form of speculation. This term is used to modify the differential between domestic and foreign interest rates.

The model can be adapted by replacing r_f in equations (10) and (11) by $(r_f + \theta\pi)$. The system can then be solved again to give:

$$\Delta' r = udjr_f + (e + j\theta)uA - udB \tag{12}$$
$$- (e + j\theta - td)C$$

$$\Delta'\pi = -(l + ub)jr_f + (ju - lt)A \tag{13}$$
$$+ (l + ub)B - (j + tb)C$$

where $\qquad \Delta' = (e + j\theta - td)(l + ub)$
$$+ (j + tb)ud > 0$$

In the very short run (the term is used without prejudice to the actual extent of elapsed time implied), a much simpler model may be applicable. It takes quite a long time for output to respond to either interest rates or the exchange rate. The very-short-run effect of the exchange rate on the current account may be small too, or even perverse, thanks to the J-curve. Instead of the rather complicated model implied by equations (12) and (13), we could look in the very short run at the following system:

$$y = A \tag{14}$$

$$B + j(r - r_f - \theta\pi) - ty = 0 \tag{15}$$

$$C = -lr + uy \tag{16}$$

or, as a 'reduced form' system, at:

$$\Delta'' r = j\theta u A - j\theta C \tag{17}$$

$$\Delta'' \pi = -ljr_f + (uj - lt)A + lB - jC \tag{18}$$

where $\qquad\qquad \Delta'' = j\theta l$

This very-short-run model is recursive: the level of output is exogenous, except for shifts in the parameter (A); together with shifts in parameter (C) this determines the domestic interest rate. Changes in the external balance, whether they are shifts in B or in the foreign interest rate, can therefore change nothing except the exchange rate. The economy is insulated.

In the models described so far, the foreign interest rate, and therefore the expected rate of appreciation or depreciation of the exchange rate, appears only in the equation for the balance of payments – in equation (6) for example, but not equations (5) or (7). In a more general case, foreign bonds would be seen as substitutes for domestic goods and for money as well as for domestic bonds. This elaboration would be especially appropriate if 'foreign' bonds are interpreted as 'tradeable' bonds which may in fact be issued by domestic residents.

In the UK there is no evidence so far as we know that changes in overseas interest rates have a *direct* effect on demand for goods. It is quite likely[5] however that there is some variation in the demand for money, especially using a broad money definition like sterling M3 (the target aggregate), resulting from variation in rates on Euro-dollar deposits and also in the exchange rate or its expected rate of change.

This complication can most easily be accommodated in the very-short-run model of equations (17) and (18). Instead of equation (16) we can substitute:

$$0 = -lr - v(r_f + \theta\pi) \tag{19}$$

(For simplicity, the terms in A and C have been dropped.)
This implies:

$$r_f + \theta\pi = \frac{l}{j(v+1)}B \tag{20}$$

and

$$r = -\frac{v}{j(v+1)}B \tag{21}$$

4 APPLICATIONS OF THE ANALYSIS

In this section we hope to demonstrate the usefulness of the rather arid analysis that has provided the bulk of the paper so far. The main topics to be considered will be an increase in foreign interest rates, reductions in public expenditure and an increase in income tax. In each case we shall consider the way the conclusions might be different if it is assumed that the abolition of exchange control has increased the mobility of capital between UK and overseas assets. We shall also refer more briefly to the implications of the initial capital outflow associated with the ending of exchange controls.

In each case the results will be discussed in terms of the consequences for UK real interest rates and the real exchange rate. Obviously these are both objects of considerable public interest, but we do not want to imply that they are, or should be, given special welfare significance or treated as if they were policy objectives. We are concerned here with the strictly positive issues of the direction, and perhaps the extent, of the consequences of political actions or external events.

The Appendix describes, very briefly, some of the main characteristics of the Treasury's macroeconomic model, and especially the treatment in that model of the balance of payments and domestic financial markets. It also contains the results of four pairs of simulations of that model, to which we shall be referring in this section.

An Increase in Overseas Interest Rates[6]

In the very short run, an increase in overseas rates will be offset by a depreciation of sterling until the market feels that the uncovered differential is exactly matched by the likelihood that sterling will recover. This is the adjustment indicated by equation (18) – or equation (20) of Section 3 above. It is also the main reason for the results of simulation 1 in the Appendix. As the equations referred to show, this result holds independently of the degree of capital mobility assumed. In the very short run the *only* significant response to the foreign rate takes the form of arbitrage on the capital account. Since it is the only adjustment, its intensity does not affect this particular issue.

In the not-so-very short run, other variables may be affected as well. Turning back to equations (12) and (13), it is clear that the depreciation of sterling remains, and that the domestic interest rate now rises – although not generally by as much as the increase in overseas rates. The depreciation of sterling can be seen as transmitting the interest rate rise from one country to another. The fall in sterling makes UK goods more competitive and stimulates output in this country. Higher output and also higher prices will mean higher UK interest rates, provided the money supply is held constant. The effect is also visible in the simulations quoted in the Appendix. Even if capital mobility is very high, the adjustment at this stage will still be split between depreciation and an increase in domestic interest rates.

The long-run results are implied by equations (2) and (3) of Section 1. We now add the requirement that expectations are realised. The adverse uncovered differential can no longer be matched by an expected recovery of sterling; if that recovery does not take place, speculators will cease to expect it – indeed, some would argue that speculators are sufficiently well-informed to anticipate the long-run equilibrium much more rapidly than this sequential account would suggest.

In the long run, if capital is very mobile between countries, the bulk of the increase in foreign rates will be added to the UK rate. The real exchange rate will be reduced, even in this case, because a higher interest rate will depress the demand for UK production. Since output is 'supply determined' in the long run the real exchange rate must fall to provide the extra demand required to balance that market. If capital is less mobile, then the adjustment even in the ultimate long run will include both an increase in the UK real interest rate and a cut in the real exchange rate.

Reductions in Public Sector Borrowing

A very similar analysis can be applied to a cut in the PSBR, taking the form of a tax increase or a public expenditure cut. Both reduce the demand for goods, whether UK produced or imported. If only UK demand is affected (perhaps by a cut in public sector employment) then the effects are those of a reduction in the parameter A. Conversely if only overseas demand is affected (perhaps by a cut in overseas procurement) then the parameter B is increased. We shall ignore the possibility of shifts in the parameter C, that is shifts in the demand for money relationship, associated with changes in private sector wealth, even though in a full analysis they would in fact be relevant.

In the very short run, equations (17) and (18), a cut in overseas spending will be reflected only in an exchange rate appreciation. If capital is very mobile even that result does not hold, since the exchange rate is effectively fixed by relative interest rates.[7] (This result must be qualified if the demand for money itself is sensitive to exchange rate changes – see equation (21).) In the intermediate case of equations (10) and (11), not only will the exchange rate appreciate but the interest rate will be reduced – as one would indeed expect from any cut in the PSBR. If capital mobility is very high however these 'intermediate-run' effects will also be very small. The same results hold for the very long equilibrium position described by equations (2) and (3).

Turning to the parameter A, it is clear that the effects of a cut in domestic spending will be quite different. In the short run the interest rate will fall (because the demand for money will be cut). The effect on the exchange rate however could go either way. The import content (and any multiplier consequences) of the expenditure cut suggest an increase in the exchange rate; on the other hand, the cut in the domestic interest rate suggests a fall. If capital mobility is high then it is the latter effect which will predominate.

The long-run results are very similar although the reasoning is rather different. A cut in domestic spending must reduce real interest rates to clear the market for goods, rather than the market for money. Similarly the real exchange rate will be reduced so as to create a better market for a given level of UK production. If the expenditure cut has no direct import content at all, there will be no long-run effect on the current account at all; the multiplier effects will be transitory if output is 'supply determined' in the long run. There is therefore no ambiguity about the effects on the real exchange rate: the cut in spending results in a real depreciation. If capital mobility is very high this is the only effect that will be observed, since the domestic interest rate will be closely linked to rates overseas.

These conclusions, based on the algebra of early sections of the paper, can be compared with the results of the simulations quoted in the Appendix. These show cuts in government expenditure at home and overseas, and an increase in income tax, each with capital mobility assumed first lower and then higher. The domestic interest rate falls in every case, to much the same extent whether the PSBR change results from external spending cuts or a tax increase, and irrespective of the degree of capital mobility.

The exchange rate effects on the other hand differ greatly between simulations. When the spending cuts are external the exchange rate rises, but rises much more if capital mobility is low than if it is high. When the spending cuts are internal, the real exchange rate falls. The effects of the tax increase however could, as predicted by the algebra, go either way. With capital mobility low the exchange rate rises, with capital mobility high it falls. The exact cross-over point between these two results will depend on all the parameters of the model: it is clearly not a point that one could hope to establish with any precision.

Concluding Comment

The abolition of exchange control has been treated in this paper mainly as a special case of an increase in capital mobility. The process of abolition itself will, however, result in a capital outflow, until such time as the stock of assets has adjusted to the new regime. This transitory outflow, which may of course take place over quite a long period of time, can be represented as a temporary shift in the parameter *B*. After that adjustment is complete, there will be continuing flow effects, of uncertain sign, as indicated in Section 2. The most interesting abiding effects of abolition, however, are probably its effects on the behaviour of the economy in response to changes in policy or circumstances. The paper has attempted to identify some of these effects.

APPENDIX: SOME SIMULATION RESULTS USING THE TREASURY MODEL

The Treasury Model

In order to illustrate the theoretical relationships, a series of simulations was run using the full Treasury macroeconomic model including its new financial sector. These simulations allow us to look at the response to policy changes over time and at a level of detail prohibited by algebraic analysis. They are particularly helpful in pointing out the effects on expectations, interest payments and other variables which are neglected in the theoretical analysis. However, these results depend quantitatively and, in some cases, qualitatively upon the coefficients used in the model. In view of the uncertainty about these parameters, the simulation results should be regarded as no more than illustrative. In particular, the timescale in which the short run merges into the long run is very uncertain.

The Medium-term Properties and the Real Sector of the Model

The qualifications are particularly relevant in the case of interest rate effects. UK researchers have found it difficult to identify ways in which interest rates affect economic activity. Treasury research has been reported in the various Technical Manuals describing the income-expenditure model which have been published annually since 1974 as well as several working papers (see, for example, the 1979 edition (HM Treasury, 1979) and the working paper by Bean (1978)).

This research has identified significant interest rate effects on investment and stockbuilding. An important interest rate effect on consumer durable expenditure has also been found – working through its effect on financial wealth. But even when taken together, these do not amount to much. It follows that the effect of interest rates working through activity and savings on the trade equations is also small. In an economy such as the UK's, which is growing slowly in real terms and with a low real propensity to save, this means that the long-run effect of interest rates on the overall balance of payments is weak. Consequently the model coefficient analogous to the parameter (*b*) of the long-run theoretical treatment is small.

In contrast, the exchange rate plays an important role in the model. The real exchange rate or competitiveness has a strong, though lagged, effect on international trade. The parameter corresponding to (*d*) is therefore positive and the parameter (*e*) in the trade equation relatively large.

Short-run Properties and the Financial Sector

The stickiness of wages and prices means that the real side of the economy cannot be analysed separately from the financial side in the short run, as noted in Section 3. This is because if prices are sticky, interest rates must clear the domestic financial markets. Interest rates will in turn affect capital inflows and, if it is floating, the exchange rate. The interactions between prices, interest and exchange rates complicate short-run policy analysis enormously, introducing many more parameters and uncertainties into the problem.

The financial sector of the Treasury model is described briefly in the 1979 version of the technical manual and more fully in a working paper (Mowl *et al.*, 1978). It should be emphasised that this part of the model is still experimental, with coefficient values which may be changed considerably in the light of further work.

In the short run, capital flows determine the behaviour of the exchange rate, as is emphasised by the model developed in Section 3, paragraph 8. This model shows that the degree of capital mobility does not affect the immediate response of the exchange rate to changes in interest rates. This depends entirely upon the way exchange rate expectations are formed.

The Model of Exchange Rate Expectations

In the financial sector, expectations are handled explicitly. The model of exchange market expectations is outlined in Bell and Beenstock, 1978. The market's view of the underlying long-term exchange rate is assumed to depend upon relative money supplies and labour costs, with the greater weight being given to the former.

This is consistent with long-run exchange rate theory which states that changes in relative money supplies or labour costs will, other things being equal, be matched by equiproportionate changes in the exchange rate in order to keep the real exchange rate unchanged. However, in the exercises reported in this paper, other things are not equal and the real exchange rate changes – arguably in a predictable way. In order to ensure long-run expectational consistency, we therefore adapted the underlying exchange rate expectation to take account of the change in the real exchange rate.

The necessary degree of adjustment was calculated by taking the ratio of the actual to the expected exchange rate averaged over the final year of a preliminary run. The simulation was then rerun after multiplying the long-run expectation by this ratio in each period, and the ratio of the actual to the expected exchange rate in the final year was then rechecked. In most cases, this two-stage process ensured expectational consistency at least towards the end of the run. However, when simulating the cut in public expenditure overseas this procedure had to be repeated several times until convergence was obtained. This was probably because this example required the largest degree of manual adjustment. For example, when low degree of capital mobility was assumed (simulation 2(a) discussed below), it was found necessary to increase expectations by 2.5 per cent relative to the value produced automatically by the model.

In the short run expectations depend upon the long-run expectation and also the current exchange rate. This allows for short-run deviations from long-term equilibrium due to, say, changes in interest rates. The model of expectations is very similar in conception to that developed by Dornbusch (1976b). This kind of behaviour is rational if goods prices are sticky so that interest rates clear the money markets in the short run. In such circumstances a change in the money supply will cause the exchange rate to overshoot the long-run solution dictated by the monetary theory of the exchange rate, since it will be accompanied by short-run changes in interest rates which will have an additional effect on the exchange rate. It is assumed that the market's short-run expectation converges upon the underlying or long-term expectation with a mean lag of one year to allow for such disequilibrium effects.

Estimates of the Degree of Capital Mobility

The short-run exchange rate effects of changes in the current account depend upon the degree of capital mobility (j) as well as the expectational parameters. Again this is clear from the model of Section 3, paragraph 8. The higher the degree of capital mobility, the smaller the effects will be. This raises the difficult empirical problem of determining the responsiveness of capital flows to changes in interest rates and expectations. Treasury research in this area goes back a long way – to the original work of Hutton (1977) and Minford (1978). The present model is based on the work of Beenstock and Bell (1979). A summary of results published for the UK is reproduced as Table 6A.1.

TABLE 6A.1. UK Capital Account Effect Changes in Domestic Interest Rates ($£$ million)

		Effect of 1 % change in:			
	Estimation period	Short-terms covered differential	Short-term uncovered differential	Long-term different-ial	All UK rates[a]
Study					
1. Branson and Hill (1971)	1960/69	120			
2. Hodjera (1971)	1963/67	921			
3. Hutton (1977)	1963/70	820	100	–	127
4. Minford (1978)	1963/71	365	–	148	–
5. Beenstock and Bell (1979)	1964/75	300	48	160	240
6. HMT 1979 technical manual		500	150	160	350

[a] With cost of forward cover endogenous.

Table 6A.1 reveals that the results have varied considerably between studies and suggests that the overall degree of mobility is low. This is almost certainly due to simultaneous equations bias. This results because the authorities have in the past tended to raise UK interest rates, in response to a loss of confidence and a capital outflow. Consequently these estimates should be interpreted as being estimates of the minimum degree of mobility.

Given the perverse short-run effect of exchange rate changes on trade flows at current prices these coefficient values are not large enough to stabilise the exchange rate (see Britton, 1970). However, an upward adjustment can be justified by the likelihood of estimation bias and the increase in the general price level and scale of financial flows since the estimation period. In order to take account of these effects and to obtain sensible simulation properties the model incorporates significantly larger estimates. Our working assumptions prior to the abolition of exchange controls are reported in the final column of Table 6A.1.

It will be some time before the effect of the abolition of exchange controls on capital mobility can be judged, even on an impressionistic basis. However, it does seem to be the case that interest rate differentials have had a significant effect on the sterling dollar rate in the period since abolition, whereas such effects have been difficult to detect before. Covered interest rate differentials between the UK and other financial centres also seem to have become much smaller.

One way to approach this problem is to look at the sensitivity of capital flows to other industrial countries which have had only minimal exchange controls. This is not as easy as it sounds, since most countries have had significant controls at one time or another during the last twenty years. Moreover, with the exception of the USA no other countries have financial systems which are as developed as that of the UK. The estimates are also subject to the same open economy biases as those for the UK, again with the possible exception of the USA. Nevertheless, these estimates are revealing and some selected examples are given in Table 6A.2.

These results suggest that in the absence of controls capital is very mobile internationally. The size and openness of the different economies can be allowed for by deflating these figures by average trade flows over the period. These figures are reported in the final column of Table 6A.2. The comparable figures for the UK are 0.95 for Hutton's study of short-term flows and 1.78 for the Beenstock–Bell estimate of the overall capital account elasticity. This very simple comparison therefore suggests that capital mobility is between 50 per cent and 150 per cent higher for countries without exchange controls than it was for the UK up to last year. We might therefore double our capital mobility estimates as a way of simulating the effect of abolishing capital controls. However,

TABLE 6A.2 Selected Estimates of the Interest Sensitivity of Capital Flows in other Countries

Study	Country	Estimation period	Effect of 1 % rise in domestic interest rates	
(a) *Short-term flows*			(a) $ million	(b) Normalised by trade[a]
Branson (1968)	USA	1959/66	$850	1.33
Branson and Hill (1971)	USA	1960/69	$1400	2.19
(b) *Total capital flows*				
Branson and Hill (1971)	USA	1960/69	$2550	3.99
Branson and Hill (1971)	Germany	1960/68	$880	2.09
Herring and Marston (1977)	Germany	1962/71	$1300[b]	2.98
Hodjera (1978)	Austria	1960/71	$118	2.46

[a] Divided by sum of (1965) imports and exports in units of $100 million.
[b] Cumulative effect on flows after three-year lag, assuming forward premium adjusts.

in order to make the results as clear-cut as possible we increased mobility by a factor of 3. The results should therefore be construed as the effect of a general increase in mobility, and not as the specific effect of abolishing the controls.

The Demand for Money in the Treasury Model[A1]

The demand for money is usually modelled directly, using an equation relating it to incomes, prices and interest rates. But a major disadvantage of handling it in this way is that speculative and other factors which affect the demand for non-monetary assests are difficult to incorporate in such a specification. In the Treasury model they are identified instead through their effects on savings and the counterparts of money in non-bank portfolios – principally gilts, overseas investment and bank borrowing. Speculative influences in the gilts market, and to a lesser extent the exchange markets, consequently affect the demand for money. It is therefore important to handle them carefully especially when simulating a regime of fixed monetary targets and floating exchange rates.

The nature of the demand for money function implicit in these relationships can be seen from model simulations. The results of an exercise investigating the effect of prices, wealth, incomes and interest rates, were described in the Treasury paper produced for the 1979 City University Conference (Middleton *et al.*, 1981). These have recently been recalculated and the results are reproduced in Table 6A.3. In view of their importance in this context we have also looked at the effect of exchange rate and gilt price expectations.

TABLE 6A.3 Partial Demand for Money Elasticities in the Treasury Model

% Effect of:	1% rise in			1% p.a. rise in			Expected 1% p.a. rise in	
on £M3 in	Real income	Price level	Net fin. wealth	Long rates	Short rates	Over-seas rates	Ex-change rate	Gilt-edged prices
Q1	−0.18	0.66	0.70	0.02	0.23	−0.36	0.31	−0.24
Q4	0.38	0.44	0.43	−0.54	−0.09	−0.38	0.21	−0.45
Q8	0.33	0.43	0.49	−1.54	−0.09	−0.38	0.20	−0.73
Q12	0.37	0.46	0.55	−2.07	−0.04	−0.44	0.19	−0.93

The effects of prices, wealth and incomes are very similar to those reported at last year's Conference and we will not go into them on this occasion. The effects of domestic interest rates have changed significantly however. The effect of a rise in long rates on the money supply has increased, largely because in the present specification this is related to the market value of the stock of gilts outstanding. On the other hand, the effect of short-term interest rates is smaller. This is partly because our estimate of the effect of short-term interest rates on bank lending has fallen. But it is also because we have assumed that the abolition of exchange controls has increased the degree of substitutability between monetary assets in the UK and overseas. A rise in the return on short-term deposits in the UK will under this assumption have the side-effect of increasing resident holdings at the expense of overseas assets. Some of these deposits are included within the definition of £M3 so that this effect will offset the reduction in £M3 that might otherwise occur, reducing the overall elasticity and perhaps even making it positive. This reflects the fact that the short-term interest rate acts partly as the 'own rate' on money, as noted in last year's paper.[A2]

The possibility of substitution between £M3 and overseas assets is also reflected in the effect of overseas interest rates and exchange rate expectations on the demand for money. Their short-run effects are similar in magnitude. Overseas interest rates have a greater effect than expectations in the longer run, however, since this is a feature of the long-term capital flows equation. This is perhaps because they cause capital revaluations which are to some extent offset by new investments in order to minimise changes in international balance sheet structures. In order to obtain the results of Table 6A.3 the capital mobility coefficients were taken to be a weighted average of those used in the high and low mobility simulations.

The effect of gilt price expectations is reported in the final column of Table 6A.3. This has a similar profile to, but is smaller than, the effect of long-term interest rates. This is largely because the current specification of the demand for gilts assumes that investors will tend to offset the effect of a rise in long-term interest rates on capital values of their portfolio by purchasing new stock. This feature of the model is discussed in Mowl *et al.* (1978).

The Model of Gilt-edged Price Expectations

In the model long-term interest rate expectations are based on a normal or underlying level which depends upon inflationary expectations and the PSBR as well as UK short-term and overseas interest rates. If long rates fall below this level this induces expectations of capital gains, a rise in gilt sales and a fall in the demand for money. This is the most important effect which interest rates have on the demand for money in the short-run since the other main effect working through bank lending appears to be subject to long lags.

As with the model of exchange market expectations, it is important to ensure long-run consistency between the interest rate which is predicted by the expectations equation and that which is implied in the rest of the model. In these runs rough consistency was achieved by adapting the expectational model to take account of any long-run changes in interest rates which emerged. As with exchange market expectations this was achieved by an iterative procedure which ensured that the expected price of gilts equalled the actual price during the final year of the simulation.

The Specification of Monetary and Exchange Rate Policy

As currently specified both the exchange rate and interest rates are formally exogenous to the model: they appear only as explanatory variables and are not dependent variables in any equation. For any given set of rates the balance of payments and the demand for money are endogenous, determined by the relationships built into the model. In order to simulate a policy of floating exchange rates and fixed monetary targets these relationships must therefore be inverted to solve for values of the exchange and interest rates which are consistent with the monetary target and balance of payments equilibrium. In practice this is achieved by an iterative method whereby the computer searches over various values of these variables in order to find the equilibrium solution. This procedure is described more fully in Mowl *et al.* (1978).

Debt Interest Effects and Debt-financed Fiscal Policy

Several of the reported simulations were designed to investigate medium- and long-term effects of a change in fiscal policy. Some care must be taken over the exact definition of fiscal policy because it is complicated by debt interest effects. A sustained reduction in any item of public expenditure will lead to a cumulative reduction in the national debt and interest rates given a fixed money supply. This will have a secondary effect of lowering debt interest payments which will themselves lower the PSBR and debt finance.

It is well known that such effects may make debt-financed fiscal policy changes unstable. This has been investigated by Currie (1976) for example. In the present context these effects also make it difficult to analyse rigorously the effect of a change in public expenditure on traded and non-traded goods. A reduction in expenditure on traded goods will, for example, lead to lower debt interest payments and therefore lower private expenditure on non-tradeables. In order to avoid these problems when simulating a change in fiscal policy we used domestic transfer payments to offset the effect of changes in debt interest payments on the PSBR. The change in the PSBR therefore only reflects the initial discretionary expenditure or tax change.

The Simulation Results

The simulation results are tabulated in Table 6A.4. Four pairs of results are shown, each set showing the effect of assuming (*a*) low and (*b*) a relatively high degree of capital mobility. The first simulation in each case uses the capital mobility coefficients reported in the 1979 technical manual and reproduced in Table 6A.1. The second shows the result after increasing these estimates by a factor of 3.

In order to help relate the simulation results to the theory of the main text it is useful to recast the theory in terms of a diagram. This is shown as

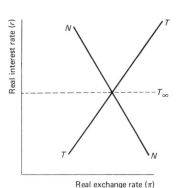

FIGURE 6A.1 Internal and external equilibrium

Figure 6A.1 and is similar to the internal-equilibrium diagram employed by Dornbusch (1976a). The real interest rate (r) is plotted on the vertical and the real exchange rate (π) on the horizontal axis. The line NN' represents the internal equilibrium condition – equation (1) of the main text – and has a negative slope because if this is to be maintained a rise in r must be offset by a fall in π. On the other hand external equilibrium requires a fall in π in this instance and so the external equilibrium line TT' corresponding to equation (2) has a positive slope. In the extreme case of perfect capital mobility this line becomes horizontal at the world real interest rate level (T_∞). These lines may on an alternative interpretation be seen as representing equilibrium in the traded (TT) and non-traded (NN) sectors.

Simulation 1: The Effect of a Rise in Overseas Interest Rates

The effect of a rise in overseas interest rates under different assumptions about the degree of capital mobility is shown by the first two simulation results. These show the effect of a one-point rise in overseas short-term rates accompanied by a half-point rise in overseas long rates. In practice, such a change might be caused by a commodity price boom or a tightening of monetary objectives, but in order to highlight the effect of interest rates *per se*, such causal factors have not been built into these simulations.

In these runs, the impact effect is felt through the external equilibrium condition. In terms of Figure 6A.1, the TT line shifts up and to the left,

TABLE 6A.4 Simulation Results

		1. Rise in overseas interest rates		2. Cut in overseas expenditure		3. Cut in domestic expenditure		4. Rise in income tax	
		(a) Low mobility	(b) High mobility	(a) Low mobility	(b) High mobility	(a) Low mobility	(b) High mobility	(a) Low mobility	(b) High mobility
Short-term interest rate (% points)	Q1	0.4	0.5	−1.2	−1.1	−1.0	−1.1	−1.3	−1.2
	Q4	0.6	0.6	−2.3	−1.7	−2.0	−1.4	−1.4	−1.1
	Q8	0.4	0.5	−2.2	−1.8	−2.4	−1.7	−1.6	−1.2
	Q16	0.6	0.7	−2.8	−2.0	−3.0	−2.1	−2.0	−1.4
	Q28	0.8	0.9	−2.7	−2.2	−2.8	−2.3	−2.2	−1.8
Exchange rate (%)	Q1	−1.4	−1.1	3.2	0.3	−0.1	−2.9	−1.6	−2.8
	Q4	−0.1	−0.2	2.5	0.7	0.6	−1.3	−0.0	−1.2
	Q8	0.1	−0.1	2.0	0.9	0.7	−1.0	−0.3	−1.2
	Q16	−0.1	−0.2	2.7	0.9	0.8	−1.0	0.3	−1.2
	Q28	−0.3	−0.2	2.8	1.0	0.8	0.2	−0.1	−0.5
RPI (%)	Q1	0.0	0.0	−0.1	0.0	−0.1	−0.1	−0.3	0.0
	Q4	0.2	0.2	−0.9	−0.4	−0.6	−0.2	−0.1	0.1
	Q8	0.2	0.2	−1.2	−0.6	−1.1	−0.5	0.0	0.3
	Q16	0.2	0.2	−1.1	−0.3	−1.5	−0.6	0.3	0.9
	Q28	0.2	0.2	−1.0	−0.1	−1.4	−1.1	0.4	0.8

The real exchange rate (%)	Q1	−1.4	−1.1	3.4	0.3	−0.1	−2.9	−1.6	−2.8
	Q4	−0.2	−1.4	2.0	0.7	+0.3	−1.3	+0.1	−0.7
	Q8	0.0	−0.2	1.2	0.6	−0.1	−1.2	−0.1	−0.7
	Q16	−0.2	−0.3	2.3	1.2	−0.4	−1.4	+1.0	0.0
	Q28	−0.3	−0.2	2.9	1.8	−0.1	−0.3	+1.3	+1.1
Competitiveness (relative unit labour costs) (%)	Q1	−1.4	−1.1	3.2	0.3	−0.2	−3.0	−0.2	−0.3
	Q4	−0.0	−0.1	2.4	0.7	−0.1	−1.9	−0.1	−0.5
	Q8	0.2	0.1	1.3	0.7	−0.6	−1.7	0.1	−0.2
	Q16	−0.0	−0.1	2.1	1.0	−1.2	−2.1	0.3	0.0
	Q28	−0.3	−0.1	2.3	1.6	−1.5	−1.2	0.4	0.5
Real GDP (%)	Q1	0.02	0.01	−0.01	0.03	−0.07	−0.66	−0.01	0.01
	Q4	0.02	0.01	0.07	0.14	−0.56	−0.50	−0.02	0.01
	Q8	−0.01	0.00	0.22	0.38	−0.04	−0.14	0.20	0.30
	Q16	0.03	0.06	−0.42	−0.17	−0.21	0.05	−0.29	−0.10
	Q28	0.05	0.03	−0.14	−0.05	0.17	0.01	−0.27	−0.33

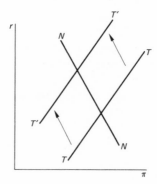

FIGURE 6A.2 Rise in world interest rate

implying a rise in the interest rate and a fall in the exchange rate. This situation is shown in Figure 6A.2. In the short run, the exchange rate falls sufficiently to induce expectations of an appreciation in later periods which balances the supply and demand for foreign exchange. This fall in the exchange rate tends to raise prices and, given the fixed money supply, interest rates. Although this effect is subject to lags, it is anticipated by the financial markets so that a large part of the rise in interest rates occurs in the first quarter. The short-run rise in domestic interest rates is larger the higher the degree of capital mobility, as we would expect from the theory set out in Section 3 above, although the differences are not marked. The fall in the exchange rate is smaller the higher the degree of capital mobility, because this has the effect of minimising the current account (J-curve) effect on the exchange rate.

Over a longer time period, balance of payments equilibrium is achieved through a rise in domestic interest rates rather than a fall in the exchange rate. As we would expect from the figure, this rise is larger the higher the degree of capital mobility, and (except in the case of perfect mobility) smaller than the rise in world rates. External equilibrium is also helped by a current account improvement which emerges because UK interest rates are higher and relative labour costs lower. These adjustments have offsetting effects on GDP and also serve to maintain internal equilibrium.

The fourth row of Table 6A.4 shows the effect on the real exchange rate, conventionally defined as the nominal exchange rate multiplied by the UK GDP deflator and divided by a world price deflator. Since world prices are fixed in these simulations, changes in the real rate are due to changes in the nominal rate and UK prices. In this simulation, the change in the real rate (and also cost competitiveness) is dominated by the change in the nominal rate. The change in the RPI reported in Table 6A.4 overstates the change in the GDP deflator because it reflects the effect of the rise in interest rates on housing costs.

Simulation 2: The Effect of Cutting Public Expenditure Overseas

Simulations 2(a) and (b) show the effect of cutting public expenditure overseas (by £ 500 m a year at 1975 prices). Debt interest effects are offset by transfer payments. Interest and exchange rates adjust to offset the effect on the money and exchange markets. This is equivalent to a downward shift in the shift parameter B in the theoretical model. This is shown in Figure 6A.3 as a downward shift in the external equilibrium line. The internal equilibrium locus does not shift since domestic expenditure is not directly affected. In this case, the exchange rate rises and interest rates fall. The degree of capital mobility plays an important role in this simulation because, in contrast to the previous example, it is the current rather than the capital account which is initially affected. In the limiting case of perfect capital mobility, the current account effect will be offset by the capital account without any change in interest and exchange rates or any other variables.

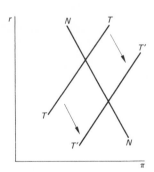

FIGURE 6A.3 Cut in overseas expenditure

These effects are clear in the simulation results. The exchange rate and competitiveness effects are much smaller in the high mobility case, both in the short and the long run. The interest rate effects are also less pronounced. The nominal exchange rate effects differ noticeably between these two cases but the effect of capital mobility on the *real* exchange rate response is less pronounced. This is mainly because domestic costs and prices fall in response to the rise in the nominal exchange rate, reducing its effect on competitiveness. It is also partly because the fall in interest rates cuts the retail prices index which in turn reduces earnings.

Simulation 3: The Effect of a Cut in Public Sector Domestic Expenditure

In this simulation, the effect of cutting public expenditure on goods without any direct import content is investigated. (The cut was of the same size as in simulation 2.) This is equivalent to a reduction in the shift parameter A in the theoretical model since domestic activity is affected directly and the balance of payments only affected indirectly by the cut. This is shown as a downward shift in the NN line in figure 6A.4. In the short run, both activity and interest rates fall, making the exchange rate effect ambiguous as noted in Section 4, paragraph 10. In the low-mobility case, the current account effect of lower interest rates dominates the activity effect and the exchange rate improves after the first quarter. In the high-mobility case, however, the interest rate effect dominates the result.

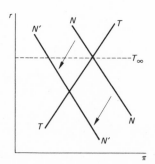

FIGURE 6A.4 Cut in domestic expenditure

In the long run, interest rates and the real exchange rate must both fall, as shown in Figure 6A.4, reflecting the equilibrium theory outlined in section 4, paragraph 11. This is necessary to offset the effect of reduced expenditure on the internal balance, whilst preserving the external balance. The degree of capital mobility does not qualitatively affect this conclusion, it only affects the distribution of the effect between the real exchange and interest rate effects. In the high-mobility variant, the fall in interest rates is smaller than in the low-mobility case and the necessary improvement in competitiveness must therefore be greater. This goes hand in hand with a better current account, matched by larger capital outflows.

The Effect of a Rise in Income Taxes

In this simulation, income taxes were reduced (again by £500 m in constant prices). Domestic expenditure and the balance of trade are both directly affected since the private sector tends to reduce its expenditure on both domestic and traded output. In terms of the theoretical analysis, parameter A is reduced and B increased. This situation is shown in Figure 6A.5, as a downward shift in both NN and TT. In addition, the various indirect effects noted in the two previous simulations will occur.

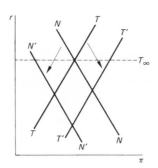

FIGURE 6A.5 Cut in income taxes

The short-run effect on the nominal exchange rate is ambiguous but these runs suggest that the effect of the lower interest rates on the capital account will dominate, causing the exchange rate to be lower. This effect occurs independently of the assumptions about the degree of capital mobility, because of lags in the response of imports to private demand.

This simulation differs from the two expenditure runs in that the long-run real exchange rate effect is ambiguous. The interest rate effect is unambiguously negative, however. The reduction in the demand for traded goods (or shift in the *TT* curve) will tend to increase the real exchange rate, whereas the fall in demand for non-tradeables (or shift in the *NN* curve) will have the opposite effect. As the degree of capital mobility is increased, this reduces the first of these effects and increases and second, making it more likely that a fall in the real exchange rate occurs. In the limit of perfect capital mobility, a fall in the real exchange rate must occur. This is because the interest rate is fixed by the external equilibrium condition at the world level (the *TT* line is horizontal and does not shift). Consequently, the fall in demand for domestic output must be offset by a fall in the real exchange rate in order to attain external equilibrium.

NOTES

1. The authors are grateful for helpful comments from colleagues at the Treasury; the paper remains their personal responsibility and should not be interpreted as expressing views on behalf of their Department.
2. We draw especially on the analysis of Dornbusch (1976a).
3. We draw here on the paper by our colleague, Chris Riley (1978).
4. Some of this ground has been covered in Turnovsky (1976).
5. See in particular paragraphs 19 and 20 of the Appendix.
6. It is worth emphasising that all other overseas variables are held constant. The increase in overseas interest rates does *not*, for example, result from higher output, higher prices or lower money supply.
7. Together with expectations of future appreciation or depreciation.
A1. The financial sector of the Treasury model is still regarded as experimental and some of the key parameters determining the demand for money are subject to frequent and substantial revision.
A2. In using the model, it is generally assumed that any change in short rates will be accompanied by a change in long rates in the same direction (and a change in expected capital gains on gilts as well). Thus, the partial elasticities quoted in Table 6A.3 are of significance only as diagnostics.

REFERENCES

Bean, C. R. (1978). 'The determination of Consumers Expenditure in the UK', HM Treasury Working Paper No. 4 (July).

Beenstock, M. and Bell, S. (1979). 'A quarterly econometric model of the capital account of the UK balance of payments', Manchester Business School (March), 47, 33–62.

Bell, S. and Beenstock, M. (1978). 'An application of rational expectations to the UK foreign exchange market', AUTE Conference volume (Croom Helm).

Branson, W. (1968). 'Financial capital flows in the US balance of payments' (North Holland).

Branson, W. and Hill, R. (1971). 'Capital movements in the OECD Area', OECD Occasional Study.

Britton, A. J. C. (1970). 'The dynamic stability of the Foreign Exchange Market', *Economic Journal*, 80, 91–6.

Currie, D. A. (1976). 'Optimal stabilisation policies and the government budget constraint', *Economica* (May), 43, 159–67.

Dornbusch, R. (1976a). 'The Theory of Flexible Exchange Rate Regimes and Macroeconomic Policy', *Scandinavian Journal of Economics*, 78, No. 2.

Dornbusch, R. (1976b). 'Exchange rate expectations and monetary policy', *Journal of International Economics* (August) 6, No. 3, 231–44.

HM Treasury (1979). 'Macroeconomic Model Technical Manual 1979.'

Herring, R. and Marston, R. (1977). 'National Monetary Policy and International Financial Markets' (North Holland).

Hodjera, Z. (1971). 'Short term Capital Movements in the United Kingdom 1963–67', *JPE* (August), 79, 739–75.

Hodjera, Z. (1978). 'Alternative approaches in the analysis of international capital movements: a case study of Austria and France' IMF Staff Papers. (December), 23, No. 4.

Hutton, J. (1977). 'A model of short term capital movements, the foreign exchange market and official intervention in the UK', *Review of Economic Studies* (February), 44(1), No. 136.

Minford, P. (1978). 'Substitution effects, speculation and exchange rate stability' (North Holland).

Mowl, C., Spencer, P., Lomax, R. and Denham, M. (1978). 'A Financial Sector for the Treasury Model', HM Treasury working paper No. 8 (December).

Middleton, P., Mowl, C., Riley, C. and Odling Smee, J. (1981). 'Monetary Targets and the PSBR', in *Monetary Targets*, B. Griffiths and G. E. Wood (eds) (Macmillan).

Riley, C. J. (1978). 'Non-traded Goods and Macroeconomic Policy under Alternative Exchange Rate Regime in an Inflationary World', HM Treasury mimeo.

Turnovsky, S. J. (1976). 'The Dynamics of Fiscal Policy in an Open Economy', *Journal of International Economics* (May), 6, No. 2, 115–42.

Exchange Rates, Interest Rates and the Mobility of Capital: A Comment

Allan H. Meltzer

In October 1979, the government of the United Kingdom removed many, long-standing restrictions on capital movements. In the following year, the pound appreciated against the dollar and other major currencies. At the time of the announcement, the dollar exchange rate stood below $2.20 per pound; a year later the dollar exchange was above $2.40. The appreciation of the pound against other currencies – for example the mark and the yen – is proportionally greater during this period because the dollar appreciated against the mark and the yen and the pound appreciated relative to the dollar.

The paper by Andrew Britton and Peter Spencer analyses the effect of increased capital mobility on the value of a currency. The paper is in two parts. The main relation between the parts is that both discuss capital mobility.

The theory section develops some short and long-term responses to a change in the mobility of capital with prices fixed. The authors justify the assumption of fixed prices on the ground that money is neutral in the long run. They neglect effects on wealth because, they say, 'the public sector is in principle nothing other than the private sector in a different guise' (p. 200). Having dismissed the political struggle over the distribution of income and the inflation tax as inconsequential for the aggregate, the authors are able to reduce the problem to one that can be handled in the standard framework.

Prices are assumed to be fixed, also, in the short run while the monetary authority achieves pre-announced targets for the growth of money. (Would that it were so.) The authors do not recognise the inconsistency or the unreality of these assumptions. The authorities have a credible policy of announcing and achieving targets for money, but the public ignores the announcements when setting prices. Expectations are ignored throughout.

The empirical section simulates responses to various changes using the Treasury's model. The model appears to suffer from many of the drawbacks of models of this kind. Some examples are: the effects of anticipated and unanticipated changes are not distinguished; anticipations are not fully rational or consistent with the model's properties; prices are fixed in the short run.

The principal problem I have with the authors' paper is that I do not think the authors' analysis captures the relevant features of the problem they address. In the following section, I discuss the model with emphasis on long-run aspects where the analytical problems are seen most easily. I then comment on some reasons for the appreciation of the pound in the recent past and suggest that part of recent appreciation is likely to persist.

THE MODEL

The authors solve their long-run model for the real rate of interest and the 'real' exchange rate, π, as functions of foreign interest rates, r_f, (fixed) real income, y, and some parameters. They do not define π explicitly, but the context suggests that π is measured in units of foreign currency per unit of domestic currency. A rise in π appreciates home currency and reduces spending on goods and services produced at home.

There are two principal equations, one for the output market and one for external balance, shown as equations (1) and (2), just as in the authors' paper.

Output:
$$y = A - br - d\pi \tag{1}$$

External Balance:
$$B - e\pi + j(r - r_f) - ty = 0 \tag{2}$$

A, B, b, d, e, j and t are parameters. The authors note that equation (2), for the trade balance, determines a flow equilibrium. There are, surprisingly, no stocks, and the long-run model is never extended to incorporate stocks. Stocks are mentioned in a later section, however, where the authors note that the removal of exchange controls increases desired holding of foreign assets by domestic residents. This, one expects, depreciates the pound sterling.

If we picture equations (1) and (2) in the π, r plane, there is a negatively sloped equilibrium relation for the domestic output market and a positively sloped equilibrium relation for external balance. A rise in the real interest rates is compensated by a depreciation of the 'real' exchange rate to maintain equilibrium in the output market, $d\pi/dr|_{(1)} < 0$, and by an appreciation of the exchange rate to maintain equilibrium of the foreign balance or the external accounts, $d\pi/dr|_{(2)} > 0$.

Removal of exchange controls is equivalent to an increase in the effective rate of interest earned by domestic residents who purchase or hold foreign assets. A rise in r_f shifts the external balance equilibrium, in the π, r plane, lowering π and raising r. At the new equilibrium, the domestic interest rate is higher, and the currency depreciates. The size of the depreciation depends on the value of $j/e(j, e > 0)$, but there is no ambiguity about the sign.[1]

The depreciation of the exchange rate is a clear implication of the model, but the authors do not draw the conclusion I draw because they analyse the problem in a peculiar way. Anyone can see from the authors' reduced form equations (3) and (4) that a rise in r_f lowers π and raises r.[2] The authors avoid this implication by treating the elimination of exchange controls as an increase in the parameter j. They argue that j measures the degree of capital mobility, and they treat the removal of exchange controls as an increase in capital mobility.

The mistake is, I believe, a confusion between the slope of a curve, j in this case, and an impulse or policy change. A change in j has an ambiguous effect that depends on the parameters of the model. A more appropriate model would analyse the impact of removing exchange controls as an increase in α (see note 1), then trace out the effects on the new equilibrium achieved when $r = \alpha r_f$ and α is nearer (or equal) to unity as a result of the policy change.

The authors' note, on page 212, that the interest differential between domestic and foreign rates narrowed after removal of exchange controls, but they do not see this change as a cause of depreciation (following an increase in α). Throughout their emphasis is on the parameter j.

Neither the authors' model nor their method of analysing the problem seems appropriate to the task. I shall not comment further on these aspects. I note, however, that in the authors' simulations, a rise in foreign rates of interest depreciates the nominal and real exchange rate, so I expect they would share my conclusion if I could persuade them to think about the effect of removing exchange controls in a different way.

APPRECIATION OF THE POUND

The reason for removing exchange controls in October 1979 may have been a desire to depreciate the pound as a means of increasing exports and reducing the (then) anticipated and (now) actual rise in UK unemployment. The appreciation of the pound does not show that these effects did not occur; the appreciation might have been greater if exchange controls had not been removed.

An argument of this kind is empty unless one can provide a reason for appreciation. In this section, I point to three real changes that have affected the exchange rate. All three imply that the appreciation of the pound is not a temporary phenomenon but is likely to persist. Of course, other factors – including removal of exchange controls and the temporary effect of unanticipated changes in monetary growth – have affected the exchange rate. I conclude, however, that it is a mistake to believe that the appreciation of 1980 is either entirely, or mainly, transitory.

One reason underlying this conclusion is that the contrary conclusion places excessive emphasis on the role of monetary policy in the appreciation of the pound. The argument for a strong monetary influence is rather weak. The market has been encouraged to use £M3 as an indicator of the stance of monetary policy. The growth of £M3 has been higher, not lower, than was announced and, I believe, higher than anticipated. Part of the excess growth followed the removal of the 'corset', so the measured growth rate is overstated. Nevertheless, there is no reason to believe that the perceived growth rate, adjusted for elimination of the 'corset' and the special deposits, is lower than anticipated at the start of the year, so there is no reason to conclude that an unanticipated decline in monetary growth is the dominant force driving the exchange rate to a temporary appreciation.

Another reason for believing the appreciation is likely to persist is that there is evidence of persistence. Appreciation has occurred in each of the last three years. From third quarter 1977 to third quarter 1978, the pound appreciated against the dollar by 12 per cent; in the following four quarters, the pound appreciated against the dollar by about 11 per cent; and in the most recent four quarters, despite removal of exchange controls, the pound appreciated by an additional 9 per cent. If we adjust the rate of appreciation for the difference in rates of inflation, using deflators for national products, the 'real' appreciation is approximately 15 per cent, 16 per cent and 19 per cent in the three years.

What, then, are the reasons for appreciation of the pound? I find three principal reasons. The first is well-known – the UK has discovered relatively large quantities of oil, and the value of the oil has increased. The second is the effect of changes in taxation – the shift in the tax burden from taxes on income to taxes on consumption. The third is the belief that the present government intends to slow the growth of the public sector and lower the rate of inflation. I discuss each in turn.

The effect of oil prices on the pound is widely recognised. Following the collapse in Iran the relative price of oil rose, so desired investment in oil wells rose. One need only compute the revaluation of oil shares on Canadian, US and UK stock exchanges in 1979 to get a quick estimate of the change. The effect of higher oil prices on the capital flow toward the

UK is, in part, offset by a higher price of net imports of oil to the UK, however.

The Thatcher government, on taking office, reduced taxes on income and increased taxes on spending. The shift of taxes away from saving appreciates the pound. One way to state the reasoning is that the tax on consumption spending reduces spending on home goods and imports, while the reduction in taxes on income increases both spending and saving. The net effect increases measured saving relative to income and reduces consumption spending relative to income. Imports fall, the trade balance becomes more positive, and this appreciates the currency. An alternative way of describing the change emphasises the increase in the after-tax return to saving. The higher after-tax return increases saving and the assets demanded by domestic residents. If the real rate of interest is equal in all countries, the higher after-tax return in the UK diverts domestic saving from foreign to domestic assets (and attracts foreign savers if they were previously subject to income tax).

It is encouraging to note, though by no means conclusive, that the ratio of saving to disposable income rose by two percentage points in 1979. The ratio is not an ideal, or even good, measure of saving, but the change is in the required direction, and the size of the change is large enough to be of interest.

A third factor appreciating the pound is the reduction in the anticipated rate of inflation. A lower anticipated rate of inflation increases the amount of real money balances willingly held.

The medium-term strategy to reduce the rate of inflation is a statement of the government's intention to pursue less inflationary monetary policies than in the past. Steps taken during the past year reinforce the belief that a change in policy has occurred. These include a three percentage point increase in the minimum lending rate (MLR) of the Bank of England in the fall of 1979 and a manifest unwillingness to reduce MLR in the summer and fall of 1980 despite rising unemployment, falling profits and a rising failure rate for firms.

The rise in the MLR at about the time exchange controls were removed, the evidence of strong commitment to anti-inflation policy, combined with the effect of the change in tax policy could easily have swamped the effect of removing exchange controls. The conclusion is strengthened if the commitment to slower growth of the public sector, smaller subsidies to state enterprises, and further tax reduction are perceived to be the start of a policy to encourage saving and incentives to produce.

In summary, there are reasons for believing that the 'real' exchange rate has increased permanently, or at least as long as there is foreign investment in North Sea oil, a higher saving rate and lower anticipated inflation. One need not search for peculiar responses to the removal of exchange controls to explain the appreciation of the pound. Nor should one believe that monetary expansion can reduce the inflation adjusted exchange rate except by reversing the progress that has been made toward a lower anticipated rate of inflation.

NOTES

1. An alternative way of incorporating the effect of exchange controls is to multiply r_f by a parameter; $1 \geqslant \alpha > 0$, that expresses the 'cost' borne by domestic investors under exchange controls. Removing all exchange controls makes $\alpha = 1$.
2. The parameters b, e, j and d are positive.

A Comment on the Paper by A. Britton and P. Spencer: 'Exchange Rates, Interest Rates and the Mobility of Capital'

George McKenzie

In a recent paper in the *American Economic Review*, Herbert Simon interpreted the principle of Occam's Razor as involving the recommendation of theories that make no more assumptions than necessary to account for the phenomena being studied.[1] Stated in this form, the principle is one which I believe we would all accept. For example, if we are concerned with identifying the determinants of the sterling exchange rate surely we do not need to explain, in the process, the determinants of the inventory behaviour of the landlord of the local pub around the corner. At the other extreme, however, it is imperative not to sacrifice logical consistency and reality for succinctness of statement. In other words, a naive Occam's Razor principle that accepts the simplest theory that works is doomed to failure. I am afraid that this is a problem that the authors of this paper have not appreciated. Let me be more specific.

First of all, it should be noted that their paper involves a curious form of induction. A long-run, reduced form type of model is posited and various scenarios are constructed to explain how such a reduced form may be generated. Then the authors work backwards to introduce a few *ad hoc* assumptions about the nature of dynamic adjustment processes. In contrast the correct application of Occam's Razor suggests that we should start with a well-specified structural model carefully explaining lagged adjustment mechanisms as they occur in the decision processes of the various economic units. We would want to distinguish carefully between traded and non-traded commodities and to specify a detailed model of the financial sector. This model need not be estimated, however. But, it can be solved out to yield a well-specified dynamic reduced form. The virtue of following this procedure is that we are assured of consistency between the structural story that we are telling and the simplified reduced form. By not approaching the problem in this way, the authors have inevitably committed a series of logical errors. Consider the following.

Their equation (1) represents the condition for internal balance. They state that

> The parameter (d) must be positive if it is defined as a compensated price elasticity. The other parameter (b) is also positive if it too is interpreted as a compensated substitution term between present and future expenditure.

An analysis of a structural formulation would have revealed that compensated price effects cannot possibly enter into the model as stated. That is, unless we are willing to assume that the UK authorities adjust taxes or social security payments so as to keep the level of social welfare constant. Clearly this interpretation is patently unrealistic and hence the alleged sign restrictions are irrelevant.

Now let us turn to equation (2) describing the balance-of-payments or external balance constraint. Both in theory and practice this should be expressed in *nominal* terms as (a) the difference between the value of domestic output and domestic expenditure (i.e. absorption); plus (b) the non-official capital account. With respect to (a), analysis of the underlying structural equations reveals that, *ceteris paribus*, equation (2) should be homogeneous of degree one in prices and the value of output. This consideration becomes extremely important when the impact and dynamic adjustment effects are being traced out. Consider a simple example. Let us suppose that the rest of the world is experiencing price inflation relative to the United Kingdom. According to (2), this will have no effect either on the balance of payments or the exchange rate. Yet what we would expect in practice is that UK demand will shift toward domestically produced non-traded goods in the short run and that this will generate either a balance of payments surplus or an appreciation of the exchange rate. In turn, this may cause the prices of non-traded goods to increase and further adjustments to take place.

Finally, let me turn to an important issue which is not discussed in the Britton–Spencer paper. Most monetarist and Keynesian discussions of macroeconomic policy in recent years have been formulated in terms of demand management. This paper shares that orientation. Yet, in practice, it is quite likely that supply rigidities will play an extremely important role in determining the dynamic adjustment processes characterising the UK economy's response to any policy change or exogenous shock. Given that Britton and Spencer are primarily concerned with analysing dynamics, it is surprising that the supply side should be so thoroughly neglected. It is difficult to think of reasons why it should be. Consider the following example. Suppose that sterling depreciates against the rest of the world's currencies. Conventional analysis would tell us that both home and world demand would shift to UK produced commodities. What happens next is crucial. If the increased demand is met out of inventories, then we can expect an adjustment process leading to increased output as producers and retailers attempt to restock. However, suppose that the initial conditions characterising the economy involve widespread bearish expectations and high interest rates. Any increase in demand will either involve higher prices or the lengthening of order books. If the business community is highly pessimistic, there may be little overall response in output. Inevitably, the increased demand will dissipate, shifting back to foreign markets.

The point here is that the impact of any change in policy or institutional organisation will depend on factors determining supply. If these are adjudged to be significant, then any demand-oriented policy must be complemented by policies designed to provide incentives to the supply side. Obviously, all relevant issues cannot be discussed in a short comment such as this. However, in my opinion, the suggestion of Professor Pieter Korteweg in his round-table presentation is highly suggestive. That is, the tax receipts forthcoming from British North Sea oil sales should explicitly be used to finance investment tax credits in traditional industrial sectors as well as those sectors exhibiting or likely to exhibit considerable innovative behaviour. Of course, such a policy is a necessary but not a sufficient condition for expanded output. Potential demand for the commodities and services being produced must exist, as must the entrepreneural initiative to take advantage of the opportunities being created. In my opinion, it is *these* issues which are of prime importance in assessing the effects of changes in interest rates and exchange rates.

NOTE

1. Herbert Simon (1979). 'Rational Decision Making', *American Economic Review*, 69, September, 493–513.

Rejoinder

Andrew Britton

It is a strange convention that failure of communication between participants at a conference should be preserved for posterity between the covers of the conference volume.

The subject of our paper is not, as Allan Meltzer assumes, the effect of abolishing exchange control on the level of the exchange rate, but the effect of greater capital mobility on the way the exchange rate is determined (as is made clear in the very first paragraph of the introduction). That is why we consider the effects of a change in the parameter j and not the effects of a change in r_f. There is no 'mistake', no 'confusion' – only a difficulty of communication. We do, in Section 2, refer briefly to the issue with which Allan Meltzer is concerned, and we derive the same standard results as he does in his comment, subject to some necessary qualifications about income or wealth effects.

George McKenzie's objections are mainly methodological. The approach we adopt in Section 1 is in fact a very familiar one for which we can claim little credit, and can accept little blame. Like most macroeconomists, we find that simple models sometimes help understanding. Those who prefer complicated models can turn straight to the Appendix.

The only logical (as opposed to methodological) shortcoming alleged is in the treatment of the external constraint. Our approach is hardly novel, and it does not have the implications suggested. Equation (2) is a condition for long-run equilibrium expressed in terms of the real exchange rate (that is the relative price of domestic and foreign goods in terms of either currency). It cannot be used to answer questions about the short-run effects of overseas inflation on the balance of payments or the nominal exchange rate.

The point is surely clear from the third paragraph of the introduction, where we explain:

> In long-run equilibrium, as we have defined it in the first two sections, the real economy can be discussed without reference to any nominal variables. It makes no difference to the equilibrium behaviour of the system whether the exchange rate or the money supply is assumed to be fixed. This dichotomy does not hold in the short run, so the behaviour of nominal variables has to be examined simultaneously with that of real variables . . .

Of course, it is a strong simplifying assumption to assume perfect dichotomisation, even in full equilibrium, but it is a defensible assumption, often made. It has not led us into any logical errors, and we are surprised that it was misunderstood.

7 Real Exchange Rate Policy

Michael Beenstock

THE NOMINAL EXCHANGE RATE

Despite the range of material covered in the conference as a whole a number of clear policy messages have emerged which have a major bearing upon exchange rate policy in general and UK policy in particular. The main message is that because the exchange market is efficient it cannot be argued that the nominal exchange rate is too high or too low. This is so regardless of the state of monetary policy, North Sea oil and suchlike. If the price of an asset, in this case foreign exchange, reflects all the available information as Frenkel argues, it is by definition at an appropriate level. The same kind of conclusion also follows from Minford's paper while Britton and Spencer also use a model in which exchange rate expectations are rational and, subject to risk, these expectations are appropriately reflected in the current spot rate.

Taken together all this evidence suggests that there is nothing wrong with the exchange rate. This implies that an active exchange rate policy is unnecessary and that the exchange rate should be no more an objective of economic policy than the price of shares or anything else.

EXCHANGE RATE INTERVENTION

In an efficient foreign exchange market exchange rate intervention will actually increase the volatility of the exchange rate and Batchelor and Wood draw our attention to the fact that exchange rates were more volatile when the authorities were more active in the foreign exchange market. The reason for this is that the unpredictable behaviour of the authorities necessarily increases the risks with which the market has to contend. Assuming that agents are risk-averse this has the effect of frightening people off and reducing the incentives to speculate in a stabilising way.

Therefore although it is intended to smooth the market, exchange rate intervention (both spot and forward) tends to have the opposite effect of increasing exchange rate volatility. In view of the evidence about the efficiency of the foreign exchange market exchange rate intervention can only be disruptive and has no positive social role to play.

REAL EXCHANGE RATE IN THE LONG RUN

There was widespread recognition (e.g. Korteweg and Minford) that the real exchange rate will be affected by real phenomena in general, and that North Sea oil would raise the real exchange rate. Such real exchange rate changes cannot be eliminated through monetary policy. Indeed, an expansionary monetary policy which is aimed at lowering the nominal exchange rate and thence the real exchange rate is bound to fail since domestic prices will rise to match the decline in the exchange rate.

It was generally recognised that such a policy could pave the way to ever-growing inflation since it would for ever be necessary to expand monetary policy in what is in any case going to be a futile attempt to lower the real exchange rate.

As Korteweg argued, we learnt the hard way in the 1960s and 1970s that monetary policy when made subservient to real phenomena such as unemployment or real interest rates brought about ever-growing inflation. The same principles apply to the real exchange rate and it would be tragic if we had to learn this lesson all over again during the 1980s in relation to real exchange rate targets.

REAL EXCHANGE RATE IN THE SHORT RUN

If the foreign exchange market is efficient and the domestic labour and product markets are inefficient a tight monetary policy will raise the real exchange rate in the short run. Indeed such behaviour is implicit in the models of Britton and Spencer, de Grauwe and van den Bergh, and Minford. The exchange rate therefore reacts more rapidly to changes in monetary policy than does the domestic price level so that the real exchange rate rises in the short run when monetary policy contracts and falls when monetary policy is expanded.

During this period the real exchange rate will be too high or too low.

But the blame, so to speak, really rests with the price level and not with the exchange rate. This is because the exchange market is efficient while the internal markets are inefficient. Therefore to blame the exchange rate for being too high when monetary policy is tightened is a miscarriage of justice. For the truth is that domestic wages and prices are too high while the exchange rate is at its appropriate level.

Therefore the basic policy question is not 'what is wrong with the exchange rate?' but 'what is wrong with domestic wages and prices?' It is frankly difficult to understand how academics, journalists and politicians have made the elementary mistake of blaming the exchange rate when it is obvious that the central issue is the setting of wages and prices domestically. The imperfections in these markets are recognised to be legion on account of labour law, price fixing and constraints on labour mobility, etc., etc. The focus of policy attention should be to improve the efficiency of these internal markets so that the short-term real exchange rate effects are minimised.

To conclude instead that monetary objectives should be abandoned to lower the nominal exchange rate takes us back to the previous conclusion that it is entirely inappropriate to make monetary policy subservient to the real exchange rate. If such recommendations were heeded it would be necessary to abandon counterflationary policies entirely. This is the logical position of those who call for an expansion of monetary policy to lower the real exchange.

If as a result of this Conference the British 'neurosis' over the exchange rate is even partially overcome it will have been worthwhile. If in addition attention is diverted instead to the efficiency of the domestic markets the prognosis will be even better.

Author Index

Subject Index